Recipes For Life!

A Collection of Recipes To Fortify Families In Both Body and Spirit!

"Just as the living Father sent me and I have life because of the Father, so also the one who feeds on me will have life because of me." John 6:57

Copyright © 2009 www.TASTEProgram.com
ISBN 0-9779582-2-1

"*Indeed, the communion of Saints consists not only of the great men and women who went before us and whose names we know. All of us belong to the communion of Saints, we who have been baptized in the name of the Father, and of the Son, and of the Holy Spirit, we who draw life from the gift of Christ's Body and Blood, through which he transforms us and makes us like himself.*" Taken from Pope Benedict XVI Homily at his installation Mass outside St. Peter's Basilica, Vatican City

"To the family is entrusted the task of striving, first and foremost, *to unleash the forces of good,* the source of which is found in Christ the Redeemer of man. *Every family unit needs to make these forces their own so that*...the family will be *strong with the strength of God*". 23 Gratissimam Sane Letter to Families from Pope John Paul II

ACKNOWLEDGEMENTS

Thank you to all the wonderful women and teachers of the TASTE Program, who donated their tried and true recipes.

GospelGifs Christian images are copyrighted and used with permission of GospelGifs.com.

A very special thank you to William Keimig for use of the pictures from ACM (Association for Catechumenal Ministry) featuring drawings of the saints by Paul Kerris, and photographs of stained glass windows by Bob Jakielski.

Cartoons on dividers used with permission Family Circus © Bil Keane Inc. King Features Syndicate.

The front and back cover were designed by Christina Dickerson, a wife and mother, who generously donated her time and talent to this project. Thank you Christina!

Our dividers were designed by Deanne Johnson. Thank you for donating your time to make this cookbook special.

Scripture texts were taken from the *New American Bible with Revised New Testament and Revised Psalms* © 1991, 1986, 1970 Confraternity of Christian Doctrine, Washington, D.C. and are used by permission of the copyright owner. All Rights Reserved.

Special thanks to the Sisters of St. Joseph for sharing their photograph of Mary and their recipe for Saintly Citrus Crosses. For more information about Mary MacKillop, visit www.sosj.org.au

We are grateful to FrassatiUSA for use of Pier Giorgio's picture. For more information on Pier Giorgio contact www.FrassatiUSA.org

With appreciation to The Society of Saint Gianna, Philadelphia, PA for use of their picture of St. Gianna. For more information contact www.saintgianna.org

www.tasteprogram.com

INTRODUCTION

What Is The TASTE Program?

The TASTE Program stands for **T**aste **A**nd **S**ee **T**ake…**E**at. It is a Catholic program designed to help Catholic woman fall completely in love with Jesus AND the Church He founded. Speakers are invited to come and teach women about Church teachings including the Bible, papal documents, the Catechism, Church history, apologetics, Faith and morals, great Catholic books, and current issues. The sessions begin with Mass followed by small group discussion based on reflection questions from the previous session. Our speakers come in for an hour to teach, and then the Sacrament of Reconciliation is offered. Each session leaves us spiritually well fed and ready to tackle the rest of our week.

TASTE began in September 2007 at St. Mary of the Mills Catholic Church in Laurel, Maryland. Women from 17 different parishes representing the Archdioceses of Washington and Baltimore came to learn more about their Catholic Faith and about the Church that Jesus founded. The program now includes women from 24 different parishes! Speakers are by invitation only and include Catholic priests and lay people on fire for their Faith. If you are in the Baltimore/ Washington area we would love to have you join us.

For more information visit our website www.tasteprogram.com.

PREFACE

What makes this cookbook special?

This Cookbook has been compiled with love from women all seeking a deeper relationship with Jesus. The following pages are filled with wonderful recipes for you and your family to enjoy. Scattered throughout these pages are *special* pages about a particular saint and a recipe that ties in with that saint. Written simply for a child to understand, they are in no way complete. You might want to get a good book on the saints and spend time reading about them.

Use your imagination as you tell the stories to spark that flame that will ignite in your heart, and in those you love, a genuine love for our Creator. If a saint was a virgin, he/she might be paired with a recipe that has white sauce or white icing to indicate purity. Prepare an Italian dish when celebrating an Italian saint or a French dish when celebrating a French saint.

When we teach our children to be holy by imitating real men and women, they develop role models that are hard to find in our society today. Teach them that we are preparing for heaven now! Use your kitchen time to steep your whole family in God. You might want to set aside a **special bowl** that you use when cooking on your "Saint Night." When you bring it out, everyone will realize that you are baking for "Saint Night" that week.

Time has a way of getting away from us all. If you use your time in the kitchen wisely, the kids or grandkids will grow up with indelible memories of their friends (the saints) who grew up with them. The bold suggestions below the biographies are just a way of tying into your week what that saint did. Feel free to use what's provided or make up your own. The important thing is to encourage everyone in your family to grow in love toward Jesus and the Church He founded.

O adorable Blood of Jesus, wash our stains, save us from the anger of the avenging angel. Irrigate the Church; make her fruitful with Apostles and miracle-workers, enrich her with souls that are holy, pure and radiant with divine beauty."

~A meditation on the Precious Blood of Jesus from the writings of St. Albert the Great.

What Can I Do To Become A Saint?

God made each one of us in His image and likeness so we are all called to be saints. We attain heaven by God's grace and by cooperating with God's grace in our lives. We can't get to heaven until we are purified and become a saint, so why not start while we are still down here? Our goal should not be getting by so we can make it to Purgatory, but trying our hardest to get to heaven so we can see God. God is on our side. He loves us and wants us to be with Him. He sent His Son down here in order to open the gates to Heaven so it's up to us to spread His goodness and love everywhere we go. So, what can we do to become like these men and women? Let's explore the possibilities.

1. Encourage people to read the lives of saints. There are biographies for every age group and they are fascinating.

"May the eyes of [your] hearts be enlightened, that you may know what is the hope that belongs to his call, what are the riches of glory in his inheritance among the holy ones."
Eph. 1:18

2. Everyone should spend at least 10 minutes a day reading the Bible, – it's fuel for the soul. It is our **B**asic **I**nstructions **B**efore **L**eaving **E**arth!

"Jesus said to them in reply, 'You are misled because you do not know the scriptures or the power of God.'" Matt. 22:29

3. Schedule a time to pray just as you would schedule soccer practice, homework or going to the grocery store. It's a must do on your "to do" list.

"In those days he departed to the mountain to pray, and he spent the night in prayer to God." Luke 6:12

4. Incorporate God into your everyday life. How? Pick something you do often (putting your hair behind your ear, crossing your legs, walking to each class, chewing, looking at a clock…whatever you do frequently add a prayer quietly. Say "Jesus, I love you" every time you… It's a habit that will change your life!

"This is my commandment: love one another as I love you." John 15:12

5. Go to frequent Confession to keep your soul clean for Jesus.

"Whose sins you forgive are forgiven them, and whose sins you retain are retained." John 20:23

6. Try to go to Mass more than once a week.

"Whoever eats my flesh and drinks my blood remains in me and I in him." John 6:56

7. Encourage a friend who doesn't attend Mass to come to Mass with your family.

"He said to them, "Go into the whole world and proclaim the gospel to every creature." Mark 16:15

8. Attend Eucharistic Adoration once a week and have a heart to heart talk with Jesus.

"But Daniel answered, 'I adore the Lord, my God, for he is the living God.'" Dan. 14:25

9. Stop gossiping and learn to build up God's kingdom. Think of gossip as worms that come out of your mouth. Once they are out they crawl everywhere.

"Never repeat gossip, and you will not be reviled." Sir. 19:6

10. Fast or abstain from something you love to do. For example no video games on Monday, no ice cream on Tuesday, no TV on Wednesday.

Remember what Jesus said though…
 "When you fast, do not look gloomy like the hypocrites. They neglect their appearance, so that they may appear to others to be fasting. Amen, I say to you, they have received their reward. But when you fast, anoint your head and wash your face, so that you may not appear to others to be fasting, except to your Father who is hidden. And your Father who sees what is hidden will repay you." Matt. 6:16-18

You can also do something for Jesus. Help mom and dad with housework. Clean your room, do the dishes, change the dog's water, pick up someone else's mess, in other words, be nice and help others out of love for God. When we cooperate with God and do His will, we become like God. Since we were made to know Him, to love Him and to serve Him, we will become very happy because we are doing what He made us for. We were made to love God. That's the secret ingredient in the recipe for life.

"And whatever you do, in word or in deed, do everything in the name of the Lord Jesus, giving thanks to God the Father through him." Col. 3:17

The Process of Canonization

Though everyone who enters heaven is a saint, the Church recognizes outstanding men and women who have gone before us and showed exemplary virtue. These men and women that we call saints were not perfect. They sinned just like we do, but they also loved God with their whole hearts and tried their best to do His will. As you read their stories, no two are alike yet they all have a common thread. These saints all had an undying love for their creator and the desire to see Him one day. Let's take a look at how the Church declares someone a saint.

The first step is an investigation into the person's life. This usually occurs from 5 - 50 years after the person has died. The local bishop is notified of this request. The group making this request must be very serious because the life of this person must be documented and scrutinized. You cannot just be a nice person but you must have gone well beyond the call of duty. You are not sinless, but you led a virtuous life.

If there are enough people to attest to your exemplary life then the bishop asks Rome for permission to form a special tribunal to investigate your life. Once this happens and everyone testifies, you are then called a Servant of God.

Now the real investigation begins. The bishop sends the documentation to Rome and it is translated into Italian. The Congregation for the Causes of Saints reads the documents and at least 9 theologians have to declare that the evidence is overwhelming and true. Next, the bishops and cardinals on the committee meet and if they approve all the documentation the person is called Venerable. One miracle attributable to the person must have taken place after death for the cause to be presented to the Pope. If you died for the Faith then no miracle is needed before you are beatified. You are considered a martyr. The Pope, if he approves, declares the person Blessed. This is done during a special Mass.

Finally if another miracle takes place after beatification then the cause goes to the Pope again and he can declare the canonization of the person to be named a saint.

Though this is a great honor to be called a saint, we are all called to be saints. Read though these pages and pick your favorite saint. Ask him or her to help you with your mission to be holy. Set yourself apart from the world. Remember what Jesus taught us:

"Do not conform yourselves to this age but be transformed by the renewal of your mind, that you may discern what is the will of God, what is good and pleasing and perfect."
Rom. 12:2

Catholic?... Get Connected!
Here are just a few things you can do to get plugged into the Catholic World!

On Your Computer:
Change your home page to www.catholicculture.org www.catholicexchange.com or www.catholic.org. It keeps you informed as to what's going on by telling you the truth.

www.dailygospel.org Sign-up for e-mail for the daily gospel and readings.

www.masstimes.org Find any Catholic church while away on vacation.

Other trusted Catholic sites include the following:

catholic.com	feminine-genius.com
catholicity.com	missionmoment.org
catholic.net	onenationundergod.org
catholicfirst.com	osv.com
catholicliturgy.com	saintjoe.com
catholicparents.org	salvationhistory.com
catholic-soe.org	staycatholic.com
catholictreasury.info	vatican.va
chnetwork.org	usccb.org
ewtn.com	zenit.org

www.catholic.org/bible ~online Bible
www.scborromeo.org/ccc.htm ~online Catechism
www.catholicreference.net ~online Catholic dictionary
oce.catholic.com (no www.) online Catholic Encyclopedia

Watch programs on EWTN Eternal Word Television Network!

Every Catholic home should have a Bible, a Crucifix, a Catechism, a Statue of Mary, a Rosary, and picture of the Sacred Heart of Jesus and the Immaculate Heart of Mary.

Trusted Authors (not inclusive)

James Akin	Peter Kreeft
Mike Aquilina	C.S. Lewis
Dave Armstrong	Fr. Lawrence Lovasik
Raymond Arroyo	Patrick Madrid
Jeff Cavins	Ralph Martin
G.K. Chesterton	Matthew Pinto
H. W. Crocker III	Stephen Ray
M. D"Ambrosio	John Salza
Thomas Howard	Alan Schreck
Thomas Dubay	Mark Shea
Jason Evert	F.J. Sheed
Rosemarie Gortler	Edward Sri
Tim Gray	Tim Staples
Fr. Benedict Groeschel	James Stenson
Kimberly and Scott Hahn	Peter Stravinskas
Fr. John Hardon	Dietrich Von Hildebrand
Thomas Howard	George Weigel
Karl Keating	Christopher West
Ronald Knox	Mary Fabyan Windeatt

Bring Catholicism into your home!

1. Catholic League for Religious and Civil Rights newsletter, **Catalyst** www.catholicleague.org
   Or call: (212) 371-3191
2. Join **Catholics United for the Faith** Order **Lay Witness** Magazine online www.cuf.org.
   Or call: (740) 283-2484
3. **The Sower** Catechetical Journal Order online at www.thesowerreview.org
   Or call: (866) 538-7426
4. **Faith & Family Magazine** www.faithandfamilylive.com Or call (800) 421-3230
5. **Magnificat** Mass readings and prayers. Order online www.magnificat.com
   Or call (866) 522-8465 Also Children's version Magnifikid for children 6–12 years old.
6. **This Rock** Explains the Catholic faith. Order online www.catholic.com/magazines/thisrock.asp Or call: (888) 291-8000

INDEX OF SAINTS BY DATES

St. Basil the Great	January 2	pg. 12
St. Elizabeth Ann Seton	January 4	pg. 198
St. John Neumann	January 5	pg. 42
St. Francis de Sales	January 24	pg. 36
St. Thomas Aquinas	January 28	pg. 82
St. John Bosco	January 31	pg. 134
St. Agatha	February 5	pg. 202
St. Josephine Bakhita	February 8	pg. 152
Our Lady of Lourdes	February 11	pg. 270
St. Peter Damian	February 21	pg. 20
St. Gabriel Possenti	February 27	pg. 154
St. Katharine Drexel	March 3	pg. 4
Sts. Perpetua and Felicity	July 10 (P)	pg. 230
	March 7 (F)	pg. 230
St. Patrick	March 17	pg. 22
St. Joseph	March 19/ May 1	pg. 228
St. Margaret Clitherow	March 26	pg. 208
St. Vincent Ferrer	April 5	pg. 130
St. Julie Billiart	April 8	pg. 168
St. Gemma Galgani	April 11	pg. 28
Blessed Margaret of Castello	April 13	pg. 8

St. Bernadette	April 16	pg. 270
St. Ludwina	April 22	pg. 268
St. Zita	April 27	pg. 140
St. Gianna Beretta Molla	April 28	pg. 112
St. Catherine of Siena	April 29	pg. 104
St. Dominic Savio	May 6	pg. 142
St. Peregrine Laziosi	May 16	pg. 178
St. Rita	May 22	pg. 122
St. Julia	May 23	pg. 222
St. Philip Neri	May 26	pg. 180
St. Anthony of Padua	June 13	pg. 98
St. Juliana Falconieri	June 19	pg. 274
St. Aloysius Gonzaga	June 21	pg. 260
St. Josemaria Escrivá	June 26	pg. 90
St. Peter	June 29	pg. 86
St. Elizabeth of Portugal	July 4	pg. 96
Blessed Pier Giorgio Frassati	July 4	pg. 190
St. Maria Goretti	July 6	pg. 74
St. Benedict	July 11	Pg. 156
St. John Gaulbert	July 12	pg. 110
Blessed Kateri Tekakwitha	July 14	pg. 162

Saint	Feast Day	Page
St. Bridget of Sweden	July 23	pg. 172
St. Peter Julian Eymard	August 2	pg. 232
Blessed Mary MacKillop	August 8	pg. 258
St. John Vianney "Curé of Ars"	August 4	pg. 70
St. Clare of Assisi	August 11	pg. 126
St. Maximilian Kolbe	August 14	pg. 26
St. Jane Frances de Chantal	August 18	pg. 170
St. Bernard	August 20	pg. 244
St. Monica and St. Augustine	August 27 (M) August 28 (A)	pg. 114
Blessed Teresa of Calcutta	September 5	pg. 132
St. Peter Claver	September 9	pg. 182
St. John Chrysostom	September 13	pg. 204
Our Lady of Sorrows	September 15	pg. 18
St. Joseph of Cupertino	September 18	pg. 152
St. Andrew Kim Taegon	September 20	pg. 158
St. Pio of Pietrelcina (Padre Pio)	September 23	pg. 164
Sts. Michael, Gabriel, and Raphael	September 29	pg. 52
St. Jerome	September 30	pg. 250
St. Thérèse of Lisieux	October 1	pg. 56
Guardian Angels Feast Day	October 2	pg. 52

St. Francis of Assisi	October 4	pg. 254
St. Maria Faustina Kowalska	October 5	pg. 24
Our Lady of the Rosary	October 7	pg. 186
St. Teresa of Avila	October 15	pg. 282
St. Gerard Majella	October 16	pg. 47
St. Martin de Porres	November 3	pg. 174
St. Brice	November 13	pg. 248
St. Elizabeth of Hungary	November 17	pg. 120
St. Cecilia (3rd Century)	November 22	pg. 240
St. Catherine Labouré	November 28	pg. 100
St. Francis Xavier	December 3	pg. 128
St. Nicholas	December 6	pg. 238
St. Juan Diego	December 9	pg. 68
Our Lady of Guadalupe	December 12	pg. 68
St. Lucy	December 13	pg. 262
St. Peter Canisius	December 21	pg. 210
St. Stephen	December 26	pg. 144

The Importance of a Recipe

Have you ever made an appetizer, main course dish or a dessert and forgotten to add something in the recipe? Even those who have done a lot of cooking may have done this from time to time. As soon as the dish was tasted, oops – something just was not quite right!

Recipes are made to follow a step-by-step instruction in order for the recipe to turn out correctly. Similarly, members in the Body of Christ are like special ingredients that God brings together at the right time to create a beautiful banquet, but only if we listen to the Holy Spirit and cooperate with His will. The Church with the sacraments is our "Recipe For Life" to help us journey toward heaven.

We eat food to sustain our bodies and to grow. In scripture, St. Paul tells us *"from whom the whole body, being fitted and held together by what every joint supplies, according to the proper working of each individual part, causes the growth of the body for the building up of itself in love."* Eph. 4:16

Everyone in our church is a part of the recipe and has an important ingredient to mix in the batch. When something is missing, the recipe is not complete and the dish is not quite right! In order for it to turn out right, everyone must do their part. Together, with Christ, we truly are blessed with tried and true RECIPES FOR LIFE! Thanks for all the ingredients you bring to the table! May God bless you!

Table of Contents

Appetizers 1
Soups and Salads 17
Bread and Breakfast 47
Vegetables and Sides 63
Main Dishes 81
Fantastic Fridays 161
Desserts 201
This and That 279
Blessings 285
Conversions and Terminology 301

Appetizers

"Our Father, who art in heaven,
how did You know
my name?"

APPETIZERS INDEX

Artichoke Dip 2
Asian Roll Ups 15
Baked Cheese Bread Dip ...1
Baked Crab Dip 7
Cranberry Dip 7
Grandma's Cheese Balls ..11
Katharine's Hot Crab Dip 5
Margaret's Spinach Balls 9
Marinated Pretzels 15
Mexican Dip 6
Olive Dip 1
Philly Chili Cheese Dip 5

Salmon Dill Sauce............ 16
Rubin Dip… 7
Salsa 10
Sausage Dip 6
Spinach & Artichoke Dip 3
Spinach Squares.............. 11
Spinachoke Dip.................. 2
St. Basil's Vegetable
  Cheese Squares 13
Sweet Corn and Pepper
  Salsa.. 10
Veggie Bars 14
Zucchini Rounds 14

Appetizers, Snacks and Beverages

Baked Cheese Bread Dip

2 cups grated sharp Cheddar cheese
2 cups grated Monterey Jack cheese
1 cup grated mozzarella cheese
2 cups mayonnaise
1 Tbsp. minced onion (dried)
2 squirts Worcestershire sauce
1 large round hard-crusted bread

Preheat oven to 350°. Trim out top of bread, and hollow out loaf. Mix all of the ingredients together and fill loaf. Place foil over the rim of the bread. Bake for 20 to 30 minutes. Serve with crackers of your choice and remaining bread, cubed.

Note: *This recipe has been passed around for years. I have modified it slightly. The more Worcestershire sauce you add, the more it gives off a "crab dip" taste.*

Olive Dip

1 (8 oz.) pkg. cream cheese, softened
½ cup mayonnaise
½ cup chopped pecans
1 cup chopped green olives
1-2 tsp. olive juice

Mix all ingredients together and chill for 6 hours before serving. Serve with whole grain crackers.

"Every time we come before the Eucharistic Heart of Jesus He touches the heart of all humanity! The Blessed Sacrament is the heartbeat of evangelization." ~ "The Sacred Eucharistic Heart of Jesus" audio tape.

Artichoke Dip

This hot dip always gets rave reviews at parties!

4 oz. chopped pimentos (reserve 2 Tbsp.)
1 (14 oz.) can artichoke hearts, drained and broken up
3 (4 oz.) cans chopped green chilies
4 oz. shredded Monterey Jack cheese
½ cup grated Parmesan cheese
1 ½ cups mayonnaise – don't use fat free

Mix all in a small baking dish. Top with the reserved 2 tablespoons pimento. Bake, uncovered, at 350° for 30 minutes. Serve with crackers.

Spinachoke Dip

16 oz. cream cheese, softened
8 oz. Monterey Jack cheese, grated
4 oz. Parmesan cheese, grated
1 can (14 oz.) artichoke hearts, drained and chopped
2 (10 oz.) cans Ro-Tel tomatoes
1 (10 oz.) pkg. spinach, thawed, drained, and chopped
1 onion, chopped
2 tsp. cumin
2 tsp. chili powder
1 tsp. garlic powder

Mix all ingredients. Bake at 350° until hot, about 30 minutes. Serve with tortilla chips, pita chips, or Fritos Scoops.

"The Eucharist is the sun that gives light, life and joy to the feasts of the Church." ~St. Peter Julian Eymard

Spinach & Artichoke Dip

1 (8 oz.) pkg. light cream cheese *(I like the texture better; regular is fine)*
1 (14 oz.) can Progresso artichoke hearts, drained and coarsely chopped
½ cup spinach, frozen chopped or steamed
¼ cup mayonnaise (do not use Miracle Whip)
¼ cup Parmesan cheese
¼ cup Romano cheese (you can use all Parmesan)
1 clove garlic, finely minced
½ tsp. basil, dry, or 1 Tbsp. fresh basil
¼ cup mozzarella cheese, grated
¼ tsp. garlic salt
Salt and pepper to taste

Allow cream cheese to come to room temperature. Cream together with mayonnaise, Parmesan and Romano cheeses, garlic, basil, and garlic salt. Mix well. Add the artichoke hearts and spinach (be careful to drain this well), and mix until blended. Store in a container until you are ready to use.

Spray pie pan with Pam, pour in dip, and top with cheese. Bake at 350° for 25 minutes or until the top is browned. Serve with toasted bread.

"Forgiveness is hard because it involves loving other people in spite of the evil that they have done to us. When we forgive, we don't deny the hurt that we have received. We don't deny that it was wrong. We don't pretend that nothing happened. But...we acknowledge that there is more to the offender than the offense. It's that more that we acknowledge when we forgive; it's that more that we love in spite of the offense."
~Bishop Daniel Pilarczyk

St. Katharine Drexel (1858-1955) *Virgin*
Feast Day ~ March 3

Katharine was born in the United States and is the second native-born American to be declared a saint. As a young child growing up in Philadelphia, Pennsylvania in 1858, her mother died and her father remarried a wonderful woman who loved God very much. The family was quite well to do and the children learned to love and care for those less fortunate. Her mother opened their home to the poor 3 times a week, and her father prayed half an hour every night. The family had an altar in their home, and they gathered together to pray there every day. Katharine's stepmother had a very serious illness that changed Katharine; she realized that all the money in the world could not take pain and suffering away. When she was 33 years old, she founded a new community of sisters called the Sisters of the Blessed Sacrament. They were missionary sisters who helped spread the message of the Gospel and the Eucharist to the poor, especially the African and Native Americans. Since Katharine inherited a large amount of money, she used it to build schools for the children, convents for the nuns and churches for the communities. Her order started Xavier University in New Orleans. She worked very hard and had 50 missions for Native Americans in 16 states. Katharine truly loved everyone and spent millions of dollars helping others. She died in 1955 and Pope John Paul II declared her a saint in 2000.

What might you do this week to declare your love for others? Katharine used her money unselfishly. Maybe you could ask your parents to do a chore that you normally don't have to do and then donate your time and any money you might earn to the poor. Remember to do it with a willing attitude and a big smile!

Philly Chili Cheese Dip

You can make this low fat by using turkey chili, fat-free cream cheese, and low-fat cheese. It tastes great either way.

1 (15 oz.) can Hormel chili with beans
1 (8 oz.) pkg. cream cheese, softened
1 cup favorite salsa
1 cup shredded cheese (Cheddar, Monterey Jack, etc.)
Sliced green onions, sliced black olives – to top dip (optional)

Spread softened cream cheese in 9-inch pie plate. Next layer chili, salsa, and cheese on top. Garnish with green onions and/or black olives if desired. Microwave on high for 8 to 9 minutes or until cheese is melted. Serve with tortilla chips.

Katharine's Hot Crab Dip

1 lb. jumbo lump crabmeat
1 cup grated pepper jack cheese
¾ cup mayonnaise
¼ cup grated Parmesan
¼ cup minced green onions
2 cloves garlic, minced
3 Tbsp. Worcestershire sauce
2 Tbsp. lemon or lime juice
1 tsp. hot pepper sauce
½ tsp. dry mustard
Salt and pepper

Preheat oven to 325°. Combine all ingredients in a casserole and gently stir until thoroughly mixed. Bake 40 minutes.

Mexican Dip

A Family Favorite!

1 (8 oz.) pkg. cream cheese, softened
1 (15 oz.) can Hormel chili without beans
1 small can (4.5 oz.) chopped green chilies
1-2 cups Monterey Jack cheese with jalapeño peppers, shredded

Spread cream cheese on bottom of dish. Spread chili, and add green chilies on top. Sprinkle shredded cheese on top. Bake at 350° for 30 minutes. Serve with corn chips.

Sausage Dip

Good for Super Bowl Sunday!

1 ½ lbs. sausage
8 oz. cream cheese
1 (14 ½ oz.) can diced tomatoes with green chili peppers

In large skillet, brown sausage and drain fat. Cut cream cheese into small cubes. Place all ingredients in microwave-safe bowl, and microwave until cheese melts. Stir and serve with crackers, chips, or pitas. The ingredients can also be placed in a slow-cooker and heated until cheese melts.

"Faith is not merely the attachment to a complex of dogmas, complete in itself, that is supposed to satisfy the thirst for God, present in the human heart. On the contrary, it guides human beings on their way through time toward a God who is ever new in his infinity." ~August 28 (Angelus address) Pope Benedict XVI

Ruben Dip

A real crowd pleaser!

1 (8 oz.) pkg. cream cheese, softened
1 (15 oz.) can sauerkraut
4 oz. Swiss cheese, shredded
½ lb. lean corn beef, chopped into small pieces
1 small bottle Thousand Island dressing

Combine all ingredients. Pour into small crockpot. Cook on high for 1 hour before serving. Serve on rye bread squares.

Baked Crab Dip

1 lb. fresh crabmeat
1 (8 oz.) pkg. cream cheese
1 cup sour cream
3 Tbsp. mayonnaise
2 Tbsp. lemon juice
1 Tbsp. Dijon mustard
2 cloves garlic, crushed
¼ tsp. red pepper
½ cup grated Cheddar cheese
1 Tbsp. Worcestershire sauce

Mix all ingredients together. Bake in a buttered casserole dish at 400° for 30 minutes. Serve with crackers on bread. *Makes 10 servings.*

Cranberry Dip

Great at Thanksgiving. You can triple for a crowd.

1 (4 oz.) pkg. cream cheese, softened
¼ cup dried cranberries (Craisins)
¼ cup chopped pecans or walnuts
⅛ cup orange juice concentrate thawed

Combine all ingredients. Chill 30 minutes. Serve with pear slices.

Blessed Margaret of Castello (1287-1320)
Feast Day ~ April 13

Born blind, crippled by a curved spine with legs that were not the same length, and with a shriveled left arm, Margaret only grew to be 4 feet tall. Her parents took her to a shrine when she was 6 years old begging for a miracle. When they did not receive one, they abandoned her. A loving couple, Venfarino and Grigia loved her very much and adopted her. As the child grew, she was full of love and helped everyone she met. She used her own problems as a way to unite her life to that of Jesus, and took on tremendous responsibilities helping the sick and suffering in her town of Castello. No one was an outcast. She visited prisoners, comforted the sick and dying, and shared her deep devotion to God with everyone. When she died, the whole town came to her funeral. The priest, who was going to have her buried in the courtyard, was challenged by the town's people. "She deserves a place in the church," they protested. As he was arguing with them, a child who was crippled struggled up to the coffin and touched it. She stood up and walked away. The priest, realizing that a great miracle had just taken place, changed his mind and had Margaret buried inside the church.

Look around this week at some of the miracles God has put into your life. Take a few minutes to discuss your blessings at dinner tonight.

Margaret's Spinach Balls

Spinach is a vegetable that is usually not liked by children. Try these. They are delicious. Margaret was not liked at first because she looked different. Eventually everyone came to love her.

2 pkgs. frozen chopped spinach	2 medium onions, finely chopped
(8 oz.) bag Pepperidge Farm Herb Seasoned Stuffing (not cubed)	¾ tsp. pepper *(if doubling this recipe, do not double the pepper)*
1 ½ tsp. garlic powder	½ tsp. thyme
6 eggs, beaten	½ cup Parmesan cheese
	¾ cup melted butter

Cook and drain spinach. Make sure you squeeze out all of the water, as you don't want these to be soggy. Mix all ingredients. Form into balls and place on cookie sheet sprayed with Pam. Bake at 350° for 20 minutes.

They're great warm, but my family eats them even when they're cold. By the way, no one likes spinach in our family, yet everyone LOVES these! You can freeze them and take them out for parties. I thaw them in the microwave! I always make a double batch so the company can have some and then there will be leftovers for the family! ☺

TRANSFORMED BY JESUS

"For it was the LORD, our God, who brought us and our fathers up out of the land of Egypt, out of a state of slavery. He performed those great miracles before our very eyes and protected us along our entire journey and among all the peoples through whom we passed." Josh. 24:17

Salsa

This is also a really good salsa to put on top of grilled chicken.

1 (16 oz.) can tomatoes, undrained *(I have mixed 2 different diced varieties with either Italian and/or Mexican spices added)*
1 (15 oz.) can black beans, rinsed and drained
1 (15 oz.) can small white beans, rinsed and drained (whatever you can find works)

1 red pepper, chopped
½ onion, chopped
Bunch of fresh cilantro, chopped
Cumin, garlic salt, pepper, hot sauce, pinch of sugar, a little olive oil

Place tomatoes, beans, red pepper, onion, and cilantro into a bowl. Then add spices and olive oil to your taste. You can also add fresh or frozen corn kernels. *Enjoy!*

Sweet Corn & Pepper Salsa

4 ears fresh corn, cut off cob, not cooked
1 red pepper, chopped
1 jalapeño pepper, chopped
1 small bunch cilantro, chopped
1 small red onion, chopped

Dressing:
½ cup lime juice
¼ cup sherry or white wine vinegar
3 cloves garlic, chopped
Salt and pepper to taste

Combine first 5 ingredients. Combine dressing ingredients. Top veggies with dressing. Chill at least 1 hour before serving. Serve with tortilla chips. The "scoops" chips work very well with this salsa. Best when fresh.

"Jesus in the Blessed Sacrament is the Living Heart of each of our parishes." ~Pope Paul VI

Grandma's Cheese Balls

1 jar Kraft Old English cheese spread
16 oz. cream cheese
6 oz. Roquefort (or blue cheese)
1 small onion, diced
1 Tbsp. Worcestershire sauce
½ cup pecans, grated fine
Chopped pecans

Let the cheeses come to room temperature and mix together. Add onion, Worcestershire sauce, and grated pecans. Form in one large ball in a bowl and refrigerate overnight or for at least 5 hours. Using waxed paper, form 3 large balls (or smaller if desired). Roll the balls in chopped pecans.

Spinach Squares

4 Tbsp. butter
3 eggs
1 cup flour
1 cup milk
1 tsp. salt
1 tsp. baking powder
1 lb. Monterey Jack/ Pepper Jack cheese shredded
2 (10 oz.) pkgs. chopped spinach

Thaw and drain spinach. Preheat oven to 350°. Melt butter in a 13x9x2-inch pan while preheating oven. Remove pan when melted. Beat eggs. Mix flour, milk, salt, and baking powder. Add to eggs. Add shredded cheese and spinach.

Pour into pan and spread evenly. (Two 8x8-inch pans may also be used.) Bake at 350° for 35 minutes. Cool for 45 minutes prior to cutting into squares. Serve warm or cold.

"Prayer is the best weapon we have; it is the key to God's heart. You must speak to Jesus not only with your lips, but with your heart. In fact on certain occasions you should only speak to Him with your heart." ~St. Padre Pio

**St. Basil the Great (329-379)
Feast Day ~ January 2**

After becoming archbishop of Caesarea (which is now southeastern Turkey), Basil kept the heretics from receiving Holy Communion because they promoted Arianism (a heresy that denied the divinity of Christ). He united Catholics, yet he was also misunderstood during his lifetime. He built a hospital known as a 'wonder of the world' which showed wealthy people how they could practically spend their money in Christian ways by helping the poor and the sick. Even as a youth, St. Basil had a heart for those less fortunate and organized famine relief and volunteered in soup kitchens. Though he had the opportunity to live with many comforts, he chose to live a simple lifestyle, eating and dressing plainly. He is known as one of the most distinguished Doctors of the Church, a title given by the Church to persons whose writings and preaching are useful to Christians "in any age of the Church." Their understanding of God and the teachings of the Church are exceptional.

How will you stand up for the truth this week? Maybe you could start saying grace in public at school or in restaurants. Don't be afraid to show the world that you love God.

St. Basil's Vegetable Cheese Squares

Great appetizer!

1 (8 oz.) can Pillsbury crescent rolls
1 (8 oz.) pkg. cream cheese, softened
⅓ cup Kraft Fat Free Ranch dressing
1 tsp. basil or dill weed
2 cups desired vegetables, chopped (broccoli, red and green peppers, carrots, cauliflower, etc.)
1 cup shredded Cheddar cheese

For crust, unroll crescent rolls and gently pat into 13x9x2-inch baking pan. Bake according to package directions. Cool.

Meanwhile, in small mixing bowl, stir together cream cheese, salad dressing, and basil or dill weed. Spread cream cheese mixture evenly over crust. Sprinkle with vegetables and gently press vegetables into cream cheese. Sprinkle with shredded cheese. If time permits, chill 1 hour before serving. To serve, cut into small squares.

"What is the mark of a Christian? That he be purified of all defilement of the flesh and of the spirit in the Blood of Christ, perfecting sanctification in the fear of God and the love of Christ, and that he have no blemish nor spot nor any such thing; that he be holy and blameless and so eat the Body of Christ and drink His Blood; for 'he that eateth and drinketh unworthily, eateth and drinketh judgement to himself.' What is the mark of those who eat the Bread and drink the Cup of Christ? That they keep in perpetual remembrance Him who died for us and rose again."
~"The Morals", St. Basil the Great, Ch. 22

Zucchini Rounds

2 medium zucchini, cut into
 ¼-inch rounds
⅔ cup Italian breadcrumbs
⅓ cup Parmesan cheese

1 cup flour
2 eggs
2 Tbsp. butter

In a shallow dish, combine breadcrumbs and Parmesan cheese. Set aside. Place flour in another shallow dish; set aside. Beat eggs in another shallow dish; set aside.

Heat butter in skillet over medium heat. Season zucchini with salt and pepper. Dredge in flour, beaten egg, and then breadcrumbs mixture. Sauté carefully until golden brown.

Veggie Bars

2 pkgs. crescent rolls
2 (8 oz.) pkgs. cream cheese
¾-1 cup mayonnaise
1 envelope Hidden Valley
 Ranch dressing

Chopped veggies: broccoli, radishes, carrots, zucchini, spring onions, mushrooms, or any other vegetable – as much or as little as you desire!

Bake rolls flat on a cookie sheet at 350° for 7 to 8 minutes.

With a mixer, blend together cream cheese, mayonnaise, and dressing. Spread mixture over the cooled crust and top with chopped vegetables. Cut into bars.

> "The Lord 'hath set His tabernacle in the sun,' says the Psalmist. The sun is Mary's heart." No! We do not see the Eucharistic Heart of Jesus! But we possess it; it is ours!
> ~St. Peter Julian Eymard

Asian Roll Ups

1 (10 oz.) can salmon, drained and flaked
1 (7 oz.) can mandarin oranges
⅓ cup finely chopped green onion
1 ½ Tbsp. peanut butter

⅛ cup low-sodium soy sauce plus 1 Tbsp., divided
½ tsp. fresh lemon juice
1-2 cloves garlic, pressed
½ tsp. ground ginger
4 tortillas (if available)
½ Tbsp. rice vinegar

Drain oranges and reserve 2 tablespoons liquid. Chop enough oranges to equal ½ cup and reserve the remaining oranges for a tossed green salad.

Place the salmon in a medium bowl. Add green onions, peanut butter, 1 tablespoon of the soy sauce, lemon juice, and garlic; mix well. Spoon a portion of the salmon filling in each tortilla and wrap it up and serve. *Makes 4 servings.*

In a small bowl, combine remaining ¼ cup soy sauce, reserved mandarin orange liquid, and vinegar; mix well to be served as a dipping sauce.

Marinated Pretzels

1 cup vegetable oil
1 pkg. Hidden Valley Ranch dry dressing mix

1 Tbsp. lemon pepper
2-3 bags assorted pretzels (small, medium, and large)

Mix oil, dressing, and lemon pepper. Break pretzels into a large container. Pour/spoon some marinade on pretzels; stir. Repeat until all marinade is used. Let pretzels sit at least 1 day to marinate.

Appetizers, Snacks and Beverages

Salmon Dill Sauce

2 Tbsp. butter or margarine
¼ tsp. dill
1 clove garlic, chopped

¼ cup sour cream
3 Tbsp. Dijon mustard
2 tsp. lemon juice

Melt together butter or margarine, dill, and chopped garlic. Stir in remaining ingredients. Serve immediately, or chill until ready to serve.

"When you have received Him, stir up your heart to do Him homage; speak to Him about your spiritual life, gazing upon Him in your soul where He is present for your happiness; welcome Him as warmly as possible, and behave outwardly in such a way that your actions may give proof to all of His Presence."
~St. Francis de Sales

"Who is Jesus to me? Jesus is the Word made Flesh. Jesus is the Bread of Life. Jesus is the Victim offered for our sins on the cross. Jesus is the sacrifice offered at holy Mass for the sins of the world and for mine. Jesus is the Word - to be spoken. Jesus is the Truth - to be told. Jesus is the Way - to be walked. Jesus is the Light - to be lit. Jesus is the Life - to be lived. Jesus is the Love - to be loved."
~Blessed Teresa of Calcutta

Soups & Salads

"When we say grace, do we look up at Heaven, or down at the food?"

SOUPS AND SALADS INDEX

Black Bean & Corn Salad......39
Broccoli Orange Salad......38
Broccoli Salad......38
Chicken Noodle Soup......30
Colorful Fresh Vegetable Salad......35
Crab Bisque......32
Crunchy Asian Salad......41
Cucumber and Onion Salad......34
DeSales Dinner Salad......37
Easy Fruit Salad......44
Easy Vegetable Soup......17
Grape Salad......46
Great Greek Salad......32
Irish Potato Soup......23
Mandarin Salad......44
Neumann's Philly Cheese Steak Salad......43
Overnight Salad......46

Pennsylvania-Dutch Cucumbers & Dressing 34
Polish Black-Eyed Pea Soup...... 25
Polish Sausage Soup...... 27
Ramen Noodle Salad...... 41
Rotini Salad...... 40
Seven-Layer Salad...... 35
Shrimp Bisque...... 31
Southwest Bean & Corn Salad...... 39
Spinach Salad...... 33
Spaghetti Salad...... 40
Spinach Salad...... 33
St. Peter's Lentil Soup...... 21
Strawberry Pretzel Salad. 45
Strawberry Spinach Salad 33
Tortellini Soup...... 29
Tortellini Spinach Salad... 40
Turkey Tortellini Soup...... 30
Vegetable Soup...... 19

Soups and Salads

Easy Vegetable Soup

1 lb. ground beef
1 cup diced onion
1 (16 oz.) can tomatoes
1 (15 oz.) can tomato sauce
1 cup sliced celery
2 cups water
2 cloves garlic, minced
5 tsp. beef bouillon granules
1 Tbsp. dried parsley
½ tsp. oregano*
½ tsp. sweet basil*
¼ tsp. black pepper*
1 tsp. salt*
1 cup frozen or fresh green beans
½ cup frozen or fresh corn

½-1 cup small shaped pasta *(Ditalini is my favorite, but sometimes hard to find. Pastina is also good. If all else fails, use elbow macaroni!)*
1 (15 oz.) can red kidney beans, undrained (optional)
2 cups shredded cabbage (optional)

*Sometimes I will use 2 tablespoons of **Sun of Italy Italian Spice Mix** instead of these four ingredients.

Brown the beef or boil it in a cup. *(I think boiling it keeps it softer.)* Drain the cooked beef, and add all the ingredients except green beans and corn (and cabbage, if using). Bring to a boil and simmer for 20 minutes; then add the green beans, corn (and cabbage). For a thinner soup, add water and salt and pepper to taste.

Cook pasta separately according to package directions. *(I personally do not add pasta to soup. I put it in individual soup bowls and add the soup to it so that it doesn't soak up all the broth in the pan.)*

Add grated Italian cheese on top of soup serving; add a loaf of bread, and *Mangia!*

Our Lady of Sorrows ~ September 15

The Seven Sorrows of Mary:

1. The prophecy of Simeon *(Luke 2:25-35)*
2. The flight into Egypt *(Matthew 2:13-15)*
3. Loss of the Child Jesus for three days *(Luke 2:41-50)*
4. Mary meets Jesus on his way to Calvary *(Luke 23:27-31; John 19:17)*
5. Crucifixion and Death of Jesus *(John 19:25-30)*
6. The body of Jesus being taken from the Cross *(Psalm 130; Luke 23:50-54; John 19:31-37)*
7. The burial of Jesus *(Isaiah 53:8; Luke 23:50-56; John 19:38-42; Mark 15:40-47)*

Soups and Salads

Vegetable Soup

Good for Fridays or abstaining on a special day as a sacrifice for Jesus! As you make this soup, there are 7 ingredients you place in the liquid – the onion, garlic, tomatoes, beans, spinach, carrots, and mushrooms. As you place the ingredients in the pot, you might want to think about each suffering Mary went through.

1 medium onion, chopped
2 cloves garlic, minced
1 tsp. olive oil
6 cups water
1 (28 oz.) can diced tomatoes, undrained
1 (14 oz.) can kidney beans, drained and rinsed
½ (10 oz.) pkg. frozen spinach

1 ½ cups baby carrots
1 cup fresh mushrooms, sliced
½ cup tomato basil rice
1 tsp. basil
½ tsp. oregano
½ tsp. salt
¼ tsp. black pepper

In a 4-quart saucepan, cook onion and garlic in oil until tender. Add remaining ingredients. Bring to a boil. Reduce heat to low; cover and simmer 45 to 50 minutes, stirring occasionally. *Makes ten 1-cup servings.*

"Behold, this child is destined for the fall and rise of many in Israel, and to be a sign that will be contradicted (and you yourself a sword will pierce) so that the thoughts of many hearts may be revealed." Luke 2:34b-35

St. Peter Damian (1007-1072)
Feast Day ~ February 21

St. Peter Damian was an orphan who had a mean brother that didn't take very good care of him. Another brother who was archpriest of Ravenna loved Peter and had Peter come live with him. Peter was an extraordinary boy and would offer up all kinds of discomforts for God. He wore a hairy, itchy shirt under his top; he wouldn't eat any treats and spent hours and hours praying to God. He joined the Benedictines and lived with another monk in a little hermitage. There he prayed and fasted so much that he hardly ever slept. This wasn't good for him and soon Peter became sick. He realized that he couldn't help others if he was too sick to pray, so he started taking better care of himself. The abbot died, and Peter took his place. He founded five hermitages and was known throughout as a peacekeeper. The Holy See called on him many times to settle disputes. He encouraged priests to pray and to live a life of poverty. He wrote many letters, some of which we still have today. Peter was declared a Doctor of the Church in 1828.

What could you do this week to encourage your family to pray more? Imitate St. Peter Damian and start a prayer-fest in your house. It doesn't have to be long but gather everyone together and say a special prayer before you eat and then have everyone tell God how much they love Him. Organize this for the whole week and be an encourager. Help your little brothers and sisters to pray too.

St. Peter's Lentil Soup

1 large onion, diced
3-4 carrots, shredded (or thinly sliced, optional)
1-2 cloves garlic, diced
Salt and pepper and Italian seasoning to taste

¼-½ cup sherry (or other alcoholic drink for cooking)
1 bag dry lentils
2 boxes vegetable broth/stock
Sour cream, apple cider vinegar (optional)

Prepare a day or two in advance by soaking lentils, changing out the water as needed (at least once a day) to allow the beans to sprout. You will know you have achieved your goal when you see tiny "tails" on the beans. *(I place my colander in a large bowl as it makes it easier to lift out the beans, dump out the water, and refill with fresh water).* Sprouted beans are nutritional powerhouses compared to their unsprouted counterparts.

When ready to make the soup, sauté onions in olive oil with salt to taste until translucent. Add garlic, and continue to cook for a minute; add sherry and shredded carrots. Allow the vegetables to steam in the sherry as it cooks down. Before it is all gone, add broth/stock and drained lentils. Bring to a boil; carefully skim foam that results. Reduce heat and let simmer until beans are tender, roughly 30 minutes or so. Use a stick blender in the pot to purée soup to desired degree. *(Could use a regular blender, too.)* Can simmer further for thicker texture, if desired. Serve with sour cream or apple cider vinegar to taste. *Makes 8 to 10 servings; add bread and salad for a complete simple supper.*

Can use this same process to make split pea soup, by replacing the type of bean (no need to presoak split peas since they can't sprout) and type of broth/stock, if desired.

❧ *"Most important of all, pray to God to set your feet in the path of truth."* Sir. 37:15

St. Patrick (385-461)
Feast Day ~ March 17

As a youth, Patrick was captured and taken to Ireland as a slave. He could have become bitter as the best years of his life were taken from him, but he used this time to come closer to God. One night, six years after he was taken captive, Patrick had a dream. It was revealed to him that he should go to the shore and escape in a boat. Free at last, Patrick wanted to become a priest. After many years of studying, Patrick asked to go back to Ireland, a very bold thing to do especially since Ireland was a pagan country. He wanted the people who had treated him so poorly to know God and love Him as he did. Patrick became bishop and was sent to Ireland. He encountered much danger but God protected him, and his sermons converted thousands. Whole villages would come to hear him speak. After 40 years of loving the Irish people, Patrick had converted Ireland into a Christian country. He performed many miracles and the people to this day revere him. He died in 461. Everyone is Irish on St. Patrick's Day!

Patrick gave up his life to do what God wanted. Pray this week that you follow God's plan for your life and not what you always want to do. Turn the TV off when you want to watch a show and spend some time praying to God. Go get a book on the saints and read it!

Irish Potato Soup

1 gallon water
2 ½ lbs. potatoes
1 Tbsp. chicken stock base
Salt and pepper to taste
2 (11 oz.) cans concentrated
   Cheddar cheese soup

1 lb. butter or margarine
1 ½ cups flour
2 cups half-and-half
Chives, bacon bits, and parsley

Bring water to boil in large pot. Add potatoes to water along with chicken stock base, salt and pepper. Cook 12 minutes, or until potatoes are about half-done. Add Cheddar cheese soup, and simmer 10 minutes.

Melt butter or margarine in a heavy saucepan. Add flour, and cook over medium heat, stirring constantly, for 3 to 4 minutes. Do not brown. Whisk flour mixture into the potato mixture and bring to a boil. Reduce heat and simmer an additional 3 to 4 minutes. Stir in half-and-half, and heat to serving temperature. Do not boil. Serve with chives, bacon bits, and parsley.

"As a result, those who suffer in accord with God's will hand their souls over to a faithful creator as they do good". 1Pet. 4:19

"For God did not give us a spirit of cowardice but rather of power and love and self-control." 2Tim. 1:7

Soups and Salads 23

St. Maria Faustina Kowalska (1905-1938)
Feast Day ~ October 5

Having nine brothers and sisters, Elena grew up in Warsaw, Poland. She only went to three years of school and then became a servant helping other families. She wanted to become a nun but was rejected several times. Finally, the Congregation of the Sisters of Our Lady of Mercy accepted her and she changed her name to Sister Maria Faustina of the Most Blessed Sacrament. There she answered the door, cooked for the sisters, and helped in the convent garden. No one knew the depths of her spirituality. She had visions and was blessed with the gift of prophecy. She also bore the invisible stigmata and suffered with Jesus. She is the nun who is responsible for having the Divine Mercy painting of Jesus with the red and white rays flowing out from Him. She kept a diary of over 700 pages, which is published now. What a joy to be able to read what Jesus said to her! The first Sunday after Easter is now designated **Divine Mercy Sunday** and a beautiful Novena to Jesus is said beginning on Good Friday every year to help us learn to trust in His mercy. We also have a Chaplet of Divine Mercy that can be said every day especially at **3 PM** to remind us of our God of Infinite Mercy.* Faustina died of tuberculosis in 1938, thirteen years after becoming a nun. She was declared a saint in 2000.

*See page 291.

What will you do this week to show Jesus you trust in His Mercy? Learn the Chaplet of Divine Mercy on pg. 291 or say, "Jesus I trust in you" everyday.

Polish Black-Eyed Pea Soup

1 Tbsp. olive oil
1 onion, chopped
½ lb. kielbasa, chopped
2 cans black-eyed peas, drained
1 can Navy beans, drained

1 cup brown rice, cooked
2 (14 oz.) cans chicken broth
1 tsp. garlic powder
½ tsp. cayenne pepper
½ tsp. thyme
Salt and pepper to taste

In a soup pot, heat oil over medium-high heat. Add onion and cook until translucent. Add kielbasa, peas, beans, rice, broth, and seasonings. Stir well to blend, and heat. Mash beans slightly to help thicken soup. Serve when hot.

I serve this with a salad and corn muffins.

"Souls have time for everything, but they have no time to come to come to Me for graces."
Jesus speaking to St. Faustina. Divine Mercy Diary (367)

"My daughter, just as you prepare in My presence, so also you make your confession before Me. The person of the priest is, for Me, only a screen. Never analyze what sort of a priest it is that I am making use of; open your soul in confession as you would to Me, and I will fill it with My light." Divine Mercy Diary (1725)

"But God, who is rich in mercy, because of the great love he had for us." Eph. 2:4

Soups and Salads

St. Maximilian Kolbe (1894-1941) *Martyr*
Feast Day ~ August 14

Raymond (Maximilian) grew up in Poland under the Russians with loving parents who were both Third Order Franciscans. They were weavers and also ran a religious bookstore. He was poor and got into trouble since he was a mischievous and wild child. When he was 12 years old, he received a vision of the Blessed Mother and his life changed. She appeared before him holding two crowns. One was red, the other white. The white one was for Raymond to be pure and the red one was for him to be a martyr. He had a choice; but he chose both crowns.

He attended the Franciscan junior seminary and loved math and physics. He wanted to join the military but listened to God and became a priest. He took the name Maximilian and became a priest at the age of 24. He had a tremendous devotion to the Blessed Mother and worked hard to spread devotion to sinners and to combat Freemasonry, which was very anti-Catholic. He went to Japan and started a magazine. A monastery that he founded actually survived a nuclear bomb. He came down with tuberculosis, which left his body weak for the rest of his life. However, sickness did not stop him.

He spread the love of the Blessed Mother everywhere he went. When the Nazis invaded Poland, he was arrested for 3 months and released. A few months later, he was arrested for publishing anti-Nazi material. While in the concentration camp, he received very harsh beatings and heavy work. He was beaten so badly that he was left for dead. The other prisoners smuggled him into the hospital where he heard confession until he recovered. He said Mass for the men and joyfully bore his sufferings. A man escaped one day and as punishment the Nazis killed 10 men for each man that escaped. A young father with 3 children was chosen to die, and he was crying that he had a wife and kids to care for. Maximilian offered to take his place and the guards consented. He died in Auschwitz joyfully giving his life to God.

Gather some flowers from your garden and go to church and place them in front of the Blessed Mother. Pray to her that she will always keep you in her mantle of love.

Polish Sausage Soup

2 Tbsp. butter or margarine
1 lb. kielbasa, sliced
1 cup chopped fresh onion
2 cups chopped celery and leaves
4 cups shredded white cabbage
2 cups sliced pared carrots
1 bay leaf
½ tsp. dried leaf thyme
2 Tbsp. vinegar
1 Tbsp. salt
1 ½ cups beef bouillon
5 cups water *(I usually put in a little more)*
3 cups cubed pared potatoes

Sauté the kielbasa, onion, and celery in the butter in a large kettle; cook until onion and celery are tender. Add remaining ingredients. Cover and cook 1 ½ hours or a little longer.

"If angels could be jealous of men, they would be so for one reason: Holy Communion." ~St. Maximilian Kolbe

St. Gemma Galgani (1878-1903)
Feast Day ~ April 11

Gemma was born in Italy to very devout parents. When she was 3 years old, her mother became ill and eventually died after a long illness. Gemma, who had learned to pray and enjoyed talking to her mother about God, was very sad. As she grew older, she went to daily Mass and tried to help out. She was loved by everyone and did well in school, but had to quit due to poor health. She prayed to the Venerable Gabriel Possenti, who later became a saint, and was cured.

Gemma received many graces as she grew. She would be given a warning that she was about to receive an unusual grace, and then it happened. Gemma received the stigmata, the marks of Jesus on her hands, feet and heart. She would bleed every Thursday evening, and by Saturday morning, all would be well. This went on for the rest of her life, except the last three years, when she was told by her spiritual director not to accept them. The scars still remained. God spoke to Gemma often and she had the wonderful privilege of being able to see her Guardian Angel. She would sit and talk with her angel and sent her angel to do errands, mostly to deliver a message to her spiritual director. She died when she was 25 from tuberculosis. Though she suffered much pain, she died with a big smile so it was hard for people to think she was dead.

This week name your Guardian Angel and then talk with your angel. You have a special angel assigned just to you by God. What will you do with your angel this week to put a smile on everyone's face?

Tortellini Soup

2 Tbsp. olive oil
2 or 3 cloves garlic, minced
1 (49 oz.) can chicken broth
1 (15 oz.) can stewed tomatoes (Italian flavored)
1 (10 oz.) pkg. frozen chopped spinach, thawed and well drained
1 (19 oz.) pkg. frozen cheese tortellini
Parmesan cheese, grated (optional)

Heat oil in a medium soup kettle. Add garlic and sauté lightly. Add broth, tomatoes, spinach, and tortellini. Simmer for 20 to 30 minutes. Add more broth if soup is too thick. Serve with Parmesan cheese on top.

Serve with a salad and fresh Italian bread. Great for Lent.

"There is a school in Heaven, and there one has only to learn how to love. The school is in the Cenacle; the Teacher is Jesus; the matter taught is His Flesh and His Blood." ~St. Gemma Galani

Turkey Tortellini Soup

1 lb. ground turkey, browned and drained
1 (10 ¾ oz.) can Campbell's French Onion soup
1 (28 oz.) can diced tomatoes, undrained
4 cups water
2 tsp. dried basil
1 cup frozen green beans
1 ½ cups frozen or dry cheese tortellini

Brown turkey in a large soup pan and drain. Add rest of ingredients and cook until green beans and tortellini are tender, about 20 minutes. Add water or tomato juice if soup gets too thick. If desired, sprinkle with Parmesan cheese while serving.

Chicken Noodle Soup

3-4 chicken breasts
4 whole carrots (slice and peel)
1 medium whole onion
4 stalks whole celery
7 or more squirts of Maggi seasoning (liquid spice found in the imported foods section of the grocery store – it looks very similar to Kitchen Bouquet seasoning for gravy)
Knorr chicken bouillon (diluted as per package instructions)
1 or 2 bags of Kluski noodles *(Tastes like Grandma's! I usually use 2 bags as I make 36 cups. Freezes well.)*

In a large pot of water, place chicken, whole carrots, whole onion, and whole celery stalks; boil until chicken is done, approximately 20 minutes. Discard the onion and celery, but save the broth and measure the amount left. Add enough water to the broth to make at least 24 to 36 cups liquid. Add correct amount of chicken bouillon necessary to make 2 cups chicken broth per bouillon cube *(Knorr brand is different dilution – it's just a personal preference!)* If you use a regular chicken bouillon cube, it is 1:1 ratio of water to cube!

Bring broth to a boil and cook noodles according to the package instructions. While the noodles are cooking, cut up the cooked chicken in nice bite-size pieces and peel and slice the carrots. Once the noodles are cooked to perfection, add the carrots, chicken, Maggi seasoning, salt and pepper.

My family loves this soup with cornbread or French baguette! Truthfully, the Maggi seasoning is the trick to making this recipe different from other chicken soups! ☺

Shrimp Bisque

1 ½ lbs. steamed spiced shrimp, peeled
2 (10 ¾ oz.) cans cream of celery soup
4 oz. sliced mushrooms (canned or in jar)
½ cup chopped onion
2 Tbsp. butter or margarine
1 cup heavy cream *(I use half-and-half)*
1 Tbsp. Worcestershire sauce
1 tsp. paprika
1 ½ soup cans of milk
¼ tsp. pepper
Dash salt

The Seafood Department at most grocery stores will steam shrimp upon request. Since I live in Maryland, and Old Bay seasoning and J. O. Spice are popular seafood spices, I ask them to spice the shrimp <u>moderately</u> before placing in the steamer! The kids can help with all the peeling at home, provided they don't help themselves to too much of the shrimp. Shrimp will be added to the soup close to serving time so they are not rubbery. You may want to cut them in half or thirds.

In a large pot, sauté mushrooms and onions in butter or margarine until onions are translucent. Add remaining ingredients, except shrimp, and cook on medium-low heat, stirring frequently until you can tell that it is heated thoroughly. (Do not bring to boil – it will scorch.) Turn burner off or on very low heat and allow bisque to steep for a while with lid on it. Add shrimp and stir so that the spice from the shrimp can blend well for a few minutes. Serve with salad, sandwiches, or before the main dish! Makes 10 servings.

Crab Bisque

3 cans tomato bisque soup
2 cans split pea soup
5 soup cans of milk <u>or</u> water <u>or</u> part milk and part water

12-16 oz. crabmeat
½ cup sherry (optional)
3 Tbsp. seafood seasoning (such as Old Bay)

Gradually stir milk and/or water into canned soup. Add crabmeat, seafood seasoning, and sherry if desired. Heat slowly over low heat, stirring frequently, until bisque is very hot. Crab bisque may be prepared in a crockery cooker for 2 to 4 hours on low heat. *Makes 12 servings.*

Great Greek Salad

Salad:
1 head romaine lettuce, cut to bite size
½ red onion, sliced
Tomatoes, cucumber (peeled and sliced), and black olives, as desired
¼ cup crumbled feta

Dressing:
3 Tbsp. red wine vinegar
3 Tbsp. olive oil
¼ tsp. salt
¼ tsp. pepper
1 clove garlic, diced or pressed

Toss the romaine, onion, tomatoes, cucumber, and olives. Combine all ingredients for the dressing in a small bowl, then toss into the salad. Top with feta cheese. *Makes 4 to 6 servings.*

☙ *"Oh, how fortunate you shall be to be able to receive every day this divine Sacrament, to hold this God of Love in your hands and place Him in your own heart!"* ~St. Margaret Mary

Spinach Salad

1 head iceberg lettuce
1 pkg. fresh spinach
2 cans mandarin oranges
1 can cashew nuts

Dressing:
⅓ cup sugar
⅓ cup vinegar
1 cup oil
1 tsp. salt
1 tsp. garlic salt
1 tsp. celery salt

Beat dressing ingredients thoroughly with electric beater. Store in refrigerator while combining salad ingredients. Pour dressing as desired over salad ingredients. *Makes 6 to 8 servings.*

Strawberry Spinach Salad

I always serve this salad at the Teacher's Appreciation Luncheon. Teachers and parents always want the recipe! It's easy to make and serve, and presents very nicely!

Salad:
1 lb. fresh spinach
1 Tbsp. dill or 1 tsp. dried dill
1 tsp. sesame seed
1 pint strawberries, hulled and sliced thin

Dressing:
½ cup Canola oil (or any vegetable oil)
¼ cup red wine vinegar
¼ cup sugar
¼ tsp. each of garlic powder, onion powder, salt, pepper, and dry mustard.

Mix salad dressing ingredients together in a small bowl. Toss spinach with dill, sesame, and strawberries; then toss with salad dressing. *Makes about 10 to 12 servings.*

☙ "The flesh feeds on the Body and Blood of Christ that the soul may be fattened on God." ~Tertullian (c. 200)

Cucumber & Onion Salad

Cucumbers, peeled
Onions

Vinegar Dressing:
1 cup vinegar
4 cups sugar
4 cups water
Salt and pepper

Slice several peeled cucumbers and onions very thin. Place in large bowl and cover with salted ice water. Soak for at least 2 hours. Drain excess liquid. Cover with vinegar dressing. Let marinate for 2 hours or longer before serving.

Vinegar Dressing: In saucepan mix all ingredients and bring to a boil over medium heat. Reduce heat and simmer for 1 to 2 minutes. Let cool and pour over cucumber and onion mixture.

Pennsylvania-Dutch Cucumbers & Dressing

Cucumbers
Onions
Salt

Dressing:
¼ cup white vinegar
½ cup sugar
1 cup water

Slice cucumbers and onions thinly. Sprinkle lightly with salt, and refrigerate while making dressing.

Combine dressing ingredients and pour over vegetable mixture. Refrigerate until served.

"Trust all things to Jesus in the Blessed Sacrament and to Mary Help of Christians and you will see what miracles are."
~St. John Bosco

Colorful Fresh Vegetable Salad

3 cups thinly sliced cucumbers
¾ cup chopped red onion
½ cup **each** chopped green, sweet red and yellow peppers

½ cup cider vinegar
2 Tbsp. sugar

In a large serving bowl, combine cucumbers, onion, and peppers. In a small bowl, whisk vinegar and sugar. Pour over vegetables; toss to coat. Chill until serving. Serve with a slotted spoon. *Makes 6 servings.*

Seven-Layer Salad

Use a 9x13-inch dish or pan.

1st Layer – Cut/tear 1 head of iceberg lettuce into dish or pan.
2nd Layer – 1 cup diced celery
3rd Layer – 4 to 5 hard-boiled eggs, sliced
4th Layer – 1 (10 oz.) pkg. uncooked frozen peas, thawed
5th Layer – ½ cup chopped green pepper and
  ½ cup chopped onion
6th Layer – 2 cups Miracle Whip mixed with
  2 Tbsp. sugar
7th Layer – 4 to 8 oz. shredded Cheddar cheese, and
  8 slices of bacon, fried and crumbled (or bacon bits)

Put all ingredients on top of each other in order of layers. Cover salad with foil and refrigerate **at least 12 hours**. Keeps 2 to 3 days.

St. Francis de Sales (1567-1622)
Feast Day ~ January 24

Francis became a lawyer at his father's insistence, but he convinced his father that he wanted to be a priest. He was placed in the Diocese of Geneva, Switzerland, which had mostly people who were Calvinists. There he preached and wrote pamphlets explaining the Church doctrine and distributed them with great success. He became bishop of Geneva at age 35 and spent his days preaching, hearing confessions and teaching the Faith to children. Though he had a temper that took him many years to control, he is better known for his gentleness and ability to preach, and he won many hearts to Christ. He believed, "A spoonful of honey attracts more flies than a barrelful of vinegar."

His famous books, **Introduction to the Devout Life** and **A Treatise on the Love of God**, were just part of his massive writings as he corresponded with many. He is known as the patron of the Catholic press. He also worked with St. Jane Frances de Chantal to establish the Sisters of the Visitation.

Try being extra kind this week. When you want to get mad think of Jesus and how He suffered and died so that the gates of heaven could be opened for you. Instead of yelling and losing your temper count to ten and take a deep breath. Then calmly ask the person your question.

DeSales Dinner Salad

3 Tbsp. nonfat plain yogurt
3 Tbsp. reduced-fat mayonnaise
2 Tbsp. lemon juice
2 Tbsp. chopped fresh mint
1 clove garlic, minced
1 tsp. honey
½ tsp. salt
1 medium zucchini, finely diced (about 2 cups)
1 large red bell pepper, finely diced (about 1 ½ cups)
1 bunch radishes, finely diced (about ½ cup)
1 (15 oz.) can chickpeas, rinsed
8 large Boston lettuce leaves, for serving

Whisk yogurt, mayonnaise, lemon juice, mint, garlic, honey, and salt in a small bowl until creamy. Toss zucchini, bell pepper, radishes, and chickpeas in a large bowl. Pour the dressing over the vegetables; toss gently. Spoon into lettuce leaves for cups and serve. *Makes 4 main-course servings or 8 side salads.*

"Give up your anger, abandon your wrath; do not be provoked; it brings only harm." Ps. 37:8

"When the bee has gathered the dew of heaven and the earth's sweetest nectar from the flowers, it turns it into honey, then hastens to its hive. In the same way, the priest, having taken from the altar the Son of God (who is as the dew from heaven, and true son of Mary, flower of our humanity), gives him to you as delicious food." ~St. Francis de Sales

Broccoli Salad

1 large head of broccoli, chopped
1 lb. bacon, cooked crisp and crumbled
1 cup sunflower seeds
1 cup golden raisins
1 small red onion, chopped

Dressing:
1 cup mayonnaise
2-4 Tbsp. sugar
2 Tbsp. white or apple cider vinegar

Mix broccoli, bacon, sunflower seeds, raisins, and onion in a large bowl. Mix mayonnaise, 2 tablespoons sugar, and vinegar in a small bowl. Add remaining sugar to taste. Stir dressing into salad right before serving.

Broccoli Orange Salad

4 cups fresh broccoli florets, cut up *(about 1 ½ lbs.)*
1 small red onion, thinly sliced and separated into rings *(I cut the rings in halves or quarters)*
½ cup raisins *(I use some Craisins, regular raisins, and white raisins)*
½ cup pecan pieces, toasted *(single layer on baking sheet at 400° for 2 ½ to 3 minutes)*
1 (11 oz.) can mandarin oranges, drained
¾ cup Hellmann's mayonnaise *(can use light)*
¼ cup granulated sugar
1 ½ Tbsp. white vinegar *(I use Tarragon vinegar)*

Combine broccoli, onion, raisins, and pecans. Set aside.

Mix dressing ingredients (mayonnaise, granulated sugar, and vinegar) until smooth. Pour dressing over broccoli, onion, raisin, nut mixture. Combine. Add mandarin oranges and mix **gently**.

Refrigerate **at least** 3 hours or can make day ahead. Holds well for several days.

Black Bean & Corn Salad

3 (15 oz.) cans black beans, rinsed and drained
10 oz. frozen corn, thawed
1 large sweet red pepper, chopped
½ sweet red onion, chopped
⅓ cup chopped fresh parsley

Dressing:
⅓ cup red wine vinegar
⅓ cup olive oil
½ tsp. pepper
3 cloves garlic, chopped

Combine beans, corn, pepper, and onion. Top with dressing. Stir in parsley.

Southwest Bean & Corn Salad

½ cup reduced-fat Ranch dressing
¼ tsp. hot pepper sauce
1 (10 oz.) bag mixed salad greens
1 (15 oz.) can black beans, rinsed and drained
1 (10 oz.) pkg. frozen whole kernel corn, thawed and drained
½ cup red pepper strips
¼ cup finely chopped red onions
½ cup 2% milk reduced-fat shredded Cheddar cheese

Mix dressing and hot pepper sauce; set aside. Toss greens with beans, corn, red pepper, and onions in 3-quart serving bowl. Add dressing mixture; toss to coat. Sprinkle with cheese.

"O Lord, we cannot go to the pool of Siloe to which you sent the blind man. But we have the chalice of Your Precious Blood, filled with life and light." ~St. Ephrem

Spaghetti Salad

1 lb. spaghetti, cooked
1 (8 oz.) bottle Italian salad dressing
1 jar Salad Supreme seasoning
4 small tomatoes, chopped
1 large green pepper, chopped
1 cup chopped vegetables (broccoli, cauliflower, or carrots)

Cook and drain noodles. Marinate in dressing overnight. Add rest of ingredients.

Tortellini Spinach Salad

2 (9 oz.) pkgs. three-cheese tortellini, cooked according to package directions
1 ½ cups chopped fresh baby spinach leaves
1 (4 oz.) pkg. crumbled feta cheese
½ small red onion, finely chopped
1 envelope Good Seasons Italian salad dressing, prepared using less oil than directions

Combine all ingredients; cover. Refrigerate several hours or until chilled. *Makes eight 1-cup servings.*

Note: Don't add spinach or feta cheese when tortellini is hot because they will wilt/melt.

Rotini Salad

1 (12 oz.) box tricolor rotini
1 (16 oz.) bottle Greek-style salad dressing
8 oz. feta cheese
1 pint grape tomatoes
1 cucumber, chopped
1 cup chopped black olives

Cook rotini until done; drain and cool slightly. Add rest of ingredients; chill and serve.

Ramen Noodle Salad

1 lb. coleslaw mix
1 pkg. ramen oriental noodles (chicken flavor), uncooked
3 oz. slivered almonds
¼ cup sunflower seeds
¼ cup chopped green onions
½ cup oil
¼ cup vinegar
2 Tbsp. sugar

In small bowl, mix oil, sugar, and flavor packet from ramen noodles; set aside. Combine remaining ingredients, breaking noodles in large bowl. Right before serving, mix oil mixture in large bowl with coleslaw mixture. Serve.

Crunchy Asian Salad

2 heads romaine lettuce
Broccoli florets (optional)

Dressing:
1 cup salad oil
½ cup cider vinegar
3 Tbsp. soy sauce
Sugar to taste – up to ¾ cup

Topping:
1 stick butter
2 bags crushed ramen noodles (You can really get your frustration out smashing these, but be careful not to break the bag! Discard the flavor packet or save for another use.)
½-¾ cup sliced almonds
½-¾ cup raw sunflower seeds

Brown noodles, almonds, and sunflower seeds together in butter. Place on top of lettuce and broccoli. Add salad dressing to taste.

When I am not making this for a party, I usually keep the dressing refrigerated in a container that I can shake to mix whenever I need to use it. It doesn't spoil quickly. When I want to use some, I put the mixture in the microwave for 20 seconds or so to warm it up so that I can spoon easily. ☺

St. John Neumann
Feast Day ~ January 5 (1811-1860)

Born in the Czech Republic, John studied in Prague and came to New York at age 25 where he became a priest. He lived there for 4 years doing missionary work until he joined the Redemptorists. His missionary work continued as he traveled to Maryland, Virginia and Ohio. The German people loved him, and at age 41, he became bishop of Philadelphia where he organized the Catholic school system into a diocesan system. The school system thrived and saw an increase – 20 times the number of students it previously had enrolled. Known for his organizational ability, John was the first American bishop to be beatified. His body is buried in Philadelphia at St. Peter the Apostle Church.

What could you do this week to organize something at your school? Ask your teachers if they could use your help to clean up your classroom. If you are home-schooled, what a great opportunity to help mom or dad with straightening up your study area!

Neumann's Philly Cheese Steak Salad

16 oz. flank steak
1 green bell pepper
1 large onion, chopped
1 (8 oz.) bottle Italian dressing

8 oz. shredded Provolone cheese
1 head iceberg lettuce
4 tomatoes quartered
1 bottle Ranch dressing (if desired)

In a covered dish, marinate the steak, peppers, and onions by pouring Italian dressing over all. Cover and refrigerate for at least 20 minutes.

In a large skillet, cook over medium-high heat the sliced steak, peppers, and onions until vegetables are tender and steak is done. Toss in tomatoes and sprinkle cheese on top of mixture.

Arrange salad on plates and pour meat mixture onto the lettuce. *Eat and enjoy!*

"Jesus has prepared not just one Host, but one for everyday of our life. The Hosts for us are ready. Let us not forfeit even one of them." ~St. Peter Julian Eymard

Mandarin Salad

1 head green leaf lettuce
1 cup chopped green onions
1 large can mandarin oranges
½ cup slivered almonds *(brown for 20 minutes at 350°)*

Dressing:
2 Tbsp. sugar
1 ½ tsp. salt
2 Tbsp. tarragon vinegar
Dash hot sauce
¼ cup oil

Toss the lettuce, onions, and oranges. Prepare dressing. Right before serving, add dressing and almonds.

Easy Fruit Salad

I usually cut up any fresh fruit – strawberries, blueberries, etc. I don't add bananas or apples until I am ready to serve it, as they tend to get brown.

When I am ready to serve the fruit, I mix in about 3 ounces of vanilla yogurt per serving. Sprinkle with cinnamon and slivered almonds, and you have a tasty good-for-you treat!

"In Cana of Galilee Christ changed water into wine, and shall we think Him less worthy of credit when He changes wine into His Blood?" ~St. Cyril of Jerusalem

Strawberry Pretzel Salad

This has been a family favorite in our home for many years!

2 cups crushed pretzels *(not too fine)*
¾ cup melted margarine
3 Tbsp. sugar
8 oz. cream cheese, softened
8 oz. Cool Whip

1 cup sugar
2 (3 oz.) pkgs. strawberry Jell-O (or one 6-oz. pkg.)
2 cups boiling water
2 (10 oz.) pkgs. frozen strawberries *(I use Birdseye brand)*

Combine crushed pretzels, melted margarine, and 3 tablespoons sugar; form a crust in a 9x13-inch pan. Bake at 400° for about 9 to 10 minutes, and then cool.

Next, blend the softened cream cheese with 1 cup of sugar. Fold in the Cool Whip. Spread this over the cooled crust. *(I place the pretzel crust with the cream cheese mixture in the fridge while making the Jell-O.)*

Dissolve the Jell-O in the boiling water; stir until well dissolved. Stir in the frozen strawberries. Refrigerate the Jell-O mixture for just 10 minutes. Remove from refrigerator and carefully pour Jell-O over the cream cheese mixture. (*Pour slowly or get splashed!* Refrigerate until set.)

"When we go before the Blessed Sacrament, let us open our heart; our good God will open His. We shall go to Him; He will come to us; the one to ask, the other to receive. It will be like a breath from one to the other." ~St. John Vianney

Overnight Salad

1 head iceberg lettuce
1 onion, sliced
1 10 oz. bag frozen peas
1 can sliced water chestnuts
½ lb. cooked bacon
Parmesan cheese

Dressing:
1 cup sour cream
¼ cup sugar
1 cup mayo
1 Tbsp. vinegar

Pull apart head of lettuce and wash. Pat dry. In large bowl layer lettuce, onion slices, peas, bacon and water chestnuts. Combine dressing ingredients and drizzle over salad half way through layering and again when you are finished. Sprinkle with Parmesan cheese and refrigerate overnight.
Great for a family get together as you prepare it before hand and it's ready to go!

Grape Salad

4 lbs. grapes *(2 lbs red 2 lbs, green)*
2 (8oz.) pkgs. cream cheese, softened

¼ cup sour cream
¼ cup sugar
1 cup brown sugar
1 cup crushed pecans

Wash and pat grapes dry or the salad will be runny. Mix cream cheese, sour cream and sugar, combine mixture with grapes in a 9x13 pan. Sprinkle brown sugar over the mixture and then the crushed pecans. Cover and refrigerate overnight.

"Like the sick who expose their diseased bodies to the healing rays of the sun, expose miseries, no matter what they are, to the beams of light streaming forth from the Sacred Host," ~from "The Holy Eucharist", ~Jose Guadalupe Trevino

Bread & Breakfast

"Mmm! Your eggs Benedict look good, Daddy! Were they named after the Pope?"

BREAD AND BREAKFAST INDEX

Absolutely Incredible Muffins 54
All-Bran Muffins 54
Angel Pumpkin Muffins 53
Banana Nut Bread 51
Banana Nut Muffins 51
Bannock Bread 49
Blueberry Muffins 55
Breakfast Casserole 60
Christmas Morning Breakfast 60

Croissant French Toast.... 57
Egg Casserole 59
Egg Lasagna 61
Herb Rolls 50
Overnight Eggs 61
St. Gerard's Delicious Dough for Shaping 48
Sticky Buns 55
Versatile Egg Casserole .. 58
Zucchini Bread (In a Can) 50

Bread and Breakfast

St. Gerard Majella (1726-1755)
Feast Day ~ October 16

Born in Italy, Gerard was a sickly child and was baptized immediately. His family was poor but they were very devout. Gerard would come home from praying at church when he was five with a loaf of bread. His mother asked him where he got the bread, and Gerard would say "a most beautiful boy" gave it to me. His sister followed him to church one day and saw Jesus come down from Mary's arms and hand her brother a loaf of bread. Gerard longed to receive Jesus, and when he was eight years old, he went up to the altar one day but was passed by. He was too young in those days to receive Holy Communion. He went home and cried, but the next day St. Michael the archangel came and gave him the Host. When Gerard was twelve, he had to leave school because his father died and he needed to work. One day the key to the house dropped down into the well, and Gerard took a statue of the Infant Jesus and tied it to a string and put it down in the well. The statue came up holding the key.

Gerard wanted to become a priest and tried 3 different times always being turned down because of poor health. The fourth time he begged and was turned down again. The priest told his mother to make sure that Gerard didn't follow them so she locked him in his room. The next day she went to check on him and he was gone. A note read "I have gone to become a saint." The priest wasn't happy but sent him to the rector of the Redemptorist's house where he thought he would be useless. Gerard loved what he did and did the work of many. Even the brothers he worked with said he was a saint. He brought many people back to the sacraments. The miracles he performed were numerous, but he is best known for saving mothers and their babies during childbirth. He died when he was just 29 years old.

Gerard loved God more than anything else in the entire world. He also loved people and saw God in everyone he met. Try looking at your friends this week and see Jesus in them. Pray that they will grow up to love God just as much as Gerard did.

St. Gerard's Delicious Dough for Shaping

2 pkgs. yeast (4 ¼ tsp.)
2 cups warm milk
1 ½ cups sugar
3 eggs

2 tsp. salt
1 ½ cups oil or butter
7 ½-8 cups bread flour, unbleached preferred

Mix the milk, sugar, 2 of the eggs, salt, oil/butter together in large bowl with a whisk. When combined, add the yeast and use whisk to dissolve and combine. When combined, set timer for 5 to 8 minutes, and do not touch! When yeast is ready, you should see foam.

Now add flour and stir together until combined. Sprinkle some flour on a counter, pull the dough out of the bowl, and continue to mix/knead on counter. When all flour has been thoroughly incorporated, put back into bowl to rest and rise for 1 hour or more, until doubled. (Slightly warmer location will speed rising; cooler location will slow rising.)

Pull out and punch down and knead again. When it feels smooth and somewhat silky, form into desired shape. This dough can be baked in regular bread pans for a regularly shaped loaf of bread, or it can be in some free-form shape of your choosing and baked on a cookie or pizza sheet to accommodate whatever structure you are creating. When you have finished, beat your final egg and add a bit of water; apply to the top and sides of your structure (if desired) before putting in oven. This will give the bread a darker, golden, slightly glossy surface when finished. Bake at 350° for approximately 45 to 60 minutes. *Makes similar volume as a "two-loaf" regular bread recipe.*

Shaping Suggestions

Crown of Thorns for Good Friday: Divide dough into 3 long strands, braid together, turn on edge, and circle them on a pizza sheet. Poke soaked toothpicks in all around.

Feast of the Immaculate Conception or Feast of the Annunciation: Shape a woman and reserve some dough for small face that you stack on the woman's "tummy."

Shape of the instrument of martyrdom for a saint's feast day.

Letters (or selected letters) to spell a name or the entire alphabet (might need more dough!).

Bannock Bread

4 cups flour
6 Tbsp. sugar
1 tsp. salt

4 tsp. baking powder
⅓ cup cold bacon fat
About 1 ¼ cups milk or water

Mix together dry ingredients. Cream in fat with fork or cut in with pastry cutter. Add water or milk until dough gathers into ball with no dry spots (not sloppy wet). Form into round cakes less than 1-inch thick. Dust top and bottom with flour. Bake in preheated oven at 400° for 25 minutes.

Herb Rolls

1 pkg. (11 oz.) refrigerated buttermilk biscuits (like Pillsbury)
¼ cup melted butter
½ tsp. dill seed
1 ½ tsp. parsley flakes
1 Tbsp. Parmesan cheese
¼ tsp. minced onion flakes

Mix herbs and butter on baking sheet. Cut each roll in half and coat with herb/butter mixture. Bake at 425° for 12 to 15 minutes.

Zucchini Bread (In a Can)

3 cups flour
1 tsp. baking powder
1 tsp. baking soda
1 tsp. salt
1 Tbsp. cinnamon
3 eggs
2 cups sugar
1 cup vegetable oil
2 tsp. vanilla extract
2 cups shredded zucchini
1 cup chopped nuts – walnuts or pecans *(optional)*
3 (1-lb.) coffee cans

Preheat oven to 350°. Combine first 5 ingredients; set aside. Combine eggs, sugar, oil, and vanilla in a *large bowl*; beat at medium speed with an electric mixer until well blended. Stir in zucchini and nuts if desired. Add dry ingredients, stirring until moistened.

Spoon batter into **3 greased and floured 1-pound coffee cans**. Bake at 350° for 55 to 60 minutes or until done *(I use a long metal cake tester to check)*. Cool in cans about 15 to 20 minutes. *(If too hot, bread will stick in can.)* Remove to wire rack and cool completely. Bread slices better when completely cool! *(You may also bake this bread in a regular loaf pan.)*

Banana Nut Bread

1 stick margarine
1 ½ cups sugar
2 cups flour
3 eggs
1 tsp. baking soda

4 Tbsp. buttermilk
1 cup chopped pecans
3 medium bananas, mashed
1 tsp. vanilla

Cream together margarine and sugar. Add remaining ingredients and bake in tube pan at 350° for 45 minutes to an hour.

Banana Nut Muffins

1 ½ cups all-purpose flour
1 cup chopped walnuts
½ cup toasted wheat germ
½ cup brown sugar
1 Tbsp. baking powder
1 tsp. cinnamon

½ tsp. salt
¼ tsp. ground nutmeg
2 ripe bananas, mashed
¾ cup milk
5 Tbsp. melted butter
1 egg

Preheat oven to 400°. Fit 12 muffin cups with paper liners. Coat each with cooking spray.

Mix flour, walnuts, wheat germ, brown sugar, baking powder, cinnamon, salt, and nutmeg in large bowl. Stir in bananas, milk, butter, and egg. Mix just until blended. Using an ice cream scoop, fill muffin cups evenly with batter.

Bake muffins until a toothpick comes out clean, 20 to 22 minutes. Cool, then remove from the muffin pan and cool on a wire rack. Makes 1 dozen muffins.

Sts. Michael, Gabriel, and Raphael
Feast Day ~ September 29
Guardian Angels Feast Day ~ Oct 2

These saints are different because they are angels. Michael's name stands for "who is like God." He protected the gates of Paradise after Adam and Eve sinned. He is the protector of us all against the devil.

Gabriel was the angel who announced to Mary that she was going to bring Jesus into the world and be His mother. His name stands for "the power of God." He also was the angel that came to Zechariah and told him that he and St. Elizabeth would have a son, John, even though they were very old.

Raphael's name stands for "God has healed." He protected Tobit when he was blind and then healed him through God's power. This is a special day when all three angels are honored.

What will you do today to show your special angel, your guardian angel that you love him? Maybe ask your angel to hug Sts. Michael, Gabriel, and Raphael and thank them for loving you! They protect us from harm. Stay close to them and pray to them.

Angel Pumpkin Muffins

2 cups packed biscuit mix
½ cup sugar
1 ½ tsp. pumpkin pie spice
¾ cup milk

½ cup canned pumpkin
1 egg, slightly beaten
2 Tbsp. oil

Thoroughly combine biscuit mix, sugar, and pumpkin pie spice. In another bowl, combine milk, pumpkin, beaten egg, and oil; then stir into dry ingredients. Fill muffin pans ⅔ full. Bake at 400° for 20 minutes (less for small muffins). *Makes 12 large muffins.*

"The Son of Man will send his angels, and they will collect out of his kingdom all who cause others to sin and all evildoers."
Matt. 13:41

"For the Son of Man will come with his angels in his Father's glory, and then he will repay everyone according to his conduct." Matt. 16:27

"But whoever denies me before others will be denied before the angels of God." Luke 12:9

Prayer To St. Michael

Composed by Pope Leo XIII in 1884 after he had a vision of the devil boasting that he would destroy the Church.
Encourage your parish to say this prayer after Mass!
What a great Confirmation project!

*Saint Michael the Archangel,
Defend us in battle.
Be our protection against the wickedness and snares of the devil.
May God rebuke him, we humbly pray;
and do Thou, O Prince of the Heavenly Host -
by the Power of God -
cast into hell, satan and all the evil spirits,
that prowl about the world seeking the ruin on souls. Amen.*

Absolutely Incredible Muffins

½ cup unsalted butter
½ cup brown sugar
½ cup granulated sugar
3 Tbsp. instant coffee granules
2 tsp. vanilla extract
2 large eggs
⅔ cup milk

1 ¾ cups flour
½ tsp. salt
1 Tbsp. baking powder
¾ cup semi-sweet chocolate chunks or bits
1 cup chopped walnuts

Preheat oven to 350°. Grease or line muffin tins.

Cream butter, sugar, coffee, and vanilla. Mix eggs and milk together. Alternately mix in wet and dry ingredients, combining gently. Add chips and nuts. Stir. Fill muffin liners to the top. Bake 20 minutes or until toothpick comes out clean. *Makes 1 dozen over-size muffins.*

All-Bran Muffins

1 ¼ cups all-purpose flour
½ cup sugar
1 Tbsp. baking powder
¼ tsp. salt

2 cups Kellogg's All-Bran cereal
1 ¼ cups fat-free milk
1 egg
¼ cup vegetable oil

Stir together flour, sugar, baking powder, and salt. Set aside. In large mixing bowl, combine Kellogg's All-Bran cereal and milk. Let stand about 2 minutes or until cereal softens. Add egg and oil. Beat well. Add flour mixture, stirring only until combined. Portion evenly into twelve 2 ½-inch muffin pan cups coated with cooking spray. Bake at 400° for about 20 minutes or until golden brown. Serve warm. *Makes 12 servings.*

Blueberry Muffins

2 Tbsp. margarine or butter, melted
2 cups biscuit mix
⅓ cup sugar
1 egg
Juice from 1 lemon, about ¼ cup
⅓ cup milk
1 cup blueberries, frozen or fresh

Mix together first 4 ingredients. Add lemon juice and milk. Gently stir in berries. Fill 12 muffin cups ⅔ full. Bake at 400° for 20 to 25 minutes.

Sticky Buns

1 pkg. frozen dough ball rolls
½ pkg. regular butterscotch pudding *(not instant)*
Cinnamon
Nuts *(I use pecans)*
1 stick margarine
½ cup brown sugar

Grease tube pan. Place frozen rolls in pan. Sprinkle with pudding mix, cinnamon, and nuts. Melt margarine. Combine brown sugar with margarine and pour over rolls. Let sit on counter overnight.

In the morning, remove foil and bake at 350° for 20 to 25 minutes. *(I watch it carefully and sometimes place foil over pan for the last 5 minutes so it doesn't burn.)* Turn out onto serving plate. Tastes better when warm.

"The Eucharist is the supreme proof of the love of Jesus. After this, there is nothing more but Heaven itself."
~St. Peter Julian Eymard

St. Thérèse of Lisieux (1873-1897)
Feast Day ~ October 1

Born in France to a father who wanted to be a monk and a mother who wanted to be a saint, her parents had 9 children but only 5 lived and they were all girls. When Thérèse was 4 years old, her mother died of breast cancer, and her sister Pauline, 16 years of age, became a second mother to her. She was a very sensitive child who cried all the time and was frequently spoiled by her father as she was the baby of the family. When Pauline turned 21 she left to become a nun, and Thérèse became very ill. Almost dying she, along with her sisters, prayed before a statue of Mary and a wonderful miracle happened. Thérèse saw Mary smile at her and she miraculously was cured.

When she was 15 years of age, she asked to be admitted into the Carmel convent where her 2 sisters already were, but permission was denied. Thérèse, determined to enter the convent, took a trip to Rome seeking the Pope's approval. When the Pope came close to Thérèse, she ran up to him with the enthusiasm of a child, begging him to let her become a Carmelite. The Vicar General was so impressed with her enthusiasm and her courage that she was admitted to the order. Life was not easy for her there. She tried hard to please God and to be humble and had incredible spiritual courage. She was often misunderstood by some of the nuns, but she took this hurt and offered it to God. It was her "little way" and all the tiny sufferings became flowers for Jesus. Added together, they were a beautiful bouquet for God. But no one recognized that Thérèse was special and many people thought she was almost too ordinary. One day Thérèse became very sick, coughing up blood, but didn't let anyone know. When she became too ill to function, some accused her of making it up because she was so joyful. When she died, she was 24 years old. Her last words were "My God, I love you." One nun said she was so ordinary there just wasn't anything to say about her. Her sister Pauline put together her writings and sent them off to other convents. She became very popular in her death, and everyone wanted to imitate her "little way." Thérèse promised to let fall a shower of roses from heaven. She wanted to spend heaven, doing good for those on earth. By 1925, she had been canonized and was declared a Doctor of the Church in 1997.

By giving up little things you can make your life holy. St. Thérèse said "What matters in life, is not great deeds, but great love." Without bragging, what could you do this week as a small sacrifice to please God?

Croissant French Toast

10 eggs, lightly beaten
2 cups milk
¼ cup + 1 Tbsp. brandy
2 ½ Tbsp. sugar
1 Tbsp. + 1 tsp. vanilla

6-12 croissants, depending on size
Butter
Cinnamon

(If using very large croissants, use 6 to 8; for medium-size, use 10 to 12.)

Beat eggs, milk, brandy, sugar, and vanilla in large bowl. Cut croissants in halves horizontally.

Spray a 9x13-inch pan generously with Pam (or grease with shortening). Place croissant halves cut side up in pan. Pour egg mixture evenly over croissants. Dot with butter and sprinkle cinnamon on top. Bake at 325° for about 30 to 45 minutes, or until puffed and set.

This may be prepared the night before and stored in refrigerator before baking. *Makes 8 to 10 servings.*

Versatile Egg Casserole

2 cups grated Cheddar cheese
2 Tbsp. instant onion
   (dehydrated onion flakes)
½ tsp. black pepper
6 eggs
3 cups milk
1 ½ cups Bisquick mix
½ tsp. dry mustard
½ cup margarine, melted

For a Mexican version, add chopped red and green pepper (about 1 cup total), 2 tsp. cumin; change cheese to 1 cup mozzarella cheese and 1 cup Cheddar.

Preheat oven to 400°. In greased 9x13-inch baking pan, sprinkle cheese, onion, and pepper on bottom (for Mexican-style, also add red and green pepper and cumin).

Beat together rest of ingredients in a bowl (to avoid lumps, place Bisquick in bowl first, then add some milk to moisten). Pour egg-milk mixture carefully over contents in baking pan. Bake 30 to 35 minutes or until the middle is firm.

"My sweetest Joy is to be in the presence of Jesus in the holy Sacrament. I beg that when obliged to withdraw in body, I may leave my heart before the holy Sacrament. How I would miss Our Lord if He were to be away from me by His presence in the Blessed Sacrament!" ~St. Katharine Drexel

Egg Casserole

6 eggs slightly beaten
½ cup evaporated milk *(calls for half-and-half, but I use evaporated)*
1 tsp. Worcestershire sauce
2 cups shredded Cheddar cheese
½ cup shredded Monterey Jack cheese *(I used with jalapeño peppers)*
1 Tbsp. flour
Meat or veggies of your choosing

(For each casserole, I doubled the ingredients.)

Add flour to Cheddar cheese; mix. Place cheese and flour mixture on bottom of ungreased 1 ½-quart Pyrex casserole dish. Sprinkle the Monterey Jack over top of the Cheddar and put to the side.

Mix eggs with milk and Worcestershire sauce. Pour over cheeses.

At this point you can sprinkle whatever meat you wish to use, or veggies, like tomatoes. I used bacon for one, mild Italian sausage for another. The last one was just cheese with tomato.

Place casserole in refrigerator overnight or for at least 8 hours. Let sit on counter for 30 minutes before putting in the oven. Bake at 350° for 40 minutes or so or until knife inserted in center comes out clean.

"Devotion to the Sacred Heart should bring us to a life of intimate union with Jesus who, we know, is truly present and living in the Eucharist." ~Fr. Gabriel of St. Mary Magdalen, O.C.D

Breakfast Casserole

1 lb. bulk Jimmy Dean sausage
6 slices diced white bread
6 large eggs (or 8 medium)
1 ½ cups grated or shredded sharp Cheddar cheese

1 tsp. salt
2 cups milk
½ tsp. pepper
1 (8 oz.) can mushrooms, drained

Brown sausage, breaking into small pieces as it cooks. While sausage cooks, cut crusts from bread and cube. Place in the bottom of a 9x13-inch dish or pan. Drain sausage and add to bread cubes. Layer the mushrooms over the sausage. Beat the eggs; add the milk, salt, and pepper. Pour over the mushrooms and top the casserole with the cheese.

Let sit in refrigerator overnight. Bake in preheated 350° oven for 35 to 40 minutes (or until egg is set).

Christmas Morning Breakfast

1 lb. sausage
6 eggs, slightly beaten
6 slices bread, cubed
2 cups milk

1 tsp. salt
1 tsp. mustard
1 cup grated sharp Cheddar cheese

Cook sausage; drain, cool, and crumble. Mix eggs, bread, milk, salt, mustard, sausage, and cheese. Put in greased baking dish. Refrigerate overnight. Bake in preheated 250° oven for 45 minutes.

Overnight Eggs

1 lb. pork sausage (maple)
12 eggs, whipped
8 slices white bread, cubed without crust
3 cups shredded Cheddar cheese
4 cups milk
2 tsp. dry mustard
2 tsp. salt
1 bag hash browns

Combine ingredients and place in large casserole pan; refrigerate overnight. In the morning, preheat oven to 350°. Bake casserole 55 to 60 minutes before cutting. *Makes 12 servings.*

Variation: You can substitute slices of crisp cooked bacon for sausage, or omit meat entirely. Can add onions or green peppers as desired. It is not necessary to refrigerate casserole overnight.

Egg Lasagna

2 cups unseasoned croutons
1 cup shredded Cheddar cheese
½ cup shredded mozzarella cheese
1 cup milk
1 cup half-and-half
½ tsp. salt
½ tsp. prepared mustard
1 tsp. onion powder
5 eggs, slightly beaten
Crumbled bacon, ham, or browned sausage (optional)

Grease an 8x8-inch pan. Layer croutons and cheeses. Combine milk, half-and-half, seasonings, and eggs together and pour over croutons. You may add crumbled bacon, ham, or browned sausage on top. Refrigerate overnight. Bake at 350° for 30 minutes.

Notes

Vegetables & Sides

VEGETABLES AND SIDES INDEX

Bail-Out Beans...................77
Broccoli Casserole............63
Carrots Supreme 64
Cauliflower Bake...............65
Cheesy Broccoli................63
Corn Pudding....................65
Deer Hunter Beans...........78
Do-Ahead Mashed
  Potatoes........................73
Elkridge Tomatoes............66
Fiore di Zucca Fritta.........64
French Fried Onions........67
Grandma's Turkey
  Dressing........................80
Grilled Portabella
  Mushrooms...................67

Harvard Beets.................. 67
Hot Potato Casserole....... 73
Juan Diego's Guacamole
  Mexican Recipe........... 69
Maria's Sweet Potato
  Crunch.........................75
Praline Topped Sweet
  Potatoes...................... 76
Quick & Easy Rice.......... 78
Roasted Red Potatoes..... 72
Savory Apple Casserole.. 79
Sweet Potato Casserole.. 76
Thanksgiving Potatoes..... 72
Vianney's Potato Bake..... 71
Yummy Corn Pudding...... 66

Vegetables and Side Dishes

Broccoli Casserole

2 (10 oz.) pkgs. frozen chopped broccoli, cooked and drained
1 cup mayonnaise *(can be light mayonnaise)*
2 eggs, slightly beaten

1 (10 ¾ oz.) can condensed cream of mushroom soup, undiluted
1 cup grated sharp cheese
Buttered breadcrumbs *(reserved for topping)*

Mix all ingredients except breadcrumbs together; pour into greased casserole. Sprinkle breadcrumbs on top. Bake at 350° for 45 minutes.

Cheesy Broccoli

4 (10 oz.) boxes chopped, frozen broccoli
1 lb. Velveeta cheese

1 ½ sticks margarine or butter, divided
1 roll/sleeve Ritz crackers

Cook broccoli as directed on package. While broccoli is cooking, cut cheese and 1 stick butter into small pieces into a lightly greased 9x13-inch casserole dish. Pour hot drained broccoli over butter and cheese. Crush crackers and mix with remaining ½ stick of butter that has been softened. Put on top of broccoli. Cook at 350° until cheese starts to come up the sides of the dish, about 20 minutes.

This recipe can be made ahead of time – don't add cracker mixture until ready to put in oven. Can also be halved or doubled, but you will not need to increase the crackers unless you are using more than one dish.

Fiore di Zucca Fritta
(Fried Zucchini Blossoms)

18 zucchini blossoms
2 cups whole milk, or, even better, a mixture of beer and milk
1 ½ cups flour *(can be adjusted to get a batter that is thicker or thinner, depending on preference)*

1 egg, lightly beaten
Mozzarella cheese, cut into small pieces to be stuffed in the blossoms
Sea salt
Olive oil *(or another suitable oil)* for frying

Trim the stems of the zucchini blossoms; remove the pistils, wash them gently, and pat them dry just as gently. Prepare the batter by combining the milk, flour, and egg.

Heat the oil in a skillet. (The oil should be just deep enough to cover the blossoms when they are placed in the pan.) Stuff the zucchini blossoms with a piece of mozzarella, allowing the petals to close around it. Lightly salt the zucchini blossoms, dredge them in the batter, fry them until golden, drain them on absorbent paper, and serve them hot.

Carrots Supreme

6 carrots (1 lb.)
½ cup cooking juice
2 Tbsp. grated onion

2 Tbsp. horseradish
½ cup mayonnaise
¼ tsp. salt and pepper

Cut carrots in strips and cook in salted water for 8 minutes. Reserve ½ cup cooking liquid. Put carrots in greased casserole and pour remaining ingredients over carrots. Sprinkle with buttered breadcrumbs and bake at 350° for 15 minutes.

Cauliflower Bake

8 oz. Pepperidge Farm Herb Seasoned Stuffing (not cubed)
1 head cauliflower
¼ cup margarine
1 tsp. dill
¾ cup water *(or vegetable broth and omit the bouillon)*
1 cube vegetable bouillon

Preheat oven to 375°. Cut cauliflower into bite-size pieces. Steam cauliflower until no longer crunchy, 3 to 5 minutes.

Melt margarine and place in a big bowl; mix with water, bouillon, and dill. Add cauliflower to bowl and stir to coat with liquid. Add stuffing and mix to allow some to stick to cauliflower. Place in greased 9x13-inch pan and bake for 40 minutes. Stir every 15 minutes to ensure most of the stuffing gets toasted some.

Corn Pudding

2 eggs
1 cup milk
1 tsp. salt and pepper
2 Tbsp. sugar
2 or 3 cups corn
A little flour
Butter

Separate eggs and beat, beating whites until stiff. Mix milk and yolks together. In a separate bowl, sprinkle corn with a little flour. Add salt and pepper and sugar. Pour mixture over milk and eggs. Fold in whites gently.

Pour into glass Pyrex baking bowl. Dot with butter. Cook at 375° for about 45 minutes to 1 hour. *Makes 4 to 6 servings.*

❧ *"The Bridegroom would not have his bride lonely while he was away. He wanted her to have a companion. And the best companion he could leave her was himself in this sacrament."*
~St. Peter Alcantara

Yummy Corn Pudding

1 stick butter, melted in microwave
2 eggs, slightly beaten
1 (8 oz.) can creamed corn, undrained
1 (8 oz.) can whole corn, drained
8 oz. sour cream
8 oz. Jiffy corn muffin mix

Mix all ingredients together. Put in a 1 ½-quart casserole dish. Spray inside of dish with Pam or similar spray oil. Bake at 375° for 35 minutes or until done. *(Do not overcook as it will be dry.)*

Elkridge Tomatoes

6 firm medium tomatoes, cut in 1-inch thick slices
⅓ cup cornmeal
⅓ cup flour
1 tsp. salt
½ tsp. pepper
4 Tbsp. bacon fat *(can substitute with vegetable oil)*
2 Tbsp. brown sugar

Combine cornmeal with flour, salt and pepper. Heat bacon fat in skillet. Dip tomato slices in the cornmeal mixture and sauté quickly on both sides in bacon fat until brown. Use more fat if necessary. Sprinkle slices with brown sugar, turn and sprinkle other side. Drain tomatoes and layer in a shallow casserole with slices overlapping. Bake at 350° for about 20 minutes until hot. Makes 4 to 6 servings.

"Lord Jesus Christ, pierce my soul with your love so that I may always long for you alone, who are the bread of angels and the fulfillment of the soul's deepest desires. May my heart always hunger for you, so that souls may be filled with the sweetness of your presence" ~St. Bonaventure

French Fried Onions

1 egg
¾ cup flour
1 onion, sliced and separated
   into rings

½ tsp. salt
½ cup milk

Beat egg, flour, salt, and milk together. Add onion rings to batter, then lower into hot fat to float. Fry until brown, about 2 minutes. Drain on absorbent paper.

Harvard Beets

⅓ cup sugar
½ tsp. salt
1 Tbsp. cornstarch
½ cup vinegar

2 Tbsp. butter
1 tsp. minced onion
1 can drained beets

Mix all ingredients and heat. Stir until sauce is smooth and thick.

Grilled Portabella Mushrooms

3-4 large portabella
   mushrooms
¼ cup olive oil

3 Tbsp. soy sauce
1 Tbsp. balsamic vinegar

Combine olive oil, soy sauce, and vinegar, and emulsify with a whisk (sauce gets thick and creamy after a few minutes). Marinate mushrooms for 1 to 2 hours. Barbeque on the grill, about 7 minutes on each side. *Can use the oven at 425° for 15 minutes on each side, but the ultimate taste sensation is when they are cooked on the grill! YUM!*

Our Lady of Guadalupe (1531) **St. Juan Diego (1474-1548)**
Feast Day ~ December 12 Feast Day ~ December 9

Mary has appeared to many different children all over the world, but this story is unusual because Mary appeared to a man who was 55 years old and a convert to the Faith. It was on December 9, 1531 that Our Lady first appeared to Juan Diego. On his way to Mass one day the Blessed Mother appeared to Juan. She asked Juan to go to the bishop and have a church built. Juan begged Our Lady to choose someone else since he wasn't important enough and would not be able to convince the bishop of anything, but Mary wanted him to do it, so he obeyed. The bishop did not believe Juan but told him to go back and ask the Lady for a sign.

A few days later, Juan tried to avoid Our Lady as he was passing Tepeyac hill. He needed to go to the priest because his uncle was sick and dying. Mary called to Juan and told him that his uncle would be fine but that she still needed him. Juan obeyed and was told to go pick some flowers and place them in his tilma (cloak); he was given strict instructions not to open the tilma to anyone except the bishop. Juan did exactly as our Lady told him, and he waited to see the bishop. As he met with the bishop, Juan opened his cloak and beautiful roses fell to the floor. This was amazing as it was in the middle of winter and all the flowers were dead, so where could Juan have found fresh flowers? But this was not what amazed the bishop. He fell to his knees and stared at Juan's tilma. There was the most beautiful image of Our Lady imprinted on his cloak. If you look closely into Our Lady's eyes it is said that you can see the image of the bishop kneeling in amazement.

This inspired thousands of people to convert. A beautiful church was built and people from all over the world go to Mexico each year to see the tilma which should have disintegrated by now (it's more than 500 years old), but is still fresh and beautiful. Miracles constantly occur there. Our Lady is always seeking to bring us closer to her Son.

This week pray to Our Lady. Ask her to hold you in her mantle of love. Get some information about St. Juan Diego (feast Day Dec. 9th), Our Lady of Guadalupe and maybe put on a play with your friends. Learn about listening to God and doing His will.

Juan Diego's Guacamole Mexican Recipe

4 ripe avocados
3 limes, juiced
½ red onion, chopped
1 clove garlic, minced
2 Serrano chilies, finely
　　chopped *(Hot)*

1 big handful cilantro, finely chopped
Extra-virgin olive oil
Salt and pepper

Cut in half and pit the avocados. Using a spoon, scoop out the flesh into a mixing bowl. Mash the avocados with a fork, leaving them somewhat chunky. Add remaining ingredients and fold everything gently together. Lay plastic wrap on surface of mix so it won't brown. Refrigerate 1 hour before serving.

Vegetables and Side Dishes 69

St. John Vianney "*Curé of Ars*" (1786-1859)
Feast Day ~ August 4

Born in 1786 in Lyons, France, John took care of the sheep in his family. Little did his family know that John would take care of thousands of lost sheep when he grew up! When John turned 18, he asked his father if he could become a priest. His dad didn't want to lose his helper, but after two years, he consented. John found school difficult, especially Latin. He became very discouraged because it was hard. He took a pilgrimage and walked 60 miles praying to St. John Francis Regis. When he came back, John still had a lot of trouble with Latin, but he tried his best. When it was time for the final examinations, they were not written but oral, and John was tested on what he had learned. He was scared and started to cry. He was such a good and holy man but was very childlike. His priest stood up for him and said that John knew his catechism and loved God very much. John was finally ordained a priest.

The priest that defended John took him in and John worked hard. When the priest died, John was sent to Ars where people didn't care about God. They never went to church, were drunk, used bad language, and worked on Sundays. John prayed, fasted and offered things up for his new parishioners. He started to see a change. His prayers were working! God was listening. People started to come to church, not only on Sunday but also during the week. They didn't curse as much. People couldn't believe that the town was so changed. Why were these people so different? The people of Ars knew that John was a saint, and they obeyed him. John spent 16 hours a day in the confessional hearing people's confession and giving them ways to improve their lives. He could tell them their sins before they even confessed them. He stayed in Ars the rest of his life for 42 years and died in 1859 when he was 73 years old. He is the patron saint of priests.

This week find some time to go to confession and clean your soul for Jesus.

Vianney's Potato Bake

St. John actually fasted on potatoes. He would boil some and hang them in a basket. He'd eat one or two, but never three as that would be excessive. When they became moldy, he ate them anyway as a penance.

4 Tbsp. margarine, melted
16 oz. sour cream
1 can cream of celery (or mushroom) soup
1 small onion, chopped

2 cups shredded sharp Cheddar cheese
1 pkg. frozen hash browns *(up to 32 oz.)*, shredded or cubed

Preheat oven to 350°. In a big bowl, mix everything but the hash browns. Add hash browns and mix well. Place in greased 9x13-inch pan. Bake for 45 minutes or until golden brown.

❧ *"All the good works in the world are not equal to the Holy Sacrifice of the Mass because they are the works of men; but the Mass is the work of God. Martyrdom is nothing in comparison for it is but the sacrifice of man to God; but the Mass is the sacrifice of God for man."* ~St. John Vianney

❧ *"There is no such thing as a bad priest. Only priests whose people have not prayed enough for them."* ~St. John Vianney

Roasted Red Potatoes with Bacon and Cheese

½ cup Kraft Light Ranch reduced-fat dressing
½ cup Kraft 2% Milk reduced-fat shredded Cheddar cheese
¼ cup Real Bacon Bits
2 lbs. small red potatoes, quartered
1 Tbsp. chopped fresh parsley

Preheat oven to 350°. Mix dressing, cheese, and bacon bits into large bowl. Add potatoes; toss lightly. Spoon into lightly greased 9x13-inch baking dish; cover with foil.

Bake 40 minutes. Remove foil; bake an additional 15 minutes or until potatoes are tender. Sprinkle with parsley. *Makes eight ⅔-cup servings.*

Substitute: Use chopped fresh rosemary in place of parsley.

Thanksgiving Potatoes

This dish can be made a day ahead – which is great for a hectic Thanksgiving Day!

10 large russet potatoes
8 oz. cream cheese
8 oz. sour cream
⅓ stick butter
Dash onion salt
¼ tsp. each salt and pepper

Peel and quarter the potatoes. In a large pot of water, boil the potatoes for about 30 minutes, until soft. Drain. Beat/mash in all ingredients until smooth.

Grease a 13x9x2-inch pan with shortening and fill with mashed potatoes. Bake, uncovered, at 350° for 30 to 45 minutes, until hot. Top with your favorite Thanksgiving gravy! *Makes 10 to 12 servings.*

Do-Ahead Mashed Potatoes

5 lbs. potatoes
8 oz. cream cheese
8 oz. sour cream
2 tsp.+ onion salt or
   McCormick's onion powder
   (California Style Blend) and
   add salt to taste

2 Tbsp.+ butter
¼ tsp. pepper
2 cups grated Cheddar cheese
Paprika *(optional)*

Peel and boil potatoes; drain well. Mash until smooth.

In a separate bowl, blend cream cheese with sour cream, onion salt, and pepper. Add mashed potatoes and adjust seasoning to taste. Place in a rectangular baking pan; cool, cover, and place in refrigerator for 12 to 24 hours before baking.

Before baking, dot with butter, lots of cheese, and top with paprika. Bake at 350° for 35 to 45 minutes. *Enjoy!*

Hot Potato Casserole

This is fantastic for company or family get-togethers. Dieters beware! Serve as a side dish along with beef, chicken, or ham.

1 (2 lb.) bag Ore-Ida cubed
   potatoes, thawed
1 (10 ¾ oz.) can cream of
   chicken soup
16 oz. sour cream

½ stick (¼ cup) butter
2 Tbsp. chopped onion
2 cups grated Cheddar cheese

Melt butter and sauté onions in microwave or on stovetop. Mix all ingredients together. Bake in a greased 13x9x2-inch dish at 350° for 60 to 75 minutes. *Makes 10 to 12 servings.*

St. Maria Goretti (1890-1902)
Feast Day ~ July 6

Maria was a beautiful young daughter of poor Italian farmers. She never went to school since her parents needed her to help on the farm. Her father died of malaria and her mother struggled to raise the children. One day when Maria was 12 years of age, a neighbor named Alessandro came to her kitchen and grabbed Maria. As he began to take advantage of her beauty, she would not give in because she knew it was a sin. Furious, Alessandro began to stab Maria. On the way to the hospital in a bumpy horse drawn carriage, Maria's mom held her daughter as she fought her pain. She looked at her mom and said, "Tell Alessandro that I forgive him." Alessandro was sentenced to 30 years in prison. For the first 8 years, he wasn't sorry for what he had done, but then Maria appeared to him in a dream, and he woke up and was sorry he had killed her. After 27 years, he was released from prison and went to Maria's mother to beg for forgiveness. Maria's mom forgave him, and when Maria was declared a saint in 1950, Alessandro was there, in St. Peter's square watching. Alessandro spent the rest of his life as a gardener in a monastery. Maria had always wanted to do whatever pleased God. When something happened to her, Maria did not blame the other person, but forgave them.

Say a special prayer this week to forgive someone who has hurt you. Ask God to soften your heart and have compassion on them.

Vegetables and Side Dishes

Maria's Sweet Potato Crunch

This dish is as sweet as little Maria was. Only 12 years old, she loved and imitated Jesus. She wanted to be pure for Him and died forgiving the man who killed her. We can all learn from her!

3 ½ lbs. sweet potatoes, peeled and cut into chunks
1 stick (½ cup) butter, softened, divided
1 Tbsp. granulated sugar
½ tsp. grated orange peel
½ tsp. pumpkin pie spice
¼ tsp. salt
1 cup corn flakes
½ cup firmly packed brown sugar
½ cup chopped pecans

Place sweet potatoes in a large saucepan; add enough salted water to cover them, and bring to a boil. Cook until tender, about 20 minutes. Drain, keeping about ½ cup cooking liquid with the potatoes.

Transfer to a large bowl; using a hand mixer, beat in ½ stick butter, granulated sugar, orange peel, pumpkin pie spice, and salt. Transfer to a baking dish. Cover and refrigerate for up to 3 days.

In a small bowl, mix together corn flakes, brown sugar, and pecans. Melt remaining ½ stick butter and stir into corn flake topping. Cover and refrigerate up to 3 days. **Note:** This is best when it is fresh. It gets chewier when in the fridge.

Remove potatoes and topping from the refrigerator and bring to room temperature. Heat oven to 375°. Heat sweet potatoes in microwave at 50% power to warm. Stir. Sprinkle topping over potatoes and bake in oven for 20 minutes. *Makes 12 servings.*

"Forgive your neighbor's injustice; then when you pray, your own sins will be forgiven." Sir. 28:2

Sweet Potato Casserole

3 cups mashed sweet potatoes
½ tsp. salt
½ cup milk (evaporated milk okay)
2 eggs, slightly beaten
½ cup sugar
¼ cup melted margarine

Topping:
1 cup chopped walnuts
⅓ cup melted margarine or butter
⅓ cup flour
½ cup brown sugar

Mix all ingredients together with electric mixer until fully blended. Pour into greased glass casserole dish. Mix all topping ingredients together and sprinkle of top of casserole. Cook at 350° for 35 minutes.

Praline Topped Sweet Potatoes

About 2 ½ lbs. sweet potatoes (or butternut squash)
4 Tbsp. butter, softened
1 tsp. salt
Dash of pepper
2 eggs slightly beaten
2 apples, peeled and chopped

Topping:
½ cup firmly packed brown sugar
½ tsp. cinnamon
3 Tbsp. butter, softened
½ cup chopped pecans

Cook the sweet potatoes until they are soft *(I usually wrap in safe plastic and microwave).* Once they are cool enough to handle, scoop out the potatoes and mix the rest of the ingredients together; then spread in a greased baking pan or casserole pan.

Combine topping ingredients and spread on top of sweet potato mixture. *(If you like a lot of topping, double the ingredients… I usually do.)*

Bake at 350° for about 45 minutes. You might want to cover with foil about half way through.

Bail-Out Beans

1 tsp. olive oil
1 large onion (for about 1 cup chopped)
1 ½ tsp. bottled minced garlic
½ large red or green bell pepper (for about ¾ cup chopped)
½ large yellow bell pepper (for about ¾ cup chopped)
1 (15 oz.) can pinto beans, rinsed and drained
1 (15 oz.) can black beans, rinsed and drained
1 (15 oz.) can black beans, undrained
1 tsp. dried oregano
1 tsp. balsamic vinegar
¼ tsp. cayenne pepper
3 oz. (about 28) low-fat tortilla chips
1 medium ripe tomato (optional)
Low-fat or fat-free sour cream (optional)

Heat the oil over medium heat in a 12-inch extra-deep nonstick skillet that has a lid. Add onions and peppers. (Reserve the remaining pepper halves for another use.) Cook until soft, about 5 minutes

Rinse and drain the pinto beans and 1 can of the black beans. Add the pintos and black beans to the skillet. Add the oregano, vinegar, and cayenne pepper. Stir and raise the heat to high, and let the mixture cook until it begins to thicken slightly, about 5 minutes.

While the beans cook, mash some of them with the back of a spoon or fork to thicken the mixture. Chop the tomato, if using, into bite-size pieces and set aside. Place 7 tortilla chips in each of 4 bowls and set aside.

When the beans are done, spoon them over the chips in each bowl. Garnish with tomato chunks and a dollop of sour cream if desired. *Makes 4 servings.*

Deer Hunter Beans

1 lb. hamburger browned and drained
1 lb. bacon, cooked and drained
3 (15 oz.) cans pork and beans
1 can lima beans, drained
1 can kidney beans, drained
1 cup ketchup
¾ cup brown sugar
1 medium onion, diced

Put it all together and bake, covered, at 350° for 1 hour. *Makes 12 servings.*

Quick & Easy Rice

1 cup rice
2 ½ cups water
½ small onion, diced
½ green pepper, diced
3-4 sliced bacon, cooked and crumbled
Water chestnuts, sliced or chopped (optional)
Soy sauce

Heat water in medium saucepan and add rice. When rice begins to absorb water, place onions and green peppers on top to steam as rice finishes cooking. Remove from heat, mix, and add bacon and water chestnuts if desired. Add a few sprinkles of soy sauce and enjoy!

"Take, O Lord, and receive all my liberty, my memory, my understanding, and my entire will. Whatever I have or hold, You have given me; I restore it all to You and surrender it wholly to be governed by Your will. Give me only Your love and Your grace, and I am rich enough and ask for nothing more."
~St. Ignatius of Loyola

Savory Apple Casserole

Serve this simple, unusual dish with holiday meals or as a main dish for a cold winter supper, with soup, pumpernickel bread, and a green salad with a mustard vinaigrette.

- 1 Tbsp. butter or canola oil
- 1 cup minced onion
- 2 tsp. dry mustard
- 1 (32 oz.) jar sauerkraut, rinsed and drained
- 6 medium-size tart apples, thinly sliced *(peeling unnecessary)*
- 2 Tbsp. unbleached white flour
- 1 tsp. cinnamon
- Pinch of cloves
- Dash of salt
- Dash of nutmeg
- 2 Tbsp. light honey or brown sugar
- ⅓ lb. medium or sharp Cheddar, grated
- ½ cup good breadcrumbs
- ¾ cup minced walnuts

Preheat oven to 375°. Have ready a 2-quart capacity casserole or an equivalent pan (a 9x13-inch baking pan will work).

Melt the butter or heat the oil in a medium-size skillet. Add the onion and mustard, and sauté over medium heat for about 5 minutes, or until the onion softens. Add the sauerkraut and cook for about 5 more minutes. Set aside.

Toss together the apple slices, flour, salt, and spices in a large bowl. Add the honey or sugar, and mix well.

Now for the fun part. Make sure the following layers are in the casserole or baking pan:

- Half the apples
- Half the onion-sauerkraut mixture
- Half the cheese
- Remaining apples
- Remaining onion-sauerkraut
- Remaining cheese

Sprinkle the top with breadcrumbs and walnuts. Cover with foil and bake for 30 minutes; then uncover and bake another 15 minutes to let the top brown. Serve hot, warm, or at room temperature. *Makes 4 to 6 main dish servings.*

Grandma's Turkey Dressing

These are approximate amounts – feel free to experiment and adjust by preference or taste. When you are ready to stuff the turkey, everything that has to be cooked has been!

- 2 boxes Uncle Ben's long grain and wild rice without the seasoning packets (or a box of brown rice, or regular rice and a box of the real wild rice)
- Sausage – get the mild and season yourself. Start with 1 lb. for a 10 lb. turkey; more never hurts.
- 2 or 3 cups chopped celery
- 2 onions, chopped – add more if needed
- 1 cup chopped pecans – add more if desired

Ahead of time, chop celery, onions, and nuts. Cook rice and simmer sausage in water. Sausage takes about 15 minutes and rice about 30 minutes. Mix all together and taste; add salt and pepper until it tastes right. Will stuff a 10 lb. turkey and maybe a little more. Put extra into a casserole; bake and freeze. It's good with chicken dishes too!

"In one day the Eucharist will make you produce more for the glory of God than a whole lifetime without it."
~St. Peter Julian Eymard

Main Dishes

"Every day God lets some of the water out so there's room to play on the beach."

MAIN DISHES INDEX

"Heavenly" Bagel Pizzas 153
Augustine's Jerk Chicken 115
Australian Meat Pie 106
Baked Maple Pork Chops ... 147
Baked Parmesan Chicken ... 109
Benedict's Italian Lasagna .. 157
Bulgoki (Korean Steak) 159
Catherine's Chili 101
Catherine's Sloppy Joe's in
  the Crockpot 105
Chicken Tetrazzini 119
Chicken Casserole 108
Chicken Franchaise 116
Chicken Pot Pie 137
Chicken Pie 138
Chicken Stew 138
Chicken Swiss 117
Chicken-Italian Dressing
  Bake 111
Clare's Chicken Casserole .. 127
Cornish Pastries 85
Crescent Roll Pizza 149
Crispy Crunchy Chicken 108
Crispy Garlic Chicken 109
Crockpot Kraut 148
Crunchy Chicken Casserole . 106
Cuban Potted Steak 84
Cuban Style Pot Roast 84
Curry Chicken 133
Dominic's Turkey Meatballs
  and Pasta 143
Easy Chicken a la King 121
Easy Feta Chicken Bake 117
Easy Layered Taco Pie 93
Easy Meatloaf 94
Easy Stromboli 151
Elegant Chicken Breasts 116
Elizabeth's Easy Beef
  Stroganoff 97
English Muffin Pizza 153
Gianna's Garlic Chicken 113
Harvest Pork Roast 146

Hearty Bosco's Chicken
  Pot Pie 135
Jambalaya 148
Josemaria's Burrito Bake 91
Layered Enchilada Bake 89
Layered Zucchini Bake 149
Marinated Flank Steak 81
Marsala Chicken with Sage 118
Meatball Stew 102
Mexican Chicken Delight ... 107
Nana's Barbecue 103
Oven Fried Chicken 108
Pasta & Veggie Bake 124
Pizza Burgers 103
Possenti's Pasta with Feta
  and Tomatoes 155
Rita's Creamy Baked
  Chicken Breast 123
Ro-Tel King Ranch Chicken 125
Rouladen
  (Stuffed Beef Roll) 95
Santa Fe Taco Casserole
  Bake 92
Shepherd's Pie 81
Simple Salsa Chicken 136
Slow Cooked Italian Chicken 119
Spaghetti Sauce 97
Spicy Beef Rolls 94
St. Anthony's Italian Noodles .. 99
St. Paul – Gyros of Corinth . 145
St. Zita's Baked Ziti 141
Steak Fajitas 88
Stuffed Chicken Crescents . 136
Swiss and Chicken
  Casserole 125
Texas Straw Hat 93
Tom's Summa Ribs Alogica .. 83
Turkey Enchiladas 107
Turkey Tortilla Casserole ... 139
Upside Down Pizza 87
Vincent's Chicken
  Enchiladas 131
Xavier's Dream Chicken
  Rice Salad 129

Main Dishes

Marinated Flank Steak

½ cup teriyaki sauce (or soy)
½ cup olive oil
2 Tbsp. honey
1 Tbsp. red wine vinegar

1 Tbsp. chopped shallot
   (or onion)
1 clove garlic, chopped
½ tsp. ground ginger
2 flank steaks, about 1 lb. each

Whisk the first 7 ingredients together. Add steak and marinate for 12 hours or overnight before grilling.

Cook about 7 minutes per side. Let stand 5 minutes after grilling and slice thin across the grain. *Makes 12 servings.*

Shepherd's Pie

3 lbs. potatoes
3 ½ cups shredded cheddar
   cheese
1 ½ lbs. ground beef
1 medium onion, chopped

½ pkg. beef stew mix
   (McCormick's)
Garlic salt, to taste
3 Tbsp. ketchup
4 Tbsp. Worcestershire sauce

Preheat oven to 325°. Brown ground beef and drain. Cook onion in same pan until tender. Cook peeled and sliced potatoes until soft and drain. Mash adding milk and butter to make creamy. Mix in 1 ½ cups of cheese. Put mixture aside.

In a medium bowl, mix browned ground beef, cooked onions, ½ pkg. of beef stew mix, garlic salt, tomato ketchup, Worcestershire sauce and 1 cup of shredded yellow cheese. Mix well. Put meat mixture in a 9" x 13" casserole and cover with the mashed potatoes. Sprinkle the final cup of cheese over the mashed potatoes and put casserole in a preheated 325° oven for 30 to 45 minutes. Watch that the cheese does not burn. If it begins to burn, just cover with aluminum foil.

St. Thomas Aquinas (1225-1274)
Feast Day ~ January 28

Thomas was born to Count Landulph and Countess Theodora and at the age of 5 was sent to the Benedictine monastery at Monte Cassino, which was customary for that time. His parents wanted Thomas to be well educated so that he could carry on their line of nobility. Thomas was smart and learned very quickly. All of his teachers were astonished. Ten years later he wanted to join the Dominican order, which worked in urban areas. His family was very disappointed and did all they could to discourage this. They had him put under house arrest and for 2 years they tried to dissuade him. They brought a beautiful woman to his room and she tried to make him sin but Thomas was faithful to God and resisted her. God rewarded Thomas and took away his desire for her. While captive, Thomas studied very hard and learned metaphysics and studied Sacred Scripture. Finally his parents saw that Thomas was serious and allowed him to study under St. Albert the Great, a Dominican. St. Albert was a man who brought a whole new level of understanding between superstition and science. Thomas became a Dominican. He directed Dominican schools in Rome and Viterbo and constantly fought to defend the Faith from heresy (false teaching). His most famous writing, The Summa Theologica, dealt with Catholic theology as a whole. He is quoted extensively in the Catechism. Thomas believed we all have the gift of reason.

We all have the ability to know God, and were created to be able to understand His teachings with the gift of faith. **Spend some time this week reading about a Church teaching you don't know very well and ask the Holy Spirit to help you understand it.**

"Jesus Lord, kind Pelican, cleanse my filth with Thy blood, one drop of which can save the whole world from all its sin."
~St. Thomas Aquinas

Tom's Summa Ribs Alogica
(the ultimate rib this side of heaven)

This is a secret recipe used for years. It's delicious!

2 Tbsp. chili powder
2 Tbsp. dried parsley
4 tsp. onion powder
4 tsp. garlic powder
4 tsp. dried oregano
4 tsp. paprika
4 tsp. black pepper
1 Tbsp. salt
5-6 lbs. country pork spareribs

Tom's Dominican Barbecue Sauce *(tangy, sweet, full of life):*
3 cups prepared barbecue sauce *(whatever is your current favorite)*
¼ cup apple cider vinegar
¼ cup honey
2 tsp. onion powder
2 tsp. garlic powder
Dash hot pepper sauce

Combine all dry ingredients in small bowl and mix well. Parboil ribs for 25 minutes (put in pot, add 1 tablespoon salt, cover with water, boil, and drain afterwards).

Roll ribs individually in the dry ingredients to cover liberally. Sprinkle on whatever is left over. Grill ribs for 15 minutes over medium heat, turning every couple minutes. Flames are okay (just pick them up until they go out and maybe turn the heat down a tad). Baste with barbecue sauce for the last 5 or 6 minutes. Alternatively you can baste with barbecue sauce and bake in a 350° oven for 15 minutes. Serve remaining sauce on the side.

Barbecue Sauce: Combine all ingredients in a bowl. Mix well. Use for basting and serve on side with ribs.

Cuban Potted Steak

⅔ lb. of top round or skirt steak, thinly sliced
2 (8 oz.) cans tomato sauce
1 medium onion, chopped
1 medium green pepper or sweet red pepper *(I use red)*, chopped
4 large cloves garlic, chopped
1 beef bouillon cube, dissolved in ¾ cup water
1 cup white wine
¾ cup sliced green olives (7 oz. jar) – you can use less or add to taste
Saffron rice

Cut steak into pieces; add salt and pepper, and quickly brown in olive oil in a large cooking pot. Remove.

Sauté garlic, onion, and pepper in same pot. Add steak, tomato sauce, beef bouillon, wine, and olives. Sauce should cover steak; if it doesn't, add more wine and/or water. Bring to a boil; reduce heat and simmer 3 hours until beef is tender/falls apart. Serve over yellow saffron rice.

Cuban Style Pot Roast

¼ lb. chorizo sausage
2 Tbsp. oil
3 lbs. chuck roast
½ cup flour
¾ cup tomato sauce
½ cup water
1 Tbsp. oregano
2 bay leaves
2 tsp. minced garlic
¼ cup chopped green olives

Remove the chorizo from the casing. Place in large ovenproof pot with lid. Cook until browned. Spoon out the meat and reserve. Add the oil to the pan and heat. Dredge roast in flour. Add to the pot and brown on both sides. Add the remaining ingredients as well as the browned sausage. Cover and bake at 325° for 2 ½ hours. Serve warm.

Cornish Pastries

These are like little individual pot pies, and are so very good on a cold, raw day.

Pie crust *(You are going to make an individual meat tart.) This recipe calls for 4 pie crusts.*
1 lb. beef chuck or top round steak, cut into ¼-inch pieces *(I use stewing beef)*
2 cups diced pared potatoes
2 tsp. salt
2 cups diced carrots
1 cup diced onion
Some canned corn, undrained
4 Tbsp. butter
Water, milk, or cream
Chili sauce or pickles

Preheat oven to 350°. Prepare pastry for four 12-inch rounds. Place each on one end of ungreased baking sheet.

On half of the circle, spoon ¼ each of the meat and potato. Sprinkle with ¼ teaspoon salt. On potato, layer ¼ each of the carrot and onion, and about a tablespoon of corn. Sprinkle with pepper and ¼ tsp. salt. Dot with 1 tablespoon butter and sprinkle with 1 tablespoon corn juice.

Brush edge of pastry with water; fold pastry half over filling. Fold and roll lower edge of pastry over top edge; seal and flute. Cut slits on top and brush with milk.

Repeat with remaining pastry rounds and filling, placing second pastry circle on other end of baking sheet and remaining 2 circles on a second baking sheet. Bake 1 hour. Serve hot or cold with relishes. *Makes 4 servings.*

"To keep me from sin and straying from Him, God has used devotion to the Sacred Heart of Jesus in the Blessed Sacrament. My life vows destined to be spent in the light irradiating from the tabernacle, and it is to the Heart of Jesus that I dare go for the solution of all my problems." ~Pope John XXIII

St. Peter (1st century)
Feast Day ~ June 29
Also **February 22, November 18**

St. Peter was chosen by Jesus to be His disciple. He was one of the 12 apostles that followed Jesus while he was on earth. Peter was a simple man, a fisherman from Bethsaida. His name was Simon, but Jesus changed it to Peter and said, *"You are Peter, and upon this rock I will build my church, and the gates of the netherworld shall not prevail against it."* (Matt 16:18) Peter was a good man but was very afraid when Jesus was arrested. He denied he knew Jesus three times but was very sorry, and Jesus forgave him. He spread the Faith and was the first Pope in our Church chosen by Jesus to lead us. Jesus gave Peter the keys to the kingdom of heaven and also taught Peter about the Sacrament of Reconciliation. Jesus said, *"I will give you the keys to the kingdom of heaven. Whatever you bind on earth shall be bound in heaven; and whatever you loose on earth shall be loosed in heaven."* (Matt. 16:19) Peter loved Jesus so much that when he was about to go to his death, he insisted to be crucified upside down because he wasn't worthy enough to die as Jesus had died.

Do you love Jesus? What will you do this week to show Jesus that you want to be His disciple and follow Him?

Upside Down Pizza

1 ½ lbs. lean ground beef
1 (15 oz.) can Italian-style tomato sauce

1 ½ cups shredded mixed pizza cheese: mozzarella, provolone, Parmesan, and Romano
1 (10 oz.) pkg. refrigerated biscuits

Preheat oven to 400°. In large skillet, brown beef; drain off fat. Stir in tomato sauce and heat through.

Transfer to an ungreased 9x13-inch baking dish. Sprinkle with cheese. Flatten each biscuit with hands; arrange biscuits on top of cheese. Bake 15 minutes, until biscuits are golden.

Note: Substitute other ingredients as you would in any pizza to create your favorite!

Steak Fajitas

1 ½ lbs. flank steak
12 (8-inch) flour tortillas
2 cups shredded Monterey Jack, Cheddar, or mixed cheese
2 Vidalia onions, peeled and sliced thin
3 peppers (red, yellow, orange), cored and sliced thin
4 oz. sour cream

Marinade:
¾ cup fresh lime juice
½ cup freshly squeezed orange juice
¼ cup tequila
¼ cup vegetable oil
4 cloves garlic, minced
3 green onions, minced
1 tsp. salt
1 tsp. Worcestershire sauce
¾ tsp. paprika
½ tsp. pepper

Trim fat from steak; place steak in a large, shallow dish or large Ziploc bag. Combine marinade ingredients and pour over steak. Marinate in refrigerator 24 hours, turning occasionally.

Remove steak from marinade; reserve marinade. In a skillet, sauté onions and peppers until browned; add ¾ of the extra marinade. Heat to boiling.

Grill steak 5 to 7 minutes per side, as desired, basting frequently with last ¼ of marinade. Slice steak diagonally across grain into thin slices. Warm tortillas by wrapping in foil and baking 15 minutes in a 325° oven. Fill tortillas with steak, onions, peppers, cheese, and dollop of sour cream. Wrap tortilla around filling and serve.

"It is not to remain in a golden ciborium that He comes down each day from Heaven, but to find another Heaven, the Heaven of our soul in which He takes delight." ~St. Thérèse of Lisieux

Layered Enchilada Bake

1 lb. lean ground beef
1 large onion, chopped
2 cups Thick 'N Chunky salsa
1 (15 oz.) can black beans, rinsed and drained
¼ cup Zesty Italian dressing
2 Tbsp. taco seasoning mix
6 (8-inch) flour tortillas
1 cup sour cream
1 pkg. shredded Mexican Four Cheese

Spray a 9x13-inch baking dish with nonstick fat-free cooking spray. Brown meat with onions in large skillet on medium-high heat; drain. Add salsa, beans, dressing, and taco seasoning powder; mix well.

Arrange 3 of the tortillas in a single layer on bottom of prepared baking dish; cover with layers of half each of the meat mixture, sour cream, and cheese. Repeat all layers. Cover with foil.

Preheat oven to 400°. Bake, covered, 30 minutes. Remove foil. Bake an additional 10 minutes or until casserole is heated through and cheese is melted. Let stand 5 minutes before cutting to serve. *Makes 8 servings.*

Serving Suggestions: Top with chopped tomatoes, shredded lettuce, and chopped cilantro.

"The soul hungers for God, and nothing but God can satiate it. Therefore He came to dwell on earth and assumed a Body in order that this Body might become the Food of our souls."
~St. John Vianney

St. Josemaria Escrivá de Balaguer (1902-1975)
Feast Day ~ June 26

Born in Spain to devout parents, he learned the basic truths of the Catholic Faith. More importantly though, Josemaria practiced the truths of our Faith by going to frequent Confession, praying the rosary, going to Mass, and giving to the poor. He endured the deaths of three younger sisters, and his father's business going bankrupt. When he was 16, he decided to become a priest so that he could be open to doing the will of God. Seven years later, Josemaria became a priest and began his ministry.

The family moved to Madrid when his father died, and he needed to support them. He went to law school, and tutored to help his family. He worked with the poor and sick as well as young children. He also had an apostolate for professional people and students as well as manual laborers who came into contact with the poor and sick that Josemaria ministered to. They learned about their responsibility to help out in society and not to just take from it. Josemaria founded Opus Dei, a lay Catholic apostolate where men first and later women had a mission. They were committed to growing in holiness by doing ordinary everyday duties in an extraordinarily virtuous way. They were all called to be holy in their everyday lives. They were to follow Christ and grow in His love. Later a priestly society developed, and now, Opus Dei is all over the world. Josemaria was canonized in 2002.

Holiness is not just for priests, but for all of us. Try and do something with a friend this week that pleases God. What could you do to separate yourself from the world and be holy? Think about it with your friend and make an effort to accomplish something!

Josemaria's Burrito Bake

1 cup Bisquick*
¼ cup water
1 (16 oz.) can refried beans
1 lb. ground beef or turkey, cooked and drained

1 avocado (optional)
1 (16 oz.) jar thick taco salsa
1 ½ cups shredded Mexican cheese
1 small container (8 oz.) sour cream

Preheat oven to 375°. Grease 10x10x2-inch pan. Mix Bisquick mix, water, and beans. Spread in pan. Layer remaining ingredients on bean mixture. Bake 30 minutes. Serve with sour cream.

Bisquick Substitute: 1 cup flour, ½ tsp. baking powder, ½ tsp. salt, 1 Tbsp. shortening, oil or melted butter.

☙ *"Sanctify yourselves, then, and be holy; for I, the LORD, your God, am holy."* Lev. 20:7

☙ *"...but, as he who called you is holy, be holy yourselves in every aspect of your conduct."* 1Pet. 1:15

Santa Fe Taco Casserole Bake

1 lb. lean ground beef
1 (1.25 oz.) pkg. taco spices and seasonings mix
2 cups chicken broth
¼ cup all-purpose flour
1 cup dairy sour cream
1 (7 oz.) can diced green chilies

1 (11 oz.) pkg. corn or tortilla chips
2 cups (8 oz.) grated Monterey Jack or Cheddar cheese
2 cups salsa, divided
½ cup sliced green onions with tops

In a medium skillet, brown meat and stir until crumbly; drain fat. Add taco spices and seasonings; blend well.

In small bowl, combine broth and flour. Add to meat mixture; bring to a boil to slightly thicken liquid. Stir in sour cream and chilies; blend well.

In a lightly greased 9x13-inch glass baking dish, place ½ of chips. Top with ½ of beef mixture, ½ of salsa, ½ of cheese, and ½ of green onions. Layer again with remaining ingredients ending with green onions. Bake, uncovered, at 375° for 20 minutes. Let stand 5 minutes before cutting. *Makes 6 servings.*

"If it were not for the Eucharist, if it were not for this marvelous manifestation of God's love, if it were not for this opportunity to place ourselves in the very real presence of God, if it were not for the sacrament that reminds us of His love, His suffering and His triumph, which indeed perpetuates for us His saving sacrifice on the cross, I am sure that I could never face the challenges of my life, my own weakness and sinfulness and my own need to reach out to the Living God." ~Archbishop Theodore McCarrick

Easy Layered Taco Pie

1 lb. lean ground beef, turkey, or chicken
1 (1.25 oz.) pkg. taco seasoning mix
½ cup water
4 flour tortillas, cut into quarters
1 cup salsa
1 cup shredded cheddar cheese
2 cups shredded lettuce
¼ cup sour cream

Brown meat in a skillet. Stir in water and seasoning mix, and cook for 3 minutes. Remove half of the meat mixture and set aside. Place 8 tortilla quarters on top of remaining meat mixture in a 9-inch microwaveable dish. Top with reserved meat mixture and remaining 8 tortilla quarters. Top with salsa and cheese. Microwave 4 minutes. Top with lettuce and sour cream just before serving.

Texas Straw Hat

1 lb. ground beef
1 cup chopped onion
⅔ cup chopped celery
⅔ cup chopped green pepper
2 (6 oz.) cans tomato paste
1 cup water
2 tsp. chili powder
1 tsp. Worcestershire sauce
½ tsp. salt
¼ tsp. dried whole thyme
⅛ tsp. pepper
Dash of hot sauce
1 (6 oz.) pkg. corn chips
2 cups (8 oz.) shredded Cheddar cheese

Combine first 4 ingredients in a large skillet; cook until meat is browned, stirring to crumble. Drain off grease. Stir in remaining ingredients except corn chips and cheese; bring to a boil. Cover, reduce heat, and simmer 20 minutes, stirring occasionally. Serve over corn chips and top with cheese.

Easy Meatloaf

1 ½ lbs. ground beef
1 cup fresh breadcrumbs
1 onion, chopped *(I use less or some powdered onion)*
1 egg
1 ½ tsp. salt
¼ tsp. pepper
1 (8 oz.) can tomato sauce

Sauce:
1 (8 oz.) can tomato sauce
½ cup water
3 Tbsp. vinegar
3 Tbsp. brown sugar
2 Tbsp. mustard
2 tsp. Worcestershire sauce

Mix first 7 ingredients together to form a loaf. Place in shallow pan. Then mix together the sauce and pour over meatloaf. Bake at 350° for 1 ½ hours.

Sometimes I make additional sauce and add carrots and potatoes in the last 30 minutes or so to cook just like a roast.

Spicy Beef Rolls

1 lb. ground beef
1 Tbsp. finely chopped onion
½ cup tomato sauce
½ cup ketchup
2 Tbsp. grated Parmesan cheese
½ tsp. garlic powder
¼ tsp. fennel seeds *(optional)*
⅛ tsp. ground oregano

6 Kaiser rolls, split
6 (3-inch) squares sliced mozzarella cheese

Garlic Spread:
2 Tbsp. butter or margarine, softened
¼ tsp. garlic powder
½ tsp. paprika

Combine ground beef and onion in a heavy skillet. Cook over medium heat until beef is browned, stirring to crumble meat. Drain. Add tomato sauce, ketchup, Parmesan cheese, and seasonings. Mix well. Simmer 20 minutes.

Spread ½ teaspoon garlic spread on insides of each roll. Spoon beef mixture evenly on bottom halves of roll. Place cheese slice over beef. Replace top halves. Wrap each sandwich in foil. Bake at 350° for 15 minutes or until thoroughly heated.

Garlic Spread: Combine all ingredients. Mix well, *Makes 2 tablespoons.*

Rouladen (Stuffed Beef Roll)

6 very thin slices of beef (scaloppini style)
Mustard
Paprika
Salt and pepper
About 4 uncooked slices of bacon, chopped
1 small onion, diced
3 dill pickles, diced
Margarine or shortening
Sturdy toothpicks or heavy thread
Brown gravy mix or homemade with flour

Tenderize each beef slice with a meat hammer. They can be placed inside a plastic bag or under waxed paper for less mess. On one side of each slice, spread mustard, then sprinkle on paprika, salt and pepper. Place a small amount of diced pickle, onion, and bacon along middle of beef slice. Fold a small amount of each beef slice edge inward on the long sides. Then begin rolling from short end until you have it completely rolled up with stuffing inside. Hold the roll together by pushing 2 toothpicks through it or tie it with heavy thread. It may be helpful to keep track of how many toothpicks are used; they will be removed later.

Melt margarine or shortening in a large pot and place beef rolls in for browning. Use tongs to turn rolls as they brown. When done, remove rolls and then remove string or toothpicks from the rolls. They will remain rolled. Use drippings to make your own gravy with flour or use a brown gravy mix. Place the beef rolls in the gravy and simmer for about 45 minutes to an hour. Serve with favorite potato dish and red cabbage.

St. Elizabeth of Portugal (1271-1336)
Feast Day ~ July 4

Though many of us may be called "Daddy's Little Princess," Elizabeth really was a princess, and she married the King of Portugal, King Denis, at the age of 12. Elizabeth loved God and went to Mass every day. Though her husband was a good ruler, he was impure, and the people all talked about him. One day a very jealous page told a lie to the king about Elizabeth and another page. The king became furious and arranged for the page to be killed. The good page did not know about this and thought he was running an errand. He quickly stopped by Mass on the way and was late so he stayed for the next Mass, too. The king, wondering if the page had been killed, sent the jealous page to find out. The jealous page, being the first to show up, was thrown into the furnace by the man waiting for the good page to arrive. When the King found out the real story, he knew that God had saved the good page, and he also knew that his wife was innocent. The king changed his life and apologized to Elizabeth. He died a holy death. Elizabeth joined the Third Order Franciscans and spent her remaining 11 years giving to the poor. She was also known as a great peacemaker in her own family as well as with nations.

Why not try and imitate Elizabeth this week? Go to a weekday Mass with your family and try to not fight with your brothers and sisters.

Elizabeth's Easy Beef Stroganoff

1 (12 oz.) pkg. egg noodles
1 ½ lbs. sirloin steak
1 tsp. dry mustard
Dash salt, pepper, garlic powder
1 onion, minced
2 Tbsp. butter
1 Tbsp. flour
2 (4 oz.) cans mushrooms, undrained
½ cup sour cream
¼ cup butter

Prepare egg noodles per instructions on package. Set aside; keep warm. Cut steak into small strips. In small bowl, combine flour, mustard, salt, pepper, garlic powder, and canned mushrooms with their liquid.

In skillet over medium-high heat, cook onion in ¼ cup butter until tender, about 5 minutes, stirring occasionally. Add steak; cook over high heat, stirring constantly, until lightly browned. Stir in mushroom mixture. Reduce heat to medium setting and continue to cook, stirring constantly, until mixture is thickened, about 5 minutes. Stir in sour cream. Heat thoroughly, but do not boil. Serve over noodles.

Spaghetti Sauce

2 lbs. ground beef
1 medium onion, diced
1 (12 oz.) can tomato paste
1 (15 oz.) can tomato sauce
2 (10 ¾ oz.) cans Campbell's tomato soup
3 whole cloves
Dash each of garlic powder, sweet basil, marjoram, oregano, salt and pepper
1 small bay leaf
2 Tbsp. brown sugar
1 (5 oz.) can evaporated milk
Margarine

Melt margarine in large pot. Lightly cook onions and add meat. Stir occasionally while meat browns. Add salt and pepper. Stir in tomato sauce, paste, and soup. Add all other spices and sugar. Simmer on medium heat for about an hour. Stir occasionally to keep sauce from sticking to bottom. Add water if sauce becomes too thick. During last 15 minutes of cooking, add canned milk. Remove bay leaf and cloves before serving. *Makes 6 to 8 servings.*

St. Anthony of Padua (1195-1231)
Feast Day ~ June 13

St. Anthony is one of the most beloved saints of the Church. He is also a Doctor of the Church. Born in Portugal, he is known for his work in Padua, Italy. He was canonized less than a year after his death at the young age of 36. He joined the Augustinian order but left to become a Franciscan when five Franciscan martyrs were brought back from Africa to be buried at his church. He too wanted to preach the Faith and become a martyr. He was sent to Italy, but an illness kept him from achieving his dream, so he spent time praying and reading the Scriptures. He worked around the hermitage but little was asked of him until one day his superiors asked him to preach at an ordination. The Holy Spirit took over and Anthony spoke so eloquently that all were astonished. He began teaching theology to the friars. Anthony was known for preaching to the heretics, and when they wouldn't listen, he would go to the river and preach to the fish. He was known as the "hammer to the heretics." When they exhumed his body some 336 years after he died, Anthony's tongue was completely incorrupt. All of his teachings had been so pure that God had preserved it. Though he is known for helping people find things, Anthony was a great lover of God and prayed to do God's will and not his own.

What will you do this week to show God that you are living for Him and not for yourself? Try and give up something special

that you really love this week and offer "your wanting it" up to God. See how happy God is when you try to please him?

St. Anthony's Italian Noodles

This makes two 9x13-inch pans, freezes well, and is good for a busy day or to take to a family with illness, new baby, etc.

2 lbs. ground beef
1 onion, diced
4 cups uncooked macaroni noodles (or 7-8 cups uncooked "larger" noodles – rotini, penne, etc.)

2 small cans mushrooms
45 oz. spaghetti sauce
¾ lb. sharp Cheddar cheese, grated
½-1 cup Parmesan cheese, grated

Bring sufficient water to boil; cook noodles al dente. Sauté onions in oil; add salt and ground beef when onions are translucent. Cook until done; add salt and pepper and Italian seasonings as desired; drain meat/onion mixture.

Mix all ingredients, including drained pasta, in a large bowl to combine. Divide into two 9x13-inch pans. (If intending to freeze one or both, can line the pan with foil to be able to remove easily and wrap for longer storage.)

Bake at 350° for 30 minutes if using right away to allow cheeses to melt and everything to combine nicely. If the dish is frozen before baking, bake at 375° for 1 hour, covered, and then 15 minutes uncovered.

⁕ *"Through him [then] let us continually offer God a sacrifice of praise, that is, the fruit of lips that confess his name."* Heb. 13:15

⁕ *"I urge you therefore, brothers, by the mercies of God, to offer your bodies as a living sacrifice, holy and pleasing to God, your spiritual worship."* Rom. 12:1

St. Catherine Labouré (1806-1876)
Feast Day ~ November 28

Catherine was born to an upper middle class family, the ninth of eleven children. She was nine years old when her mother died and she ran to her room and took the picture of the Blessed Mother off the wall and kissed it. "Now, dear Lady, you are to be my mother," she said. After receiving her first Holy Communion she woke up every day at 4 a.m. and went to Mass several miles away. One day she had a dream where she saw an old priest saying Mass. He motioned for her to come closer and as she did he said, "My child, it is a good deed to look after the sick; you run away now, but one day you will be glad to come to me. God has designs on you; do not forget it."

She went on with her life, but one day she saw a picture on the wall of the hospital and asked who the man was. It was St. Vincent de Paul, the same man in her dream. Catherine joined the Daughters of Charity and was given the honor of seeing Jesus' heart outside the tabernacle. One night as she went to bed a voice of a child awakened her and told her to go to the chapel. She obeyed and the angel opened the locked door. The chapel was aglow with candles. Catherine walked up to the altar and knelt down. She heard a rustling of a dress and saw the Blessed Mother in a chair. She knelt next to her with her hands in Mary's lap. She was told she would be given a mission.

100 Main Dishes

Several months later, she had another vision, and Our Lady asked that she have a medal made. When Catherine asked what the light coming from her fingers was, Our Lady explained that they were all the graces that fell to the ground that no one asked for. Catherine obeyed and told her confessor about the medal, but it took two years to have it made. The medal was called the Miraculous Medal because so many miracles happened to people wearing one. Catherine kept the secret for 46 years and told no one that she was the one Our Lady had come to. Right before she died, she told the nuns. Her body is incorrupt in the chapel where she saw Our Lady in Paris, France.

This week remember to pray to Mary and to Jesus, her Son, and ask them for the graces you need to be a great Catholic. Pray that God blesses your whole family and makes them strong. As a present to Jesus, why not get a shoebox and cut up several pieces of paper and place them in a dish. Every time you do a good deed, place one piece of shredded paper in the box. As the box fills with paper, imagine that it's straw for the baby Jesus to lay his head on Christmas morning. Encourage everyone to fill the box.

Catherine's Chili

Quick and easy to make this warms you up after a cold day. You can prepare it ahead of time and reheat it quite easily.

1 ½-2 lbs. ground beef
1 medium onion, chopped
1 Tbsp. ground thyme
1 Tbsp. chili powder
4 (10 oz.) cans condensed tomato soup
4-5 stalks celery, chopped and cooked separately
1 (14-16 oz.) can red kidney beans
1 cup elbow macaroni

Brown ground beef and onion in large pot. Drain all fat. Add thyme, chili powder, celery, soup, kidney beans, and 1 to 2 cans of water. Mix well and heat. Simmer for 15 minutes.

Meanwhile, cook macaroni. Add cooked macaroni when done. If you want to freeze this, do not add the macaroni until you serve it, as macaroni doesn't freeze well.

Meatball Stew

1 ½ lbs. ground beef
1 cup soft breadcrumbs
¼ cup finely chopped onion
1 egg, beaten
1 tsp. salt
½ tsp. marjoram leaves
¼ tsp. thyme leaves
⅛ tsp. pepper

2 (10 ¾ oz.) cans tomato soup
2 (10 ½ oz.) cans beef broth
4 medium potatoes, pared and chopped into pieces
4 carrots, cut in 1-inch cubes
8-15 small white onions
2 Tbsp. chopped fresh parsley *(optional)*

Combine first 8 ingredients. Mix lightly but well. Shape into meatballs. Brown meatballs in hot oil. Remove as they brown.

Drain oil from pan used to brown meatballs. Add soups and heat, scraping loose pieces of meat and browns. When soups are combined and heated, add potatoes and carrots*. Cover and cook slowly until veggies are tender. Add onions last ½ hour. Makes 6 to 8 servings.

At this point you can put the stew into a crockpot and cook on low 8 hours or until veggies are cooked. Add onions last ½ hour to cook until tender but not falling apart.

"As I read the sad statistics... that only 30% believe what the church teaches on the Real Presence of Christ, my mind went back to an earlier heresy - the Protestant Revolt. It was not the so called "selling of indulgences" that caused the painful break in our family. It was... [those] who no longer believed in the Real Presence..."

"When Catholics are asked, 'Do you have a personal relationship with Jesus Christ?' they should answer a resounding YES! There is no closer union with Jesus than when you receive Him in the Eucharist. You too can say with St. Paul, '...and the life I now live is not my own CHRIST IS LIVING IN ME.' (Gal 2:20)"
~Rev. Msgr. Richard L. Carroll, V.F.

Nana's Barbecue

3-4 lbs. pork or beef roast
(inexpensive cut)
1 envelope onion soup mix
Barbeque sauce

Sauce:
½ cup vinegar
½ cup Worcestershire sauce
½ cup ketchup
½ cup mustard
½-1 cup brown sugar
1 (8 oz.) can tomato sauce
1 cup reserved liquid

Place cut of meat into crockpot with dry onion mix poured over top. Cover with lid and cook 8 hours on high. Shred meat and cool. Reserve 1 cup of liquid from crockpot.

Combine sauce ingredients and simmer for 10 minutes. Add shredded meat and warm up. Serve on hamburger buns.

Pizza Burgers

2 lbs. ground beef
2 (6 oz.) cans tomato sauce
   + 1 can water
⅔ cup grated Parmesan cheese

¼ cup minced onion
½ cup chopped green pepper
2 tsp. salt
½ tsp. basil
Mozzarella cheese

Brown meat and drain. Add remaining ingredients except cheese, and simmer. Place mixture on split English muffins. Grate mozzarella cheese over top. Broil 10 minutes.

"By our little acts of charity practiced in the shade we convert souls far away, we help missionaries, we win for them abundant alms; and by that means build actual dwellings spiritual and material for our Eucharistic Lord." ~St. Thérèse of Lisieux

St. Catherine of Siena (1347-1380) *Virgin*
Feast Day ~ April 29

Catherine was the 25th child born to a family in Italy. Her father was a wool dyer. She was just a little girl of 6 when she started seeing her Guardian Angel. She wanted to become a nun, but her parents wanted her to marry, so she cut off her long beautiful hair to make herself unattractive. She was given the heaviest and dirtiest housework, but she did her work happily. Finally, her parents realized that this child of theirs was not going to back down. This stubbornness held Catherine in good stead, as she would need it for later in life. One night when she was alone in her room, Jesus and His Mother Mary appeared to Catherine. The Blessed Mother lifted Catherine's hand as Jesus put a ring on her finger. She belonged to Jesus.

Catherine had no formal education, but she was brilliant theologically. She lived in hard times and was determined when she knew she was right. She wrote to kings and queens begging for peace and avoiding war. She even wrote to the Pope asking him to leave Avignon, France and come back to Rome where he belonged. She wrote that it was God's will, and the Pope listened to her. For the last five years of her life, Catherine had the pain of the stigmata, though few knew about it until it appeared after her death. She died in 1380 when she was only 33 years old. Fifty years later, her body was found to be incorrupt. She is a Doctor of the Church.

This week look around at your world. Is there something going on that doesn't honor God's law or Church teaching?

Why not try and be like Catherine and explain the truth. One person can change the world. Catherine did!

Catherine's Sloppy Joe's in the Crockpot

This recipe can be doubled using a large crockpot depending on how many you need to feed. Catherine was the youngest of 25, so you can imagine how much her mom had to make!

2 lbs. ground beef or turkey, cooked and drained	1 cup barbecue sauce
1 large onion, chopped	1-2 Tbsp. vinegar *(optional)*
1 medium red or green pepper chopped	1-2 Tbsp. Worcestershire sauce *(optional)*
2 cups ketchup	1 Tbsp. prepared mustard

Place beef, onion, and pepper in slow cooker in an even layer. Combine all other ingredients in a medium bowl. Pour over beef and vegetables. Cook on high 4 to 5 hours or until vegetables are tender.

"Be brave and steadfast; have no fear or dread of them, for it is the LORD, your God, who marches with you; he will never fail you or forsake you." Deut. 31:6

"Wait for the LORD, take courage; be stouthearted, wait for the LORD!" Psa. 27:14

"See, then! The LORD has chosen you to build a house as his sanctuary. Take courage and set to work." 1Chr. 28:10

"O You who are mad about Your creature, true God and true Man, You have left Yourself wholly to us, as food, so that we will not fall through weariness during our pilgrimage in this life, but will be fortified by You, celestial nourishment."
~St. Catherine of Siena

Australian Meat Pie (Family Size)

1 ¾ lbs. lean ground beef
1 cup finely chopped mushrooms
1 cup finely chopped onion
1 tsp. dry parsley
½ tsp. salt
Dash of pepper

1 Tbsp. butter
2 Tbsp. olive oil
1 cup beef stock
2 Tbsp. cornstarch
1 tsp. Worcestershire sauce
1 tsp. tomato paste
1 egg, beaten

1 pkg. of (2) 9-inch pie crusts

Melt butter with oil in a large pot and sauté mushrooms and onions with parsley, salt and pepper until onions are translucent. Mix in beef, breaking it apart until well blended and browned. In separate bowl combine beef stock, cornstarch, Worcestershire sauce and tomato paste, stir well and add to pot. Continue to stir, bring to a simmer and cover on medium low heat for 15 minutes, stirring regularly to bring liquid to a thick gravy. Continue to simmer and stir for 15 more minutes uncovered. Remove from heat and cool for 20 minutes. Line one pie crust in pie dish, gently fill with meat filling and cover with other pie crust. Moisten edges with egg wash, fold extra dough under bottom crust and crimp. Brush top with egg and cut 4 vents for steam. Bake at 400° for 30 minutes and let sit for 15 minutes. Serve the Australian way with tomato sauce (ketchup). Also makes 4 individual mini pies.

Crunchy Chicken Casserole

5 cups cubed cooked chicken
2 cups celery
1 (8 oz.) pkg. cream cheese, softened

1 cup mayonnaise
½ tsp. salt
½ onion finely chopped
1 ½ cups potato chips, crushed (or more if desired)

Preheat oven to 350°. Mix chicken, celery, salt and onion. In separate bowl mix mayonnaise and cream cheese together. Fold into chicken mixture. Place mixture into greased 9x13-inch baking dish and sprinkle with crushed potato chips. Heat in oven for 30 minutes until browned.

Mexican Chicken Delight

5 cups cubed cooked chicken
1 can tomatoes w/green chilies
1 (10 ¾ oz.) can cream of mushroom soup
1 (10 ¾ oz.) can cream of chicken soup
4 oz. taco sauce
½ cup chicken broth
1 pkg. taco chips
1 ½ cups Mexican blend cheese grated

In a saucepan, combine and heat tomatoes, soups, taco sauce and broth. Line bottom of casserole dish with taco chips. Place chicken on top of chips and pour sauce over chicken and chips. Top with grated cheese. Bake at 350° until bubbly and hot.

Turkey Enchiladas

⅓ cup peanut oil
½ cup onion, finely chopped
2 cloves garlic, crushed
½ cup flour
13¼ oz. chicken broth
1 ⅔ cups water
½ cup enchilada sauce
1 Tbsp. chili powder
5 oz. shredded cheddar cheese
2 lbs. ground turkey, cooked
¼ cup black olives (optional)
Eight 7-inch corn tortillas

Preheat oven to 350°. Brown ground turkey in pan and drain. Heat oil in a saucepan over medium heat; add onion and garlic and cook until tender. Stir in flour, mixing until smooth. Gradually add chicken broth, water and enchilada sauce, mixing until smooth. Stir in chili powder. Cook over medium heat stirring constantly until thick. Reserving ½ cup cheese, mix remaining cheese with cooked turkey and ½ cup sauce mixture. Dip tortillas in sauce to lightly coat. Spoon 3 heaping Tbsp. into each tortilla and roll up. Place seam side down in shallow greased baking pan. Pour remaining sauce over tortillas. Bake at 350° for 15 minutes. Sprinkle with remaining cheese and heat an additional 10 minutes.

Chicken Casserole

4 cups cubed cooked chicken
2 cups celery
2 cups croutons
8 oz. Swiss Cheese
1 cup Miracle Whip
½ cup milk
¼ cup chopped onion
1 tsp. salt
¼ tsp. pepper
¼ cup chopped walnuts

Preheat oven to 350°. Mix all ingredients and spoon into 2 qt. casserole dish. Sprinkle with walnuts. Bake 40 minutes.

Oven Fried Chicken

1 cup Italian-seasoned breadcrumbs
¼ cup grated Parmesan cheese
½ cup mayonnaise
½ tsp. salt *(optional)*
½ tsp. poultry seasoning
¼ tsp. ground red pepper
8 skinned and boned chicken breast halves

Stir together breadcrumbs and Parmesan cheese in shallow dish. Stir together mayo and next 3 ingredients. Brush both sides of chicken with mayo mixture, then dredge in breadcrumb mixture.

Place on aluminum foil-lined 15x10-inch jelly roll pan coated with vegetable cooking spray. Bake at 425° for 20 minutes or until done.

Crispy Crunchy Chicken

1 pint sour cream
4 tsp. lemon juice
4 tsp. Worcestershire sauce
2 tsp. celery salt
2 tsp. paprika
1 tsp. garlic salt
¼ tsp. pepper
8 boneless chicken breasts
Pepperidge Farm bread stuffing
½ cup melted butter

Mix first 7 ingredients together. Dip chicken breasts into mixture and roll in stuffing. Arrange in a greased shallow baking dish and pour melted butter over all. Bake, uncovered, at 350° for 1 hour until chicken is done.

Crispy Garlic Chicken

2 chicken breasts, split, deboned, and skin removed
1 stick butter
2 Tbsp. garlic powder
Fresh breadcrumbs
Parmesan cheese

Melt butter in microwave dish with lid. Add garlic powder to melted butter. Then add Parmesan cheese until it becomes a thick paste.

One at a time, put both sides of chicken in butter mixture, then in breadcrumbs. Place in baking dish. Bake at 350° for 1 hour. Enjoy!

Baked Parmesan Chicken

1 cup dry breadcrumbs
1/3 cup grated Parmesan cheese
1/4 tsp. oregano
1/4 tsp. pepper
Salt
1 clove garlic, minced
3/4 cup melted butter, divided
6 boneless chicken breasts

Combine breadcrumbs, cheese, oregano, pepper, and salt; set aside. Lightly sauté garlic in 2 tablespoons butter; stir in remaining butter. Dip chicken in garlic butter, then roll in crumb mixture.

Place chicken in a 9x13-inch pan. Sprinkle with remaining crumb mixture and pour on remaining garlic butter. Bake at 350° for 55 minutes.

"The guest of our soul knows our misery; He comes to find an empty tent within us - that is all He asks."
~St. Thérèse of Lisieux

St. John Gaulbert (993-1073) *Abbot*
Feast Day ~ July 12

Born in Florence, Italy to a rich non-Christian family, John had one brother. One day his brother, Hugo, was murdered by one of his friends, and John set out to avenge his brother's death. He arranged to meet the murderer on Good Friday in a narrow alley where there was little room for escape. He charged at the man who killed his brother, but the man fell to his knees and begged in the name of Jesus for mercy just as John was about to kill him. John was so touched by this that he ran to a monastery and begged God to forgive his sins. As John knelt crying, Jesus on the crucifix bowed his head. He felt that God had forgiven him, and he asked to join the monastery. His father couldn't believe this and threatened to burn down the monastery, but John cut his hair, put on a borrowed habit, and went out to meet his father. His father, taken back at how his son had changed, consented to having him join the monastery. John gave his life to God. He especially loved working with the poor. God blessed him with the gift of working miracles, and even Pope Leo IX sought out his guidance. John was about 80 years old when he died.

When you get in a bad mood this week try and think about St. John. Just stop and realize that God is watching you and pray for a sense of peace. Control your temper and let your anger flow out of you.

Chicken-Italian Dressing Bake

½ cup Italian-seasoned breadcrumbs
¼ cup grated fresh Parmesan cheese
⅛ tsp. salt

4 skinless, boneless chicken breast halves
¼ cup Italian salad dressing
Vegetable cooking spray

Combine breadcrumbs, cheese, and salt in a plastic bag; shake to mix. Dip chicken in salad dressing. Place 1 piece of chicken in bag and shake to coat. Repeat procedure with remaining chicken.

Place in lightly greased pan. Bake at 400° for 15 minutes. Spray chicken with cooking spray and bake an additional 5 to 10 minutes or until done. *Makes 4 servings. Recipe can be doubled.*

"But now, do forgive me my sin once more, and pray the LORD, your God, to take at least this deadly pest from me."
Ex. 10:17

"May the God of peace himself make you perfectly holy and may you entirely, spirit, soul, and body, be preserved blameless for the coming of our Lord Jesus Christ."
1Th. 5:23

"Keep on doing what you have learned and received and heard and seen in me. Then the God of peace will be with you." Phil. 4:9

St. Gianna Beretta Molla (1922-1962)
Feast Day ~ April 28

Gianna was born near Milan, Italy. She grew up in a very Christian home with loving Catholic parents. When she was in medical school, her parents died four months apart. She studied hard and became a doctor, opening up a clinic very soon after she graduated. She was involved in Catholic action groups always helping the less fortunate, especially the youth organizing retreats, hiking, and social events.

Her future husband, Pietro, was impressed and wanted to marry her. Gianna had to pray about this because she was also thinking of becoming a nun. She talked with her priest, and he encouraged her to become a wife and mother. They had 3 children and were very happy. Gianna learned that she was going to have a fourth child, but after 2 months of being pregnant, there were complications and Gianna was found to have a tumor in her uterus. She was insistent that they do nothing to hurt the baby. She would wait and have the surgery after the baby was born.

She delivered a healthy baby girl on Holy Saturday, April 21, 1962. By this time, Gianna knew that she was going to die. She was a doctor and knew the risk of not going in to remove the tumor. In spite of pain, she refused pain medication because she wanted to meet Jesus having suffered for her sins. She died seven days later saying, "Jesus I love you. Jesus I love you."

She was beatified on April 24, 1994 with her "little" girl, 32 years old, at the ceremony. She was canonized on May 16, 2004. She is the patron saint of mothers and physicians, and the Pro-Life movement has adopted her as a woman whose choice changed the world. Her daughter is now a physician in Italy.

This week when something doesn't go the way you want it to, say to Jesus, "Jesus, I love you," just as Gianna did. Learn to love God no matter what happens to you in good times and in bad times.

Gianna's Garlic Chicken

½ cup olive oil
8-10 cloves garlic, minced
1 tsp. red pepper flakes
3-4 cups freshly ground breadcrumbs

½ cup Parmesan cheese
Salt and pepper to taste
4 or 5 chicken breast halves

Combine first 3 ingredients and warm in microwave for a minute to marry flavors a bit. Cut chicken breasts in half and tenderize a bit. Pour oil mixture over chicken and allow to marinate for at least 2 hours.

Mix breadcrumbs with cheese and seasonings. Remove chicken from oil mixture and dredge in breadcrumbs. Place on a baking sheet and bake at 400° for 25 minutes or until golden brown.

"The LORD, your God, will circumcise your hearts and the hearts of your descendants, that you may love the LORD, your God, with all your heart and all your soul, and so may live." Deut. 30:6

St. Monica (322-387)
Feast Day ~ August 27

Monica was born into a Christian family in Tagaste, North Africa. Her parents arranged a marriage for her to an ill-tempered and unfaithful pagan named Patricius, and together they had 3 children. Her life was difficult because her mother-in-law, who also lived with them, criticized Monica and told lies about her. Through much prayer, she eventually converted them both. Two of her children entered religious life, but Augustine was a difficult child. Monica prayed and prayed, begging prayers from the priests and holy ones for her son to repent of his wild ways. When her husband died, she was left to bear the burden, and many tears were shed. Seventeen years later, Augustine was baptized by St. Ambrose. St. Monica teaches us never to give up on our prayers for those needing conversion. Monica died that same year shortly after her son's conversion. She is the patroness of wives and abuse victims.

Pick a special person in your family to pray for this week. Pray every day for them and ask God to protect them from harm!

Augustine's Jerk Chicken

St. Monica prayed for her wayward son, St. Augustine, for almost 30 years begging God to help him. He finally converted to Catholicism, and a few months later his dear mother died. He became a great saint!

1 cup coarsely chopped washed fresh cilantro leaves and stems
½ cup cayenne pepper sauce
⅓ cup vegetable or olive oil
6 cloves garlic, coarsely chopped
¼ cup fresh lime juice *(juice of 2 limes)*
1 tsp. grated lime peel
1 tsp. ground turmeric
1 tsp. ground allspice
4 Tbsp. brown sugar
4-6 boneless chicken breasts

Take all ingredients (other than chicken) and mix together in a large mixing bowl. Reserve ½ cup or so of the mixture for a side marinade at the table.

Wash chicken breasts, pound to flatten if desired, and submerge into liquid. Cover bowl with plastic wrap and place in refrigerator to marinate for several hours (or overnight).

Grill over medium heat until done, turning regularly, approximately 8 to 12 minutes for flattened chicken breasts, 15 to 20 minutes for regular chicken breasts, depending on heat. Serve with the reserved marinade.

"LORD, protect us always; preserve us from this generation."
Ps. 12:8

Elegant Chicken Breasts

8 boneless chicken breasts
Salt and pepper
1 cup butter
8 slices mozzarella cheese
2 Tbsp. chopped parsley
⅛ tsp. sage
¼ tsp. rosemary and thyme
½ cup flour
½ cup breadcrumbs
¾ cup white wine
2 eggs, beaten

Turn chicken breast with smooth side down; sprinkle with salt and pepper. Dot each breast with butter. Place a slice of cheese and roll up jelly roll fashion. Secure with toothpicks. Melt remaining butter and add parsley, sage, rosemary, and thyme. Roll chicken in flour, then egg, then in breadcrumbs.

Place side by side in a baking dish. Pour butter and spice mixture over chicken. Bake at 350° for 30 minutes. Pour wine over chicken and bake an additional 30 minutes.

Chicken Franchaise

4-6 boneless chicken breasts
1 egg, beaten
Flour
½ cup white wine *(cooking or regular table wine)*
Lemon juice

Pound (tenderize) chicken breasts. Coat chicken in egg, then lightly flour. Sauté in butter until <u>lightly</u> browned (do not let butter get too hot or burned). Simmer until chicken is no longer pink.

A minute or two before removing from pan, add about ½ cup white wine with a little lemon juice – or squeeze a little fresh lemon once chicken is on serving dish.

Chicken Swiss

8 boneless chicken breasts
8 pieces Swiss cheese
1 (10 ¾ oz.) can cream of celery soup + ¼ cup water
1 ½ cups stuffing mix
1 stick (½ cup) butter, melted

Layer in 9x13-inch pan. Bake at 350° for 45 minutes.

Easy Feta Chicken Bake

6-8 boneless, skinless chicken breast halves
2 Tbsp. lemon juice, divided
½ tsp. salt *(optional)*
¼ tsp. pepper
1 cup (4 oz.) crumbled feta cheese
¼ cup diced red pepper
¼ cup diced fresh parsley

Preheat oven to 350°. Arrange chicken in a 9x13-inch baking dish. Drizzle with 1 tablespoon lemon juice. Season with salt and pepper. Top with feta cheese. Drizzle remaining 1 tablespoon lemon juice on top. Bake 35 to 40 minutes or until chicken is done. Sprinkle with red pepper and parsley.

"Do you realize that Jesus is there in the tabernacle expressly for you - for you alone? He burns with the desire to come into your heart...don't listen to the demon, laugh at him, and go without fear to receive the Jesus of peace and love." ~St. Thérèse of Lisieux

Marsala Chicken with Sage and Cremini Mushrooms

2 Tbsp. all-purpose flour
Coarse salt and ground pepper
4 boneless, skinless chicken breast halves (6 to 8 oz. each)
1 Tbsp. olive oil
10 oz. cremini mushrooms *(or any kind)*, trimmed and thinly sliced
1 shallot minced
1 Tbsp. finely chopped fresh sage, plus more for garnish
½ cup sweet Marsala wine
¼ cup heavy cream
1 Tbsp. butter

Place flour in shallow bowl; season generously with salt and pepper. Dredge each piece of chicken in flour, shaking off excess.

In a large skillet, heat oil over medium heat, add chicken, and cook until golden on the outside and opaque throughout, 8 to 10 minutes per side. Transfer to a plate and cover with aluminum foil to keep warm (reserve skillet).

Add mushrooms, shallot, sage, and ¼ cup water to skillet; season with salt and pepper. Cook, tossing frequently until mushrooms are tender 3 to 5 minutes. Add wine and cream; simmer over medium-high until slightly thickened, 3 to 5 minutes. Remove from heat and stir in butter; season again with salt and pepper. Top chicken with mushroom sauce and garnish with sage. *Makes 4 servings.*

☙ *"Mass is not an opportunity to relax and daydream, to let our minds wander wherever they might. We are called to participate with our hearts, minds, and bodies. Such participation must be internal and spiritual; it requires periods of silence and listening, but above all it requires prayer."* ~Cardinal George Pell, Archbishop of Sydney, Australia, May 2005

Chicken Tetrazzini

1 (10 ¾ oz.) can cream of mushroom soup
½ cup milk
¼ cup grated Parmesan cheese
¼ cup sour cream or plain yogurt
1 ½ cups cubed cooked chicken or turkey
1 small onion, chopped
½ cup sliced mushrooms
1 ½ cups cooked spaghetti
1 clove garlic, minced

Preheat oven to 350°. Cook spaghetti (about ½ cup uncooked makes 1 ½ cups).

Sauté onions, mushrooms and garlic until onions are translucent. Stir together soup, milk, sour cream or yogurt, cheese, onions, mushrooms, garlic, chicken or turkey, and spaghetti. Spoon into a 2-quart casserole and bake for 30 minutes or until hot.

Slow Cooked Italian Chicken

3 lbs. boneless, skinless chicken breast pieces
1 pkg. dry Italian dressing mix
1 (10 ¾ oz.) can 98% fat-free cream of mushroom soup *(I also get the low-sodium along with fat-free)*
1 (4 oz.) can mushrooms, drained *(I skip this, but it is in the recipe)*
8 oz. fat-free sour cream or fat-free plain yogurt *(I think the sour cream tastes better)*

Place chicken in crockpot. Mix together Italian dressing mix, soup, and mushrooms; then stir into chicken. Cook on low 6 to 8 hours.

With slotted spoon, lift chicken out of cooker. Place in a covered dish and keep warm. Combine cooking juices with sour cream or yogurt in slow cooker. Cover and heat until warmed through. Ready to serve on rice or noodles.

St. Elizabeth of Hungary (1207-1231)
Feast Day ~ November 17

Elizabeth was the daughter of a king and her husband was chosen for her at the age of 4. She grew up with him and led a very holy life but had many tragedies occur. Her mother was killed by Hungarian nobles, her husband-to-be was killed, and his brother was next in line to marry her. She married Ludwig who was 21 and she was 14 years old. He was very devoted to her and allowed her to do many pious acts even holding her hand at night while she prayed. While her husband was away, she took over and distributed alms to the poor and built a hospital to care for the sick. She oversaw 900 people daily. Her husband returned but soon left and was killed in battle. She delivered her third child not knowing that he had died. Upon learning of his death, Elizabeth said, "The world with all its joys is now dead to me." She was 20 years old.

Elizabeth learned about St. Francis of Assisi and followed his teachings. She later helped her spiritual director found a monastery in Eisenach and filled her life with his rule, which was to lead a life of prayer, humility, chastity according to your state in life, and to practice patience, and charity. She became a Third Order Franciscan and devoted herself to the sick. She died in 1231 at the age of 24. St. Elizabeth is the patron saint of bakers, widows and brides.

Help out this week by not being *asked* to do something. Look around at what needs to be done and just do it. You can pretend you are in charge of your house and give orders to yourself: go and clean your room; do the dishes; straighten up the family room. Show God how much you love Him.

Easy Chicken a la King

1 lb. boneless, skinless chicken breasts, cut up
1 onion, chopped
1 tsp. ground garlic *(optional)*
1 cup chopped celery
Salt and pepper to taste
2 Tbsp. olive oil or margarine
1 can (10 ¾ oz.) cream of chicken soup
1 cup milk
Chinese noodles

Brown chicken in 1 tablespoon olive oil or margarine; push to sides and brown the onion and celery. Add soup and milk; simmer for 25 minutes. Serve with rice. Top with Chinese noodles. *Makes 4 servings.*

"For kindness to a father will not be forgotten, it will serve as a sin offering — it will take lasting root." Sir. 3:14

"He does a kindness who lends to his neighbor, and he fulfills the precepts who holds out a helping hand." Sir. 29:1

"Thus says the LORD of hosts: Render true judgment, and show kindness and compassion toward each other."
Zech. 7:9

**St. Rita (1381-1457)
Feast day ~ May 22**

Born in Italy in 1381, St. Rita had always wanted to become a nun but her parents arranged a marriage to a man who was mean and had a harsh temper. Rita had two sons who followed in their father's footsteps. One night, her husband was killed in a fight. Rita had prayed for him, and he repented before he died. Her 2 sons were also killed shortly afterwards, and Rita was free to become a nun. She tried to join the Augustinian order, but they wouldn't accept Rita because she was a widow. Eventually, she succeeded and led a life of prayer, fasting and great love for God. She wanted to become as close to God as possible so she asked Him to have her suffer as He had suffered. Rita received a deep puncture wound on her forehead as though from Christ's crown of thorns. This caused her great pain, yet she still joyfully prayed to God, suffering with Him. She is known for being the patroness of impossible causes.

What could you do this week to offer to Jesus a little suffering of your own?

> **"As a result, those who suffer in accord with God's will hand their souls over to a faithful creator as they do good."**
> *1Pet. 4:19*

Main Dishes

Rita's Creamy Baked Chicken Breast

In honor of St. Rita, why not make two of these dishes and give one away to a friend who is ill?

8 chicken breast halves, skinned and boned
8 (4-inch) slices Swiss cheese
1 (10 ¾ oz.) can cream of chicken soup, undiluted
¼ cup dry white wine
1 cup herb-seasoned stuffing mix, crushed
¼ cup butter or margarine, melted

Arrange chicken in lightly greased 13x9x2-inch baking dish. Top with cheese slices.

Combine soup and wine; stir well. Spoon evenly over chicken; sprinkle with stuffing mix. Drizzle butter over crumbs; bake at 350° for 45 to 55 minutes. *Makes 8 servings.*

☙ *"...and if children, then heirs, heirs of God and joint heirs with Christ, if only we suffer with him so that we may also be glorified with him."* Rom. 8:17

☙ *"For to you has been granted, for the sake of Christ, not only to believe in him but also to suffer for him."* Phil. 1:29

Pasta & Veggie Bake

8 asparagus spears
5 mushrooms
1 red bell pepper
1 yellow or orange pepper
2 Tbsp. olive oil
3 cloves garlic, minced or pressed
Salt and pepper to taste

2 Tbsp. fresh basil
3 cups (8 oz.) pasta *(spirals, rigatoni, penne)*
¾-1 cup whipping cream
½-1 cup grated Italian cheese *(Parmesan, Romano, etc.)*
½-1 lb. cooked chicken pieces

Preheat oven to 425°. Cook pasta al dente according to package directions. Snip basil, add to pasta.

Prepare vegetables. Remove ends of asparagus and cut in 1½-inch pieces. Cut peppers into small slices; cut mushrooms in halves or quarters. In a large bowl, add vegetables, garlic, olive oil, salt and pepper. Mix well. Pour into a baking dish (stoneware works best). Bake 10 to 12 minutes until vegetables are CRISP.

In a small saucepan, simmer whipping cream to thicken slightly. You can add up to ½ cup of cheese to it if you like.

When vegetables are done, add pasta, warmed chicken, and whipping cream, and toss. Top with remaining cheese and basil.

"Receive Communion often, very often...there you have the sole remedy, if you want to be cured. Jesus has not put this attraction in your heart for nothing." ~St. Thérèse of Lisieux

Swiss and Chicken Casserole

4 cups chopped cooked chicken
2 cups sliced celery
2 cups croutons
2 cups or 8 oz. Swiss cheese
1 cup Miracle Whip

½ cup milk
¼ cup chopped onion
1 tsp. salt
¼ tsp. pepper
¼ cup chopped walnuts to sprinkle on top

Mix all ingredients. Spoon into a 2-quart casserole. Sprinkle with walnuts. Cook in preheated 350° oven for 40 minutes.

Ro-Tel King Ranch Chicken

¼ cup margarine
1 medium green bell pepper, chopped
1 medium onion, chopped
10 ¾ oz. can cream of mushroom soup
10 ¾ oz. can cream of chicken soup

1 can extra-hot or milder Ro-Tel* tomatoes
2 cups cubed cooked chicken
12 tortillas, torn into bite-size pieces
2 cups (8 oz.) shredded cheddar cheese

Preheat oven to 325°. In large saucepan, cook pepper, onion, and margarine about 5 minutes. Add soups, Ro-Tel tomatoes, and chicken, stirring until well blended.

Lightly grease a 9x13-inch baking pan and alternately layer tortillas, soup mixture, and cheese, repeating for 3 layers. Bake 40 minutes or until hot and bubbly.

*Ro-Tel is a brand of canned chopped tomatoes with chili peppers or jalapeños.

Saint Clare of Assisi (1193-1253) *Virgin*
Feast Day ~ August 11

Just like St. Francis, Clare came from a wealthy family, but material things didn't have meaning for her. She loved God and felt called to serve Him. One day, St. Francis came to her church to preach during Lent. She heard him and begged to belong to his order. St. Francis had her sent to a Benedictine convent because he had not yet established a Franciscan convent. Her father was furious and to make matters worse, her sister, Agnes, joined her 16 days later followed by many other holy women. She eventually became Abbess of Francis' new second order called the Poor Clares. Clare was so prayerful that she interceded for the people of Assisi while lying in bed sick. She raised a ciborium with consecrated hosts in it, as men scaled the walls of San Damiano, and they fell backwards and ran fleeing the monastery. This would happen again, and Clare gathered her women and prayed. A storm arose spreading the men's tents wildly; they were so terrified, they fled. Years later, as she lay dying, Clare was no longer able to go to Mass. She turned toward the Chapel on the other side of the wall in her room and suddenly the wall disappeared and Clare was able to see her Jesus in the consecrated host. For this reason, she is known as the patroness of TV as well as embroiderers and eye disorders.

This week try praying very hard for our country, our President and for all elected officials that they take their office very seriously and work for God and not themselves.

Clare's Chicken Casserole

2-3 lbs. boneless, skinless chicken breasts
1 (10 ¾ oz.) can cream of chicken soup
¾ cup light sour cream
½ cup chicken broth
¼ cup white wine

¼ lb. margarine
6-8 thin slices Swiss cheese
1 sleeve Ritz crackers, crushed*
Poppy seeds

Poach chicken in boiling water to cover, until done, about 20 minutes. Cool. Cut into bite-size pieces.

Preheat oven to 350°. Grease 9x13-inch baking dish with margarine. Mix together soup, sour cream, broth, and wine. Put cut-up chicken in a layer in baking dish. Place cheese slices on top of chicken. Pour soup mixture evenly over chicken.

Melt margarine. Crush crackers to make 1 ¼ cups coarse crumbs. Sprinkle crumbs in a layer over soup mixture. Drizzle melted margarine over crumbs. Sprinkle generously with poppy seeds. Bake at 350° for 45 minutes.

*I used Keebler's Multi-Grain Crackers in place of Ritz.

"What is more beautiful to gaze upon than Jesus in the Blessed Sacrament?"
~St. Clare, patroness of the televised media

"They say that we are too poor, but can a heart which possesses the Infinite God be truly called poor?" ~St. Clare

"For through the law I died to the law, that I might live for God. I have been crucified with Christ." Gal. 2:19

St. Francis Xavier (1506-1552)
Feast Day ~ December 3

Francis, a great missionary, was born in Spain in a town called Navarre. When he was nineteen, he went to Paris to study and there he met St. Ignatius. The two became friends and Ignatius taught Francis about God and convinced him to leave his worldly ambitions and join the Society of Jesus. He did and Francis earned his degree and devoted himself to God. He was asked to go to far away lands and preach the Gospel, which he willingly did and converted thousands of people. He taught children about the Catholic Faith and baptized so many people that he could hardly hold his hands up. He was on fire for his Faith and wanted to go to China and spread the Faith there. Unfortunately, he died before ever reaching the coast of China. When he was canonized, he had some very good company: St. Ignatius, St. Teresa of Avila, St. Philip Neri, and St. Isidore the Farmer were all canonized with him.

Why not try and imitate St. Francis this week and go out and tell someone what Jesus did for all of us? You can tell people but you can also show them by doing good deeds in the name of Jesus. Discuss what you might do together as a family to spread your Faith.

Xavier's Dream Chicken Rice Salad

This is a wonderful main dish to make ahead. It also makes a great dish to take to friends who would appreciate a homemade meal. St. Francis never made it to China, though it was his dream to evangelize there.

1 (13 ¾-14 ½ oz.) can chicken broth	2 cups diced cooked chicken, turkey, or pork*
1 cup Uncle Ben's converted rice	¼ lb. fresh bean sprouts
¼ cup vegetable oil	¼ lb. fresh mushrooms, sliced
2 Tbsp. soy sauce	4 green onions with tops, sliced
2 Tbsp. toasted sesame seeds	1 (2 oz.) jar diced pimentos

Add enough water to chicken broth to make 2 ½ cups liquid. Cook rice in broth mix according to package directions. Transfer to large bowl.

Combine oil, soy sauce, sesame seeds; mix well. Stir this into hot cooked rice. Cover and chill (easy to do overnight). Add remaining ingredients before serving.

*I use 4 boneless chicken breasts and cut into ½-inch pieces, then stir-fry until just cooked – only a few minutes.

 "Neglect not to visit the sick — for these things you will be loved." Sir. 7:35

 "Do not neglect to do good and to share what you have; God is pleased by sacrifices of that kind." Heb. 13:16

St. Vincent Ferrer (1350-1419)
Feast Day ~ April 5

Born in Valencia, Spain in 1350, Vincent had a great love for the Blessed Mother. He wanted to be a priest and studied hard. At the age of 17, he joined the Dominicans and excelled in his studies. He became a teacher at different colleges but eventually became ill. While recovering, St. Dominic and St. Francis appeared to him in a vision asking him to go preach. When Vincent got better, he traveled all over Spain and France telling everyone about the Catholic Faith. Many lives changed as the people gathered to hear about the wonderful truths and what Jesus had done just for them. Vincent knew it was God speaking through him, but one day, he heard that a very important nobleman was coming to hear him preach. Vincent spent a long time making sure his sermon was perfect, and he preached that day forgetting to pray beforehand. The nobleman wasn't impressed and left. Vincent was very sad as he realized he had relied on himself and not God. Then one day, the nobleman came back, but Vincent was unaware that he was in the crowd. He had prayed beforehand and preached from God's inspiration. The message that Vincent gave really touched the nobleman's heart.

It is important for us to always remember that we are God's instruments. We need to let God use us as He wants to and not the way we want to be used. Pray this week that God will help you become more like Him. What might you do to imitate Jesus this week?

Vincent's Chicken Enchiladas

15-18 tortillas
1 (6 oz.) can enchilada sauce
1 (4.5 oz.) can chopped green chilies
2 cups cream *(I use half-and-half)*
6 cups shredded chicken
1 cup finely chopped onion
2 (8 oz.) pkgs. cream cheese *(I use ⅓-less fat)*
1 cup Monterey Jack cheese
1 cup Cheddar cheese

Cook chicken and shred it. *(This is a great recipe to use for leftover chicken.)*

Combine cooked chicken with green chilies, cream cheese, and onions. Place small amount of chicken mixture across each tortilla and roll up into logs. Place each log into a 9x13-inch pan, side by side. *I use 2 pans.*

After all tortillas are rolled, pour combined cream and enchilada sauce over them. Cover and bake at 375° for 30 to 40 minutes; then remove and sprinkle cheese over entire mixture. Return to oven until cheeses are all melted. Serve immediately.

🕊 **"Beloved, we are God's children now; what we shall be has not yet been revealed. We do know that when it is revealed we shall be like him, for we shall see him as he is."** 1John 3:2

🕊 **"No disciple is superior to the teacher; but when fully trained, every disciple will be like his teacher."** Luke 6:40

Blessed Teresa of Calcutta (1910-1997)
Feast Day ~ September 5

This modern day saint is an inspiration for all of us. She was born in 1910 in Skopje, Macedonia. Her real name was Agnes, and she loved God very much. By the time she was 12, she knew that God wanted her to be a nun, but she waited until she was 18 to leave her mother and travel all the way to India to join the Loreto Sisters. In Calcutta she taught geography to wealthy children. She loved teaching and became principal of the school, but it troubled her that the children being taught were from rich families while the poor children were not allowed an education. God spoke to Teresa many times. She went through many rejections before she was allowed to go out and help poor children learn. She was scared to give up all of her comforts and live like the poor lived, but she knew that God was calling her to do this, so she cheerfully obeyed.

Unknown to almost everyone, including all the women who flocked to be a part of Mother Teresa's order, the Missionaries of Charity, she had to suffer a great deal. It is said that a nun complained that she didn't have time to pray in front of the Eucharist for an hour each day because of all the other work that had to be done. Mother looked at her and said, "I think we need to increase our prayer in front of the Eucharist for two hours each day." She established convents all over the world and was given the Nobel Peace Prize in 1979. All of her work was attributed to God. She told people that there were different kinds of poverty. There is spiritual poverty as well: America has spiritual poverty, for we are starving for God.

What can you do this week to bring others to God? Do you have a friend that doesn't know about God? Is there a family that doesn't go to church on your street? Why not invite them to your church this Sunday?

Curry Chicken

Curry is used in many Indian dishes. Mother Teresa went to India when she was 18 years old and lived there the rest of her life.

- 3-4 chicken breast halves, cut into bite-size pieces
- 1 (10 ¾ oz.) can cream of chicken soup
- ⅓ cup milk *(I fill ⅓ of the soup can with milk so the can gets rinsed)*
- ⅔ cup mayonnaise, light or fat-free
- ½ Tbsp. lemon juice
- 3 Tbsp. breadcrumbs
- 1 Tbsp. Parmesan cheese
- ½ tsp. curry powder

Put chicken in bottom of 2-quart casserole dish. Sprinkle with salt and pepper. Mix milk, soup, curry powder, mayonnaise, and lemon juice. Pour over chicken. Top with Parmesan cheese and breadcrumbs. Bake, uncovered, at 350° for 45 minutes. Serve over rice. *Makes 6 to 8 servings.*

"For the time will come when people will not tolerate sound doctrine but, following their own desires and insatiable curiosity, will accumulate teachers and will stop listening to the truth and will be diverted to myths. But you, be self-possessed in all circumstances; put up with hardship; perform the work of an evangelist; fulfill your ministry."
2Tim. 4:3-5

"People ask me: 'What will convert America and save the world?' My answer is prayer. What we need is for every parish to come before Jesus in the Blessed Sacrament in Holy Hours of prayer."
~Blessed Teresa of Calcutta

**St. John Bosco (1815-1888)
Feast Day ~ January 31**

John became a priest in 1841, and befriended an orphan boy. He began teaching him about the Eucharist so that he could make his First Holy Communion. Soon many children came to learn about Jesus and what the Church taught. After opening an Oratory for boys which he named for St. Francis de Sales, several wealthy families contributed money toward expanding it, and he was able to start a shoemaking and tailoring class. John was like a father to these boys and they learned to unite their spiritual life with their working life. Things went so well that they eventually added a printing press in order for them to print pamphlets explaining the Faith. John is the patron of young apprentices and Catholic publishers. He eventually founded the Order of the Salesians who focused on education and mission work for men, and he organized the Salesian sisters to help girls, too. He believed that God wasn't just for Sundays but for everyday.

Why not begin a prayer circle after dinner and have everyone in your family say a prayer to Jesus thanking Him for what happened during the day.

Hearty Bosco's Chicken Pot Pie

5 large chicken breasts
1 lb. carrots, peeled and cut up
Several sticks of celery, cut up
3 lbs. potatoes
1 (10 ¾ oz.) can cream of celery soup
2 Tbsp. poultry seasoning
1 ½ cups milk
1 ½ cups chicken broth

Pie Crust:
2 ⅔ cups all-purpose flour
1 tsp. salt
1 cup Crisco shortening
7-8 Tbsp. cold water

Boil chicken breasts *(save some broth)*. Watch the chicken when you boil it. Remove it immediately when done and pour cold water on it to stop it from cooking further. It is tender and juicy this way.

In another large pot, cook the potatoes, celery, and carrots until tender. Do not overcook. Combine remaining ingredients (the liquid and seasonings) and pour over chicken and vegetables in a 9x13-inch pan. Cover with pie crust. Bake at 400° for 25 minutes. *I also put pie crust on the bottom, as my family loves the crust.*

Pie Crust: Place flour and salt in large bowl and cut in shortening using a pastry blender. Once crumbly, add a few tablespoons of <u>ice cold</u> water. *The colder the water the flakier the pie crust!* Keep adding water until the dough is the right consistency (usually about 8 tablespoons). Knead a few times, but if you touch pie crust too much it gets tough.

Roll out on floured surface and place into pan. Add chicken mixture. Make another batch of crust and place on top. Slit the pie crust to allow steam to escape. Roll edges together and bake as directed above.

"Trust all things to Jesus in the Blessed Sacrament and to Mary Help of Christians and you will see what miracles are."
~St. John Bosco

Stuffed Chicken Crescents

2 pkgs. crescent rolls
1 (8 oz.) pkg. cream cheese
4 cups chicken, cooked and cut in small pieces
5 Tbsp. margarine
½ tsp. salt
4 Tbsp. milk
2 Tbsp. onion, finely diced
Parmesan cheese

Mix together cream cheese, chicken, salt, onion, and milk. Separate into 8 squares. Fill each with ½ cup chicken mixture. Fold edges up to center and pinch seams together. Brush with melted margarine, and sprinkle with Parmesan cheese. Bake at 350° for 20 to 25 minutes.

Simple Salsa Chicken

2 boneless, skinless chicken breast halves (5 oz. each)
⅛ tsp. salt
⅓ cup salsa
2 Tbsp. taco sauce
⅓ cup shredded Mexican cheese blend

Place chicken in a shallow 2-quart baking dish coated with nonstick cooking spray. Sprinkle with salt. Combine salsa and taco sauce; drizzle over chicken. Sprinkle with cheese.

Cover and bake at 350° for 25 to 30 minutes or until chicken juices run clear. *Makes 2 servings.*

"He himself bore our sins in his body upon the cross, so that, free from sin, we might live for righteousness. By his wounds you have been healed." 1Pet. 2:24

Chicken Pot Pie

2 (10-inch) pie crusts
2 medium potatoes, cut in ½-inch cubes
1 cup sliced carrots
½ cup peeled and halved pearl onions
1 cup frozen peas
2 cups cooked chicken, cut into ½-inch chunks

3 Tbsp. butter
3 Tbsp. flour
2 cups chicken stock (3 bouillon cubes)
1 cup milk
Salt, pepper, dill, parsley, and basil to taste
1 egg white
Paprika to taste on top crust

Preheat oven to 350°. Line a 10-inch pie pan with crust; prick bottom with fork and bake for 10 minutes. Set aside to cool.

In a large pot of boiling water, add potatoes, carrots, onions, and peas. Cook for approximately 8 minutes. Drain water, add cooked chicken, and set aside.

To prepare sauce, melt butter in a large saucepan. Add flour, and heat for 1 minute, stirring constantly to keep sauce from sticking to bottom of pan. Slowly add chicken stock, stirring constantly. Bring to a boil, reduce heat, and simmer until the sauce thickens. Add milk and salt, pepper, dill, parsley, and basil to taste. Sauce should be slightly thicker than heavy cream.

Fill pie crust with chicken and vegetables. Pour sauce on top. Cover with unbaked crust. Brush with egg white and paprika. Raise oven temperature to 375° and bake for 10 minutes. Lower to 350° and bake for 45 minutes. *Makes 4 servings.*

Note: *I usually triple the recipe for the sauce and double the rest so we can have plenty of leftovers!*

"Ask Jesus to make you a saint. After all, only He can do that. Go to confession regularly and to Communion as often as you can," ~St. John Bosco

Chicken Pie

1 cooked chicken, cut up
1 can (10 ¾ oz.) cream of
  chicken soup
1 can (10 ¾ oz.) cream of
  celery soup
1 can mixed vegetables,
  drained
1 can mixed vegetables,
  drained
1 cup milk
1 stick (8 Tbsp.) melted oleo
1 cup flour

Mix first 4 ingredients together and pour in a 9x13-inch pan. Mix remaining ingredients together and pour on top. Bake at 350° for 1 hour.

Chicken Stew

1 lb. boneless skinless thigh
  meat
1 cup stewed tomatoes, diced
  (if you can get them)
2 cans (10 ½ oz.) chicken
  broth
1 pkg. frozen okra or 1 bag
  frozen gumbo vegetables
  (i.e., okra, corn, and
  peppers)
1 sweet onion, chopped
Salt and pepper to taste
1 Tbsp. gumbo filet (in the
  spice section)
1 cup white rice, cooked

Throw all ingredients, except rice, in a crockpot and cook for 6 hours. Serve over cooked white rice.

"Christ held Himself in His hands when He gave His Body to His disciples saying: 'This is My Body.' No one partakes of this Flesh before he has adored it." ~St. Augustine

Turkey Tortilla Casserole

½ cup chopped onion
½ cup reduced-sodium chicken broth
¼ cup chopped celery
3 cups chopped cooked turkey or chicken
10-12 (6-inch) corn tortillas, torn into bite-size pieces
1 (4 oz.) can diced green chili peppers, drained
1 (10 ¾ oz.) can reduced-sodium condensed cream of chicken soup
1 tsp. pepper
1 cup (4 oz.) shredded Cheddar cheese
1 cup (4 oz.) shredded Monterey Jack cheese
1 cup salsa

In a medium saucepan, combine onion, chicken broth, and celery. Bring to boiling; reduce heat. Simmer, covered, for 5 to 10 minutes or until vegetables are just tender.

In a large bowl, stir together **undrained** onion mixture, cooked turkey or chicken, corn tortillas, chili peppers, soup, and pepper. Reserve ½ *cup* of each cheese; set aside. Stir remaining cheese into tortilla mixture.

Transfer mixture to a lightly greased 13x9x2-inch baking dish. Top with salsa and reserved cheeses. Bake at 350° for about 30 minutes or until heated through. Let stand 5 minutes before serving.

"Holiness is a disposition of the heart that makes us humble and little in the arms of God, aware of our weakness, and confident -- in the most audacious way –in His Fatherly goodness." ~St. Thérèse of Lisieux

St. Zita (1212-1272)
Feast Day ~ April 27

Zita was born in Italy to wonderful parents who had a great love for God and loved the Church. They were poor and needed money, so when Zita was 12 years old, she was sent to a rich family to do housework. This family, the Fatinellis, were kind and good. They loved Zita and Zita loved them, too, and did all she could to earn money to send back to her parents. Some of the other housekeepers made fun of Zita because she always tried her best. Zita didn't complain. She found time to pray and got up early to go to Mass. Eventually her hard work paid off and Zita was asked to be the head housekeeper and to look after the children. Many housekeepers came and left, but Zita stayed with the same family until she was 60 years old. She died in 1272.

St. Zita lived a life of service and did it with her whole self. She always tried to do her best even though some people laughed at her. Do you try your hardest? What could you work on this week to improve yourself?

"Attend to yourself and to your teaching; persevere in both tasks, for by doing so you will save both yourself and those who listen to you." 1Tim. 4:16

St. Zita's Baked Ziti

1 lb. ground turkey
1 pkg. turkey Italian sausage
1 large onion, diced
2 green peppers, diced
2 (28 oz.) cans petite diced tomatoes
1 (29 oz.) can tomato sauce

2 Tbsp. Italian seasoning
1 Tbsp. basil
2 cloves garlic, crushed
8 oz. provolone cheese
8 oz. mozzarella cheese
1 ½ boxes ziti cooked as directed

In a large pot, brown turkey and sausage. No one will be able to tell it's turkey. Cook chopped onion and peppers, and add to the drained meat. Add spices, tomatoes, and sauce. Cook the ziti and drain in colander. Place ziti in large pot and mix with sauce.

Spoon half the mixture into a large casserole dish and put half the provolone cheese and half the mozzarella cheese on top. Add the remaining mixture and then more cheese. If your pan is too small, make 2, because it will bubble while in the oven. Place in oven for about 20 minutes to melt the cheese and get hot.

"They strengthened the spirits of the disciples and exhorted them to persevere in the faith, saying, "It is necessary for us to undergo many hardships to enter the kingdom of God."
Acts 14:22

St. Dominic Savio (1842-1857)
Feast Day ~ May 6

Dominic was the son of peasants in Italy. He loved God and at age 4 was seen by his mom praying and knowing all of his prayers. He became an altar boy at age 5 and couldn't wait to make his first Holy Communion at age 7. He was known as an ordinary boy who had an extraordinary love of God. He attended a school run by St. John Bosco. One day while Dominic was at school, he stopped some children from looking at pictures in a dirty magazine though they claimed they were just having some fun. Dominic didn't back down and told them, "You are preparing yourselves to go to hell." They were ashamed. He also stopped a fight between two boys by getting between them, holding up a crucifix and telling them that Jesus had forgiven his executioners. He said that if they were going to stone each other, then they would have to throw the stones at him.

Dominic started a special group dedicated to Mary called the Company of the Immaculate Conception. They took special care of the school sweeping and tending to the children who needed help, as well as encouraging devotion to Our Lady. Dominic died when he was 15 years old. Though he lived a short life, he knew God and served Him well. Dominic is the patron saint of choir boys and falsely accused people.

What will you do this week to show God that you love Him? Bring one of your Catholic friends to Confession with you.

Dominic's Turkey Meatballs and Pasta

Coarse salt and ground pepper
¾ lb. ground turkey, 93% lean
   (dark meat = more tender)
¼ cup plain dried breadcrumbs
2 cloves garlic, minced
1 large egg, lightly beaten
¼ cup grated Parmesan cheese
½ cup chopped fresh parsley
2 Tbsp. butter
1 pint grape tomatoes, halved
8 oz. orecchiette or other short pasta
20 balls of bocconcini *(small mozzarella cheese balls)*

Boil a large pot of salted water. In a large bowl, combine turkey, breadcrumbs, garlic, egg, 2 tablespoons Parmesan, ¼ cup parsley, 1 teaspoon pepper; mix to combine. Using a level 1-tablespoon measure for each, form mixture into meatballs (about 24).

In a large skillet, heat 1 tablespoon butter over medium-high heat. Add meatballs and cook, turning occasionally, until browned all over, 5 to 7 minutes. Add 1 ½ cups water; simmer, stirring occasionally, until meatballs are cooked through and liquid is reduced to about ½ cup, approximately 10 to 12 minutes. Add tomatoes; cook until they begin to soften, about 1 minute.

Meanwhile, cook pasta in boiling water until al dente, according to package instructions, Drain, return to pot, and place on the still-warm burner. Add bocconcini, meatballs and sauce, remaining ¼ cup parsley, remaining 2 tablespoons Parmesan, and remaining tablespoon butter. Season with salt and pepper and toss until combined. *Makes 4 servings.*

Nothing seems tiresome or painful when you are working for a Master who pays well; who rewards even a cup of cold water given for love of Him. ~St. Dominic Savio

St. Stephen
Feast Day ~ Dec 26

Stephen was the very first martyr of the Church. The name Stephen means crown. His story is in the Bible in Acts 6, 7 and 8. Stephen loved God with his whole heart and spent his days preaching the Gospel to all who would listen. He changed many people's hearts and performed many miracles. Some of the people were jealous of Stephen and his preaching so they twisted his words and said he had blasphemed. Blasphemy is saying bad things about God or sacred things. A court, called the Sanhedrin, convicted him of blasphemy against Moses and God. Though this was not true, he was condemned to death. They brought him outside of the town of Jerusalem and killed him. As they were stoning him, Stephen looked up to heaven and asked God to forgive his attackers. One of the men who stoned Stephen was Saul who later repented and became a great saint himself, **St. Paul**. See how God brought good out of something evil.

This would be a good week to read the story of Stephen in your Bible. Pray to St. Stephen and ask him to help you to be able to forgive others as he did. Ask St. Stephen to help you share the Gospel with your relatives and friends; maybe visit your families or visit a nursing home? Try and sit with an older person and tell them how God is helping you to do the things you do.

St. Paul - Gyros of Corinth

Pita Bread:
1 pkg. active dry yeast
½ cup warm water
1 cup warm water
3 cups flour
1 ¼ tsp. salt
1 tsp. sugar

Gyros:
1 medium onion
2 lbs. ground lamb *(shoulder/ veal)*
1 Tbsp. garlic
1 Tbsp. marjoram
1 Tbsp. rosemary
2 tsp. salt
½ tsp. black pepper

Tzatziki Sauce:
2 cups plain yogurt
1 cup cucumber, peeled, seeded, and chopped
4 cloves garlic, finely minced
8-10 mint leaves, finely minced
1 Tbsp. olive oil
2 tsp. red wine vinegar
Pinch of salt

Pita Bread: *(I start this about 4 hours before I plan to serve it.)* Dissolve yeast, sugar, and ½ cup water together and let sit until frothy. Combine flour and salt in a large bowl, then add frothy yeast mixture. Slowly mix in 1 cup warm water. Mix with spatula until combined and elastic/sticky. Knead for 10 to 15 minutes. Coat a large bowl with vegetable oil and place dough in bowl. Turn dough to coat. Let rise in a warm place until doubled, about 2 to 3 hours.

Once dough has doubled, roll into long rope; then divide rope into 12 pieces and form into balls. Place each ball on floured surface and let rest for 10 minutes. Preheat oven to 500°. *(Optional – place pizza stone onto bottom-most rack of oven and let preheat with oven.)*

Roll out each ball into a 5- to 6-inch circle, about ¼-inch thick. Bake each on hot pizza stone or baking sheet for 2 minutes or until they "puff" up; then flip and bake another 2 minutes. Remove from oven, deflate the puff, and store immediately in storage bags. *(Continued next page)*

Gyros: Preheat oven to 350°. In food processor, chop onion for about 10 seconds. Turn out onto a clean kitchen towel, gather up the ends, and squeeze out juice. Return to food processor and add garlic and spices. Process another 10 seconds. Add lamb and process again for about a minute or until it resembles a thick paste.

Place mixture into loaf pan and bake for 1-1 ¼ hours. Drain juices and let rest for 15 minutes. If desired, weight down the loaf with another nesting loaf pan filled with cans of soup. This will help to create the proper gyro meat texture.

Tzatziki Sauce: *(I start this while pita dough is rising.)* Place yogurt in a clean kitchen towel. Gather up edges and secure with a rubber band. Suspend over a container in the fridge for 2 hours to collect the liquid. (You can stick a chop stick or skewer through rubber band and balance it across the container rim.)

Sprinkle cucumber with salt to allow water to seep out. Squeeze out excess water. In a medium mixing bowl, combine garlic, olive oil, vinegar, and mint. Mix lightly, then add cucumber and toss. Finally, add drained yogurt and stir. Serve with gyros.

Harvest Pork Roast

2 lb. pork tenderloin *(I cut it into 4-6 pieces)*
2 Tbsp. Canola oil
3 cups apple juice
3 Granny Smith apples
1 cup fresh or dried cranberries
¾ tsp. salt
½ tsp. black pepper

Brown roast on all sides with Canola oil in skillet. Add remaining ingredients and place in crockpot. Cover and cook on low for approximately 6 to 8 hours.

Baked Maple Pork Chops with Spiced Butternut Whip

4 center-cut pork chops, 1-inch thick

Marinade:
⅓ cup maple syrup
⅓ cup Dijon mustard
2 Tbsp. cider vinegar
1 tsp. ground cumin
Salt and pepper to taste

Spiced Butternut Whip:
2 butternut squash, 1 ½ lbs. each
3 Tbsp. unsalted butter
1 ½ Tbsp. honey
½ tsp. ground mace
Salt and pepper to taste

Combine marinade ingredients in a bowl. Add chops and set aside for 30 minutes to marinate, turning twice.

Preheat oven to 350°. Place chops in a shallow roasting pan to fit. Bake 30 minutes, basting occasionally with the marinade, turning once. Divide among 4 plates and serve with Spiced Butternut Whip.

Spiced Butternut Whip: Peel, seed, and cut the squash into large cubes. Place in a large, heavy pot and cover with cold water. Bring to a boil and simmer, uncovered, until tender, 15 to 20 minutes. Drain well and remove to a bowl. Add the remaining ingredients and mash with a fork. Serve immediately.

Note: Butternut squash is difficult to cut and peel, so I suggest you work carefully with a sharp knife and a vegetable peeler, or buy squash already peeled and cubed.

"And because Jesus is the Eucharist, keeping Him in the center allows all of the rich doctrines of the Church to emanate from Him, just as the beautiful gold rays stream forth from the Host in the monstrance." ~Kimberly Hahn

Crockpot Kraut

3 strips bacon *(I use more, to taste)*
1 ½ Tbsp. flour
3 lbs. sauerkraut
2 small firm apples, cubed
3 Tbsp. dark brown sugar
1 ½ tsp. caraway seeds
3 lbs. Polish sausage, cut in 1 ½-inch pieces
½ cup beer

Fry bacon (or put in microwave oven) until crisp; drain. Sift flour into bacon drippings and blend well. Stir in sauerkraut; mix well.

Place sauerkraut mixture and bacon pieces in electric slow cooker. Add all other ingredients; stir together thoroughly. Cover and cook on low for 7 to 9 hours or on high for 3 to 4 hours. Makes 8 servings.

Jambalaya

2 cups converted rice *(I use Uncle Ben's Long Grain)*
1 (10 ¾ oz.) can beef broth
1 (10 ¾ oz.) can onion soup
1 (16 oz.) can tomato soup
½ cup chopped green pepper
3 bay laves
2 Tbsp. parsley
1 tsp. cayenne pepper
1 small onion, chopped
1 lb. sausage or kielbasa, cut into small pieces
1 lb. shrimp
1 can mushrooms, undrained

Mix all ingredients in Dutch oven. Bake at 350° for 1 ½ hours. Stir every ½ hour. *Great for a large crowd.*

"The culmination of the Mass is not the consecration, but Communion." ~St. Maximilian Kolbe

Layered Zucchini Bake

Bacon *(enough to cover the top of your baking dish)*
1-2 cups shredded Cheddar cheese
Breadcrumbs

1 zucchini, sliced
1 yellow squash, sliced
1-2 tomatoes, sliced
1 sweet onion, sliced

Line the bottom of a casserole dish with breadcrumbs *(I use an Italian style, but any kind will do)*. Place a layer of sliced zucchini on top of breadcrumbs. Next layer the sliced squash and cover with some cheese. Layer sliced tomatoes, sliced onion and a little more cheese. Sprinkle bacon on top.

Bake at 350° for about an hour. Bacon should be crispy. You can also cover with foil if you see bacon getting too crispy. The juices from all the veggies and bacon will seep down and keep everything moist.

Crescent Roll Pizza

This reminds us of Our Lady of Guadalupe, standing upon the crescent moon!

2 cans crescent rolls
1-2 cups tomato sauce
1 can pineapple tidbits, drained
1-2 cups sliced ham

2 cups shredded pizza cheese
(any mix of mozzarella, Provolone, Romano, Parmesan, etc.)

Preheat oven to 375°. Spray a cookie sheet with nonstick spray. Unroll the dough of the crescent rolls onto the sheet, pressing the dough together to make a large rectangle. Spread the sauce over the dough. Top with pineapple and ham. Sprinkle the cheese over the top. Bake 12 minutes or until lightly browned. Let sit a few minutes before slicing and serving.

St. Josephine Bakhita (1868-1947)
Feast Day ~ February 8

Taken from her parents as a young child in Sudan, Bakhita never knew about God, yet while crouched in a hut, she felt a presence that comforted her. That presence turned out to be the Blessed Mother. Bakhita was a slave to many different men. One master marked her with razor cuts. An Italian man bought her and brought her back as a slave for his wife in Italy. His friend's wife was pregnant, and he felt guilty so he gave Bakhita to his friend for her to take care of the baby. Bakhita raised the child, and when it was time for the child to go to school, Bakhita took her to school and also learned along with her. Bakhita loved her life, but her owner wanted to take her back to Africa and trade her in. The Italian government intervened, since you could not own a slave in Italy. So Bakhita went to live with the nuns, finished her education there and became one of them. She never saw her family again, but she had many who loved her. She performed her chores with great zeal and spoke about coming to know God and serving Him. Bakhita is a perfect example of not knowing about God, yet still knowing that there is someone out there greater than oneself.

What will you do this week to make others aware of God? Maybe you could tell the story of St. Bakhita to someone who has stopped going to church. Encourage them to love God.

Easy Stromboli

St. Bakita left Africa as a child and spent the rest of her life in Italy! This can also be made without the pepperoni on Fridays.

2 frozen loaves of bread *(Rich's Bread Dough)*
½ lb. pepperoni
16 oz. mozzarella cheese
2 Tbsp. olive oil
3 egg yolks (save whites)

1 Tbsp. Parmesan cheese
1 Tbsp. parsley flakes
½ tsp. garlic powder
1 tsp. oregano
¼ tsp. pepper

Remove bread from package and thaw overnight on a cookie sheet or several hours before dinner. Cover top with plastic wrap sprayed with Pam so it doesn't stick. As dough thaws, it rises. Spread each loaf flat (and long) on cookie sheet (greased). Mix all ingredients except pepperoni and mozzarella cheese. Spread oil/spice mixture on both, lay meat and cheese on top just like you are making pizza. Roll up jelly roll style. (length-wise) Place seams down, tuck ends in. Brush with egg whites and bake at 350° for 25 minutes or until done. Both fit on one cookie sheet.

Main Dishes 151

St. Joseph of Cupertino (1603-1663)
Feast Day ~ September 18

Born in 1603 to poor parents in a small Italian village, Joseph's mother treated him badly. He was a bother to her so Joseph, not feeling loved, became very withdrawn and wandered about the village. He was mad at the world and didn't have any friends. He tried to become a shoemaker but was slow and couldn't learn how to do it. He tried to join the Franciscans, but they rejected him. He went to the Capuchin Order but after eight months, they asked him to leave. Joseph went back home, but his mother didn't want him with her so she managed to get him a job at the Franciscan monastery as a servant. He wore the habit and cared for the horses. Joseph began to mature, and as he grew he started to pray more. His temper was no longer a problem, and he became humble and kind. He began to offer things up and soon he was accepted into the order to begin his studies to become a priest. Though he had great difficulty, God protected Joseph and he was ordained a priest. Joseph was so in love with God that when he prayed, he experienced great happiness. Sometimes while saying Mass, he would float up to the ceiling. God worked miracles though Father Joseph. People saw him hover above the ground as he was praying. He died in 1663 when he was 60 years old, a beloved, wise, and holy priest.

Sometimes do you feel like you aren't worth much? In God's eyes we are always special. After dinner tonight everyone can pick someone else and write down 5 special things about that person. Afterwards you can share with them what your wrote.

"Heavenly" Bagel Pizzas

This is a quick and hearty recipe that anyone can make for lunch or dinner.

2 plain bagels, split
½ cup pizza sauce
20 slices pepperoni
¾ cup diced fully cooked ham
¼ cup real bacon bits
¼ cup chopped onions
1 cup mozzarella cheese

Place bagels on a baking sheet. Spread with pizza sauce. Arrange 5 slices of pepperoni on each, covering the bagel hole with one slice. Top each with ham, bacon, onions, and cheese. Bake at 400° for 6 to 8 minutes or until cheese is melted.

English Muffin Pizza

English muffin halves
Mozzarella cheese, sliced or shredded
Pizza sauce
Black pepper, oregano *(or Italian blend)*, and Parmesan cheese
Finely chopped onion and green pepper *(optional)*

Toast English muffin halves. Top each slice with shredded or sliced mozzarella cheese. Spread 1 to 2 tablespoons pizza sauce over the cheese. Sprinkle with black pepper, oregano (or Italian blend), and Parmesan cheese.

Bake on greased cookie sheet at 375° for 10 minutes. Serve immediately but be careful not to burn fingers or mouth. *Servings: variable.*

Note: May add finely chopped onion and green pepper before the sauce.

"If Christ did not want to dismiss the Jews without food in the desert for fear that they would collapse on the way, it was to teach us that it is dangerous to try to get to heaven without the Bread of Heaven." ~St. Jerome

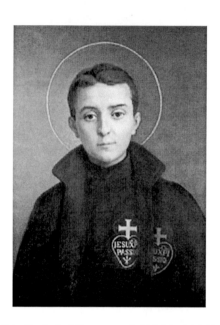

St. Gabriel Possenti (1838-1862)
St. Gabriel of Our Lady of Sorrows
Feast Day ~ February 27

Born in Assisi, Italy and named after the famous St. Francis of Assisi. Francis Possenti was raised by a governess after his mother's death. Twice he suffered severe illness as a child and promised Our Lady that if God made him well, he would join a religious order. Both times he got better but failed to keep his promise. He loved to have a good time and was the life of the party. One day he was attending a procession and a picture of Our Lady was being carried by, and Francis looked at the picture of Our Lady of Sorrows and felt that Mary was looking at him. A message went straight to his heart, "Francis, the world is not for you anymore." He listened this time and went to the Passionist monastery. This is where he received his name *Gabriel of Our Lady of Sorrows*. He was obedient to his superiors. His great love for Mary and the Eucharist flowed from him and caused him much joy. He loved to offer things up for Jesus. Just 4 years after becoming a priest, Gabriel started coughing, and it was discovered that he had tuberculosis. He died when he was only 24 years old, but it was not a sad time for he had spread his joy to all who met him. He suffered silently, and when he died, he went home to Jesus.

This week try listening to your parents the first time they tell you something and then go do it right away. Encourage others to do the same with a joyful attitude. Pick up your things for Jesus!

Possenti's Pasta with Feta and Tomatoes (Chicken Optional)

Olive oil
4-5 cloves garlic, minced
4-5 plum tomatoes, quartered
½-¾ lb. pasta (spirals or penne work best)

Feta cheese *(to taste – I like lots)*
Sons of Italy Italian seasoning

Cook pasta and set aside. Sauté garlic in olive oil for a few minutes. Add tomatoes and sprinkle with Italian seasoning. When tomatoes are soft, add pasta and crumbled feta cheese. Stir until pasta is hot again and feta melts a bit.

If you want to add chicken, it's easy to add the already-cooked pieces before the tomatoes.

"Our perfection does not consist of doing extraordinary things but to do the ordinary well" ~St. Gabriel Possenti

"I will attempt day by day to break my will into pieces. I want to do God's Holy Will, not my own" ~St. Gabriel Possenti

St. Benedict of Nursia (480-543)
Feast Day ~ July 11

St. Benedict's name means blessed. He had a twin sister, St. Scholastica and they were born to Roman nobility in Italy. He studied in Rome and at 14 was disappointed that his fellow students did not take their studies seriously so he went off to live as a hermit for 3 years. Men were so impressed that they asked him to lead them at their abbey. Some monks didn't like him because his ways were too strict so they tried to poison him. He went back to his cave and followers still sought him out. He destroyed a pagan temple and brought many back to their Faith. He founded a monastery at Monte Cassino, the birthplace of Western monasticism, where he wrote his famous Rule for the Monastic Communities. The Rule can be summed up as "Pray and work." Benedict was given great gifts from God and he used these gifts to help his people. He could read people's souls. He is known for rebuking the devil, as he was greatly tempted and overcame his temptation causing the devil to flee from him. He foretold many things including his own death.

Years later, a young boy was bitten by a poisonous snake. On the verge of death, he saw a brilliant ladder reaching toward heaven. On the ladder was an old monk, St. Benedict, who took the cross he was holding and touched Bruno's face with it. Instantly, the boy was cured. This young man later entered the Benedictine order and in 1048 became Pope Leo IX.

Discuss some of the gifts that God has given to you at dinner tonight. Are you understanding? Do you have patience? Do you speak up and have courage if someone says a bad word? Do you have a kind heart? Work on using your gifts all week long to show God how much you love Him.

Benedict's Italian Lasagna

1 lb ground beef/turkey
½ lb ground Italian sausage
1 large sweet onion, chopped
2 green peppers, chopped
6 fresh mushrooms (sliced)
1 (28 oz.) can tomato sauce
1 (28 oz.) can petite diced tomatoes
2 Tbsp. Italian seasoning
1 Tbsp. basil
2 cloves fresh garlic
Grated cheese
8oz bag shredded Mozzarella cheese
8 oz bag shredded Provolone cheese
1 box lasagna noodles (12)

Cook and drain meat. Cook onion and green peppers and set aside. Cook mushrooms in separate pan with a bit of butter and add to the onion and peppers. Combine tomato sauce, diced tomatoes and seasonings in large pot and add cooked meat. Stir. Cover and simmer after adding the onions, peppers and mushrooms. Cook noodles and drain in cold water. In a 9X13 pan place a small amount of sauce to coat the bottom so that the noodles won't stick and line the bottom of pan with three noodles. Spoon sauce onto noodles and sprinkle with grated and mozzarella cheese. Layer three more noodles, sauce, grated cheese and provolone cheese. Layer three more noodles, sauce, grated cheese, Mozzarella AND Provolone cheese. If there is room you may add a fourth layer. Cover with foil and bake for ½ hour at 350°. Remove foil and bake 10 more minutes.

St. Andrew Kim Taegon (1821-1846)
Feast Day ~ September 20

Andrew Kim Taegon was baptized at the age of 15. His parents were both converts and his father was martyred because it was illegal to practice the Faith in Confucian Korea. He studied for nine years to become a priest and went back to Korea to preach and evangelize. He was Korea's first priest! You had to practice the Faith in secret because the rulers of Korea persecuted and killed anyone who loved God. That didn't stop the Korean people as their love for God kept the Church alive. Masses were held in secret, but many Catholics were arrested and murdered. Andrew Kim Taegon was deeply in love with Jesus and wanted to bring Jesus to all the people of Korea. Thousands of Catholics were martyred including Andrew Kim Taegon who died in 1846 at the age of 25.

His last words were*: "This is my last hour of life, listen to me attentively: if I have held communication with foreigners, it has been for my religion and for my God. It is for Him that I die. My immortal life is on the point of beginning. Become Christians if you wish to be happy after death, because God has eternal chastisements in store for those who have refused to know Him."*

During Pope John Paul's trip to Korea in 1984 Andrew Kim Taegon along with 103 other Korean Martyrs were canonized.

Do you sometimes take Jesus for granted and go to Mass because you *have* to and not because you want to? This week, be enthusiastic as you go into your church and thank God that we can worship Him without any fear of being punished because of our love for Him.

Bulgoki (Korean Steak)

5 Tbsp. soy sauce
4 Tbsp. sugar
2 Tbsp. sesame seeds
1 Tbsp. sesame oil
¼ tsp. pepper

4 Tbsp. green onion
1 Tbsp. minced garlic
5 Tbsp. water
Flank steak or London broil, cut on the diagonal

Combine first 7 ingredients and pour over sliced meat. Marinate for 1 to 3 days. Grill for 1 to 2 minutes on each side.

"O You who are mad about Your creature, true God and true Man, You have left Yourself wholly to us, as food, so that we will not fall through weariness during our pilgrimage in this life, but will be fortified by You, celestial nourishment."
~St. Catherine of Siena

Notes

Fantastic Fridays

"Then Jesus fed a whole bunch of people with just five slices of bread and two fish sticks!"

FANTASTIC FRIDAYS INDEX

Baked Haddock with Mushrooms 189
Baked Tomatoes with Orzo and Olives 165
Blessed Kateri Tekakwitha Sweet Corn Cakes 163
Bridget's Vegetable Lasagna Bake 173
Butter Herbed Baked Fish 188
Cheesy Broiled Flounder 192
Crab Casserole 196
Disciplines of True Fasting 200
Fish Marinade 197
Frassati's Fish Piccata 191
Greek Quesadillas 176
Grilled Rosemary Salmon Kabobs 194
Heavenly Stuffed Zucchini 161
Homemade Spaghetti Sauce 179
Jane's Creamy Vegetable Lasagna 171
Mac & Cheese 187
Macaroni Casserole 184
Martin's Black Bean Lasagna 75

Mexican-Style Cheese Tortillas 177
Nutritional Yeast Gravy .. 188
Penne with Fresh Tomato Sauce, ... 185
Phillip's Light Fettuccine Alfredo 181
Poor Man's Lobster 193
Salmon Patties 194
Salmon with Brown Sugar & Mustard Glaze 193
Savory Sole 189
Scalloped Oysters 196
Shrimp & Lobster Casserole 195
Shrimp Stir-Fry 195
Spaghetti and Sand 184
Spicy Tuna Melt 197
St. Elizabeth's Old Bay Fish Batter 199
St. Julie's Quickie Quiche 169
St. Peter's Shrimp 183
Taku Grilled Salmon 192
Vegetarian Pot Pie 167
Vegetarian Shepherd's Pie 167
Zucchini Casserole 166

Fantastic Fridays

Heavenly Stuffed Zucchini

This is a delicious, colorful, and low-fat dish! The chopping does take a little time, but the dish can be prepped at least a day ahead of time. A food processor helps, just don't over-process and make the filling mushy (unless you like it that way).

4 medium zucchini
2 large carrots, peeled and chopped
2 tsp. grated fresh ginger
2 cloves garlic, crushed
Salt and pepper to taste
1 Tbsp. olive oil
½ lb. asparagus, chopped *(optional)*
½ cup sliced almonds, toasted

Preheat oven to 350°. Slice each zucchini in half lengthwise and scoop out most of the zucchini insides to make "boats." Chop the scooped zucchini into pea-sized pieces. Finely chop the carrots and asparagus.

Heat the oil, garlic, and ginger in a big skillet. Add chopped veggies and cook until slightly tender. Add salt and pepper to taste. Turn off heat and mix in almonds.

Place zucchini boats into baking pans, and fill each boat with the cooked vegetable stuffing (heaping is fine). Gently add water to pan so that the zucchini are halfway submerged. Cover with foil and bake for 35 to 45 minutes, depending on how soft you prefer your vegetables. *Makes 4 servings.*

Blessed Kateri Tekakwitha (1656-1680) *Virgin*
Feast Day ~ July 14

Kateri, from Auriesville, New York, was the first person born in the United States to be beatified. Her mother, a Christian, was taken captive and given to a Mohawk chief. Her parents and brother died in a smallpox epidemic which she survived, but she was left disfigured and her vision became impaired. Her uncle, the chief's brother, became chief and was a very mean man. He didn't like the "black robes"- the missionaries that came to minister to the people. Kateri refused to marry a Mohawk brave when she was 19 because she wanted to become a Catholic, which was forbidden. Kateri loved God and risked her life to be baptized on Easter Sunday. She took the Christian name of Catherine. She lived in danger and was treated as a slave. She didn't do any work on Sunday and because of this, she did not receive any food. Her life was getting harder but her faith in God was strong. Though almost blind, she took the advice of a priest and walked 200 miles to a Christian Indian village near Montreal, Canada. There she grew in holiness and spent many long hours in prayer. At 23 she promised God that she would never marry even though her future depended on being married. She trusted in God totally. She often fasted for her people. When she died on Holy Thursday in 1680, her disfigured face became radiant with a faint smile to her lips.

Fasting is a sacrifice we do to show God that we love Him. Sometimes we give up something delicious and other times we give up watching television, playing computer games, or some other activity that we really enjoy. Try and give something up this week and offer it up to Jesus.

Blessed Kateri Tekakwitha Sweet Corn Cakes

½ cup butter, softened
⅓ cup Mexican corn flour
   (or fine cornmeal)
¼ cup coarse cornmeal
¼ cup water

1 ¼ cups frozen corn, or
   1 (14 oz.) can creamed corn
⅓ cup white sugar
2 Tbsp. milk or cream
¼ tsp. salt
½ tsp. baking powder

In a medium bowl, beat butter until it is creamy. Add the cornmeal/corn flour and water and beat until well mixed. Using a food processor, process thawed corn, but leave chunky. Stir into the butter mixture.

In a separate bowl, mix sugar, milk, salt, and baking powder. Add to corn flour mixture and stir to combine. Pour batter into an ungreased 8x8-inch baking pan. Smooth batter and cover with aluminum foil. Place pan into a 9x13-inch baking dish that is filled a third of the way with water. *(This will prevent it from cooking too quickly around the edges.)*

Bake in a preheated 350° oven for 50 to 60 minutes. Let cool for 10 minutes.

St. Pio of Pietrelcina (Padre Pio) (1887-1968)
Feast Day ~ September 23

Francesco, named after St. Francis of Assisi, was born in a small Italian village to peasant farmers. As a child he wanted to be a priest, and at age 16 became a Capuchin novice. Eventually he became a priest taking the name Padre Pio. Eight years later Padre Pio was praying in front of a very large crucifix when he received the stigmata, the wounds of Christ. He was the very first priest to receive the stigmata. He wore gloves but his hands still oozed blood. These wounds caused him great pain but he offered his sufferings up to God. People said that he smelled of roses (a sign of the Blessed Mother's presence). He also had the gift of bilocation where he could be in 2 places at the same time. Many people witnessed this. He spent many hours in the confessional, and had the gift of being able to read penitents souls. Upon his death at the age of 81, over 100,000 attended his funeral.

This week consider praying in front of a crucifix and imagining what Jesus went though having nails hammered through his feet and hands. Thank Him for loving you and opening the gates of heaven. Do this for 10 minutes every day this week.

Baked Tomatoes with Orzo and Olives

4 large tomatoes, halved, hollowed
3 cups cooked orzo
¼ cup chopped olives
3 Tbsp. chopped basil or parsley
1 tsp. minced garlic
3 tsp. toasted pine nuts
1 Tbsp. olive oil
¼ cup Parmesan cheese

Preheat oven to 350°. Halve and hollow tomatoes; place in baking dish. Mix the rest of the ingredients, except the cheese, together in a small bowl and season with salt and pepper to taste. Carefully stuff the tomatoes and sprinkle with cheese. Bake for 20 minutes and serve. *Makes 8 servings.*

"Eli, Eli, lama sabachthani?" which means, "My God, my God, why have you forsaken me?" Matt. 27:46

"In this way the love of God was revealed to us: God sent his only Son into the world so that we might have life through him." 1John 4:9

"It would be easier for the world to survive without the sun than to do so without the Holy Mass." ~St. Padre Pio

Fantastic Fridays 165

Zucchini Casserole

3 medium unpeeled zucchini, ends trimmed, coarsely grated *(about 4 cups total)*
1 ¼ cups Bisquick mix
½ medium onion, finely grated *(about ⅔ cup)*
½ cup freshly grated Parmesan cheese
4 large eggs
¼ cup vegetable oil
½ tsp. salt
¼ tsp. freshly ground black pepper

Preheat oven to 350°. Have ready a 9x13-inch ovenproof casserole dish. A food processor can be used to grate the zucchini and the onion.

Combine the zucchini, Bisquick, onion, and Parmesan cheese in a large mixing bowl. In a large measuring cup, whisk together the eggs and oil. Add to the zucchini mixture, mixing well to combine; season with salt and pepper.

Spread the mixture evenly in the casserole dish and bake for 30 to 35 minutes, until the edges are lightly browned and the casserole is slightly puffed. Cut into squares, if desired. And serve hot. *Makes 8 servings.*

Make Ahead: The casserole tastes best fresh out of the oven, but it can be baked 1 day in advance, then covered and refrigerated (it will fall once it has cooled). Cover loosely with aluminum foil and reheat in a 325° oven for 20 to 25 minutes.

Vegetarian Shepherd's Pie

This dish requires some preparation ahead of time, but it really is easy to make overall.

4-5 cups mashed potatoes (make ahead of time)
1 ½ cups Nutritional Yeast Gravy (make ahead of time – see recipe pg. 188)
2 cups frozen corn kernels

12 oz. vegetarian burger crumbles *(I prefer Morningstar Farms Meal Starters Grillers Recipe Crumbles)*
1 medium onion
2 tsp. paprika

Preheat oven to 350°. Chop onion and cook in a pan until soft. Add vegetarian "burger" crumbles to pan and heat until thawed. Add gravy to onion and "burger."

Place the burger/gravy into a 9x13-inch pan. Sprinkle the corn on top. Spread the mashed potatoes on top (easier to spread if heated up a bit in microwave) and sprinkle with paprika. Bake for about 1 hour or until heated through.

Vegetarian Pot Pie

2 frozen 9-inch pie crusts
1 ½ cups Nutritional Yeast Gravy – see recipe pg. 188
1 tsp. salt
Pepper to taste

3 cups any combination of vegetables, cut into bite-size pieces. Try:
- Tofu or other vegetarian meat alternative
- Corn, peas, green beans, spinach, zucchini
- Potatoes, carrots, celery, onion

Preheat oven to 350°. If choosing fresh vegetables, cook them a little bit beforehand to soften. Bake pie crusts until slightly cooked, about 6 minutes.

Mix gravy, seasonings, and tofu/vegetables together. Place mixture into a pie crust and top with the other pie crust, sealing edges. Bake for 45 minutes.

St. Julie Billiart (1751-1816)
Feast Day ~ April 8

Julie was a happy child who loved her parents. Her favorite thing to do was to play school. She loved to teach and soon began to teach others about God. Back when Julie lived, you made your First Holy Communion when you were 13 years of age. The priest recognized Julie's love for God and allowed her to make her First Holy Communion four years earlier at the age of nine. She grew in her love for God and never missed an opportunity to talk to others about Jesus.

When Julie became sick and was paralyzed, she offered her sufferings to Jesus. As the war broke out in France, Julie let priests hide out in her home. She also had to hide herself and hid in different homes. Many young women looked up to Julie since she was such an inspiration. One day, a priest came to her town and asked her to pray a novena for nine days; during the novena, Julie took her first step and was cured after 22 years! Julie could walk.

She eventually founded the Sisters of Notre Dame de Namur. God showed her a vision of the sisters and Julie knew that this was what God wanted her to do. She gathered a few friends and they began the order. She helped nurse the wounded men from the war and eventually died helping others in 1816.

Julie never gave up. Even though she couldn't walk she still found a way to help others. Do you have an obstacle in your way that makes it hard to help others? Why not imitate Julie this week and help someone even though it may be hard to do.

St. Julie's Quickie Quiche

3 eggs
½ cup Bisquick
½ cup melted butter or margarine
½ cup milk
¼ tsp. salt
Dash pepper
1 cup shredded Swiss cheese
½ cup bacon, ham, or onion bits

Beat eggs lightly with fork. Add Bisquick, butter, milk, and seasonings. Pour into 9-inch pie plate. Sprinkle on shredded cheese and any other ingredients. Bake at 350° for 45 minutes. Let sit 10 minutes before serving. Top should be delicately brown.

"The Eucharist is really a glimpse of heaven appearing on earth. It is a glorious ray of the heavenly Jerusalem which pierces the clouds of our history and lights up our journey"
~Ecclesia De Eucharistia

Not 100 in the United States hate the Roman Catholic Church, but millions hate what they mistakenly think the Roman Catholic Church is. ~ Bishop Fulton J. Sheen

To keep a lamp burning we have to keep putting oil in it.
~Blessed Teresa of Calcutta

St. Jane Frances de Chantal (1572-1641)
Feast Day ~ August 18

Jane married a man who had just inherited the title of baron, so one would think that Jane would have been well off. This was not the case since she also inherited quite a lot of debt. She took charge of the estate and at 20 years of age turned things around. Her employees loved her, and she and her four children were devoted to each other. Jane loved to help poor people. They were never turned away, no matter how many times they returned. Her beloved husband was killed in a hunting accident. He forgave the man before he died, but Jane had a hard time forgiving him. She was heartbroken. She prayed to God for the grace to forgive him, but it was hard. After much prayer she was able to pass him on the street and greet him. This was not enough, she had to be able to truly forgive, just as Jesus had forgiven. Eventually, she could truly say she had forgiven him and even became a godmother to one of his children. St. Francis de Sales became her spiritual director and they wrote many letters to each other. Jane founded the Visitation Order. She allowed sick women and older women to join, something that was unheard of at the time. She was known for her gentleness and caring ways.

"Once we have humbled ourselves for the faults God allows us to become aware of in ourselves, we must forget them and go forward. God is merciful, even if you sin 50 times a day, get up and try again." ~St. Jane Francis de Chantal

Give yourself to Him totally and let God work in you! How will you trust in God this week?

Jane's Creamy Vegetable Lasagna

White Sauce:
4 ½ cups milk
½ cup butter
½ cup flour
2 tsp. salt
¼ tsp. pepper
½ cup Romano cheese, grated
¼ tsp. nutmeg

Lasagna:
10 oz. fresh spinach
2 cloves garlic, crushed
3 medium carrots, peeled and grated
Olive oil
16 oz. ricotta cheese
1 egg
1 pkg. no-boil lasagna noodles (about 16)

White Sauce: Warm milk in a pot. In a big pot, melt butter and then whisk in flour. Stir for 1 minute and then slowly whisk in the warmed milk. When thickened, add the rest of the ingredients.

Lasagna: Cook the spinach and garlic in olive oil until spinach is wilted; drain. Cook carrots in olive oil until tender. Mix in bowl: spinach, carrots, ricotta, and egg.

In 9x13-inch pan, spread ¾ cup of white sauce on bottom. Make 3 filled layers by placing noodles to cover pan, spreading ⅓ of cheese and veggies, and spreading 1 cup of white sauce. (**Note:** Don't let no-boil noodles touch the edge of the pan – they will get crispy and tough.) Place one last layer of noodles on top and spread remaining white sauce on top.

Cover with foil, bake at 400° for 40 minutes or until noodles are done. Let cool for a few minutes before serving.

> "We cannot always offer God great things, but at all times we can offer God little things with great love."
> ~St. Jane Francis de Chantal

St. Bridget of Sweden (1303-1373)
Feast Day ~ July 23

Born in Sweden in 1303, Bridget was raised in a devout family. Her father made Fridays special because they belonged to Jesus in remembrance of His crucifixion. The children learned to do little acts of mortification out of love for what Jesus did for them. When Bridget was 14 years old, she married a holy man who was a prince, and they had 8 children—the last one is now a saint, too, St. Catherine. They joined the Franciscan Third Order and helped the King and Queen of Sweden to live holy lives. Bridget was blessed to have visions of our Lord and visited kings and queens to help them. She was not proud or boastful but always remained humble. Upon her husband's death, she put away all her rich clothes and lived a very simple life as a poor nun. Jesus continued to reveal many things about His passion to her, which were written down and published after her death.

When someone praises us for doing a good job, we feel happy inside. This week when you receive a compliment thank Jesus for giving you the graces to be good and for allowing you to serve Him. Why not imitate St. Bridget and make Fridays in your house special remembering Jesus' crucifixion. How? Make little sacrifices and offer them to Jesus. Give up something you like to eat or do something that you don't like to do. We can all benefit from abstaining from meat!

Bridget's Vegetable Lasagna Bake

Why not imitate St. Bridget and make Fridays special to remember what Jesus did for you. Below is a yummy recipe without meat!

12 lasagna noodles
2 Tbsp. olive oil
2 heads fresh broccoli, chopped
2 carrots, thinly sliced
1 large onion, chopped
2 green bell peppers, chopped
2 zucchini, sliced
3 cloves garlic, minced
½ cup all-purpose flour
3 cups milk
¾ cup Parmesan cheese, divided
½ tsp. salt
½ tsp. pepper
1 (8 oz.) container small curd cottage cheese
24 oz. ricotta cheese
1 ½ cups shredded mozzarella cheese, mixed
1 ½ cups shredded Provolone cheese, mixed

Preheat oven to 375°. Grease a 9x13-inch casserole dish.

Bring a large pot of lightly salted water to a boil. Add lasagna noodles and cook for 8 to 10 minutes or until al dente; drain.

Heat oil in a large cast iron skillet over medium heat. When oil is hot, add broccoli, carrots, onions, bell peppers, zucchini, and garlic. Sauté for 7 minutes; set aside. *I cook the zucchini separately as there isn't enough room. I also use a nonstick pan and don't use oil.*

Place flour in a medium saucepan and gradually whisk in milk until well blended. Bring to a boil over medium heat. Cook 5 minutes or until thick, stirring constantly. Stir in ½ cup Parmesan cheese, salt and pepper; cook for 1 minute, stirring constantly. Remove from heat. In a small bowl, combine cottage and ricotta cheese; stir well.

Layer noodles, ricotta mixture, vegetables, 1 cup mozzarella and 1 cup Provolone cheese, ending with noodles Top with ½ remaining cheese and ¼ cup Parmesan cheese. Bake in preheated oven for 35 minutes, or until lightly browned on top. Cool for approximately 10 minutes before serving.

Saint Martin de Porres (1579-1639)
Feast Day ~ November 3

Martin was born to a Spanish nobleman and a freed slave in Lima, Peru. He was illegitimate and poor. He apprenticed with a surgeon-barber and learned how to care for the sick. He was made fun of and ridiculed by the townspeople, but Martin offered his humiliations to God as sacrifices. When Martin was 15, he became a servant in the Holy Rosary Dominican Priory in Lima, Peru. Drawn through compassion to the sick, he began working in the monastery infirmary, finding ingenious ways to keep the sick well supplied. He was also put in charge of the town's poor people and many would come for food and money. Through many miracles, Martin was able to feed and give money to these needy people. Martin eventually became a Dominican. He lived frugally and gave his money to the poor. He would wear one habit until it was completely worn out before he would purchase another one. Martin often spent time in prayer surrounded by a great light. He loved praying before the Blessed Sacrament and at times levitated while praying. Though Martin never sought out fame, people from all over started coming to him, for they recognized his holiness. He knew if a person was sick or if they were dying and he took great care to comfort them all. When he died, he was given the funeral of a high ranking official, as he had touched so many people's hearts. They realized that Martin was a great saint who had spent his life doing God's will.

Help clean out your closet this week. Gather up good clothes that don't fit you anymore and give them away. As a special

treat, give away something you can do without, but still really like. See how happy you feel when you give something away with love.

Martin's Black Bean Lasagna

9 lasagna noodles
2 (15 oz.) can black beans, rinsed and drained
Nonstick cooking spray
½ cup chopped onion
½ cup chopped green pepper
2 cloves garlic, minced
2 (15 oz.) cans tomato sauce
¼ cup snipped cilantro (optional)
1 (12 oz.) container low-fat cottage cheese
1 (8 oz.) pkg. reduced-fat cream cheese, softened
¼ cup light sour cream

Cook noodles; drain. Mash 1 can of beans; set aside. Spray large skillet with coating; add onion, green pepper, and garlic. Cook and stir over medium heat until tender but not brown. Add mashed beans, unmashed beans, tomato sauce, and snipped cilantro if desired; heat through.

In large mixing bowl, combine cottage cheese, cream cheese, and sour cream; set aside. Spray 9x13-inch baking dish with cooking spray. Arrange 3 noodles in dish. Add ⅓ bean layer and ⅓ cheese layer. Repeat twice. Bake, covered, at 350° for 40 to 45 minutes. Let stand 10 minutes. *Makes 8 main dish servings.*

The kindly man will be blessed, for he gives of his sustenance to the poor." Prov. 22:9

"He who gives to the poor suffers no want, but he who ignores them gets many a curse." Prov. 28:27

"The secret to evangelization is a longing for sanctity, contemplation of the face of Christ, and a desire to share him with others." ~Pope Benedict XVI.

Greek Quesadillas

1 small onion
1 tsp. olive oil
2 cloves garlic, minced
1 (7 oz.) pkg. fresh baby spinach, or 1 (10-oz.) pkg. frozen chopped spinach, thawed and drained
4 oz. (1 cup) crumbled feta cheese
3 oz. cream cheese, softened

½ cup ricotta cheese
1 tsp. fresh lemon juice
¼ tsp. ground cumin
¼ tsp. salt
¼ tsp. pepper
⅛ tsp. nutmeg
4 (8-inch) flour tortillas
Prepared salsa *(optional)*

Sauté onion in hot oil in a large nonstick skillet over medium-high heat for 6 minutes or until tender. Add garlic, and sauté 1 minute; add spinach, and sauté 3 to 4 minutes or until spinach is slightly wilted. Drain mixture on paper towels; cool slightly. Wipe skillet clean and set aside.

Stir together feta cheese and next 7 ingredients until blended. Gently stir in spinach mixture. Spoon mixture evenly onto half of each tortilla. Fold in half, pressing gently to seal.

Heat skillet over medium heat. Add quesadillas in 2 batches, and cook 2 to 3 minutes on each side or until they are slightly browned. Serve with salsa, if desired.

"If we but paused for a moment to consider attentively what takes place in this Sacrament, I am sure that the thought of Christ's love for us would transform the coldness of our hearts into a fire of love and gratitude." ~ St. Angela of Foligno

Mexican-Style Cheese Tortillas

1 avocado, diced
1 medium tomato
1 small onion, finely chopped
1 tsp. cumin

½ tsp. chili powder
Dash salt
8 flour tortillas *(burrito size)*
12-16 slices provolone cheese

Cut tomato in quarters and remove the seeds and watery pulp. Chop tomato into small pieces. Combine avocado, tomato, onion, and spices; mix well.

Lay out 4 tortillas on baking sheets and place 3 to 4 slices of provolone on each. Evenly divide avocado mixture onto tortillas and spread. Top each with another tortilla.

Bake at 400° for 6 to 8 minutes, until edges start to brown. Slice and serve. *Try it topped with sour cream and/or salsa!*

It is there in His Eucharist that He says to me: "I thirst, thirst for your love, your sacrifices, your sufferings. I thirst for your happiness, for it was to save you that I came into the world, that I suffered and died on the Cross, and in order to console and strengthen you I left you the Eucharist. So you have there all My life, all My tenderness."
~Mother Mary of Jesus, foundress of the
Sisters of Marie Reparatrice.

St. Peregrine Laziosi (1260-1335)
Feast Day ~ May 16

Peregrine belonged to an anti-papal party and was rebellious. He was listening to St. Philip Benizi, the head of the Servite order, when he became furious and hit Philip in the face. Philip simply turned his face to the other side and prepared to be hit again. Peregrine's heart softened at that moment, and he decided to change his ways and listen to what the priest was saying. He became a priest and was known for his preaching and service to the sick and poor. He offered penances to God like standing when he could sit. His legs developed varicose veins, and he was diagnosed with cancer of the foot. After going to the doctor and receiving all sorts of medical treatment, the doctors decided that his leg had to be amputated. Peregrine stayed up all night praying to Jesus on the cross. As he prayed, he fell asleep and dreamed that Jesus came down off the cross and healed his leg. When he awoke, his leg was restored, and Peregrine had no pain. He lived for many more years doing the will of God. He is the patron saint of those suffering from cancer and other serious diseases.

What could you do this week to change your heart to be more like Jesus? Pray to Jesus and ask him what He wants of you. Listen well!

Homemade Spaghetti Sauce

10 garden tomatoes
1 cup water
1 Tbsp. oregano
1 Tbsp. basil
2 Tbsp. Italian seasoning
1 Tbsp. Worcestershire sauce
1 tsp. soy sauce
1 onion

2 celery stalks, chopped
1 carrot, sliced
4 cloves garlic, minced
2 Tbsp. olive oil
4 mushrooms, sliced
1 large green pepper, chopped

In crockpot, boil down the tomatoes with 1 cup of water added. After several hours, add remaining ingredients. Let cook for at least another hour. *The secret ingredients are the Worcestershire and the soy sauce.* Serve with spaghetti.

"I am the bread of life. Your ancestors ate the manna in the desert, but they died; this is the bread that comes down from heaven so that one may eat it and not die. I am the living bread that came down from heaven; whoever eats this bread will live forever; and the bread that I will give is my flesh for the life of the world." John 6:48-51

Jesus said to them, "Amen, amen, I say to you, unless you eat the flesh of the Son of Man and drink his blood, you do not have life within you. Whoever eats my flesh and drinks my blood has eternal life, and I will raise him on the last day. For my flesh is true food, and my blood is true drink. Whoever eats my flesh and drinks my blood remains in me and I in him." John 6: 53-56

St. Philip Neri (1515-1595)
Feast Day ~ May 26

Born in Florence, Italy, Philip was called "good little Phil" by his friends. As a teenager, he went to Rome to study theology and philosophy. He worked hard to help poor children and had great compassion for the sick. He was known for his cheerfulness and great love of God. He started an organization for needy pilgrims, which became a famous hospital in Rome. While praying during a visit to the catacombs, Philip received a vision of a globe of fire. As the globe entered his chest he experienced a great joy and felt his heart swell.

A priest who befriended Philip realized the young man was bringing people to God, and suggested that he should become a priest. Philip listened, and in 1551 he was ordained at the age of 36. People flocked to him. He became their confessor, spending hours in the confessional with lines growing longer and longer each day. Father Philip was never rushed and spent needed time with each child of God. He often seemed able to read their minds. God chose to work miracles through Phillip as well. He founded the Oratorians, a society of priests that helped renew the entire city of Rome with tremendous faith and devotion. When Philip died, they found that his heart was enlarged, swelled with his love for God.

When you pray this week use your heart to pray to Jesus. Imagine a beam of light flowing from your heart to heaven. Jesus is sending down His love to you and when the beams of light meet, they shoot back down into your heart and it swells with love. Try to be alone this week and pray to God with your whole heart!

Philip's Light Fettuccine Alfredo

8 oz. uncooked fettuccine
1 Tbsp. butter
2 cloves garlic, minced
1 cup evaporated milk
3 Tbsp. grated Romano/Parmesan cheese, mixed or singularly
2 Tbsp. fresh or 1 tsp. dried basil
$1/8$ tsp. nutmeg
$1/4$ cup chopped fresh parsley
Coarsely ground black pepper to taste

Cook fettuccine as directed on package; drain. Return to pot. Add butter and garlic. Toss to coat. Stir in milk, cheeses, basil, and nutmeg. Blend well. Cook over medium-high heat until just thickened, about 5 minutes, stirring constantly. Sprinkle with parsley and pepper. Serve immediately. *Makes 6 servings.*

"When you pray, do not be like the hypocrites, who love to stand and pray in the synagogues and on street corners so that others may see them. Amen, I say to you, they have received their reward. But when you pray, go to your inner room, close the door, and pray to your Father in secret."
Matt. 6:5-6

Fantastic Fridays

St. Peter Claver (1580-1654)
Feast Day ~ September 9

Born in Spain in 1580, Peter was poor though his parents were from distinguished families. While studying to become a priest at a Jesuit college, Peter had a burning desire to go to South America. When he was 30, he traveled to Cartagena, which is now called Columbia. Peter would watch as huge ships would come in, carrying slaves who were sick and hungry. He wanted to help them. He brought them food and medicine and taught them about God. He tried to talk to their masters about treating them better. Peter worked among the slaves in South America for 40 years. He baptized 300,000 people. Though he was criticized, he persevered since he knew that God loves all people, no matter what color their skin is. He became sick and was unable to even leave his room for the last 4 years of his life. No one seemed to care, but Peter didn't get discouraged for he had done what God wanted him to do. He hadn't done it for recognition, but for God. When he died, suddenly the whole town realized that Peter had been a saint right in front of them and they hadn't realized it until he was dead. Now he is honored as a saint in heaven.

This week why not do something for God in secret so that no one knows that you were kind to someone and give God a big present!

St. Peter's Shrimp in Angel Hair Pasta Casserole

1 Tbsp. butter
2 eggs
1 cup half-and-half
1 cup plain yogurt
½ cup shredded Swiss cheese
⅓ cup crumbled feta cheese
1 tsp. dried oregano leaves, crushed
⅓ cup chopped fresh parsley
¼ cup chopped fresh basil, crushed
1 (9 oz.) pkg. uncooked fresh angel hair pasta
1 (16 oz.) jar mild, thick and chunky salsa
1 lb. medium shrimp, peeled and deveined, or you can use ½ lb. shrimp and ½ lb. scallops
½ cup shredded Monterey Jack cheese

With 1 tablespoon butter, grease 9x13-inch pan. Combine eggs, half-and-half, yogurt, Swiss cheese, feta cheese, parsley, basil, and oregano in medium bowl; mix well.

Spread ½ of pasta on the bottom of prepared pan. Cover with salsa. Add ½ of the shrimp. Cover with remaining pasta. Spread egg mixture over pasta and top with remaining shrimp. Sprinkle Monterey Jack cheese over top. Bake in preheated 350° oven for 30 minutes or until bubbly. Let stand 10 minutes. *Great dish for entertaining. Enjoy!*

"Can a man hide in secret without my seeing him?" says the LORD. "Do I not fill both heaven and earth?" says the LORD.
Jer. 23:24

Spaghetti and Sand

Red bell peppers
Olive oil
Garlic

Breadcrumbs, plain
Spaghetti

Clean and cut red bell peppers into 1-inch squares or strips *(2 peppers per 3 people)*. Sauté them in olive oil with garlic. Remove and set aside.

Sauté breadcrumbs in olive oil. Cook spaghetti in salted boiling water; drain. Mix peppers and breadcrumbs. Combine with pasta.

Macaroni Casserole

8 oz. macaroni
1 lb. small curd cottage cheese
8 oz. sour cream
1 egg, beaten

2 cups shredded Cheddar cheese
Salt and pepper to taste

Cook macaroni until tender; then mix with all other ingredients. Pour into a baking dish and sprinkle top with paprika. Bake at 350° for 40 minutes.

Penne with Fresh Tomato Sauce, Arugula & Cheese

Even though this is meatless, I have added chicken sometimes. Also have added Italian sausage, also mushrooms.

2 lbs. ripe juicy tomatoes
2 Tbsp. olive oil
1 cup chopped onion
1 ½ tsp. minced garlic
3 tsp. kosher salt
¼ tsp. red pepper flakes
1 lb. penne pasta
¾ cup Parmigiano-Reggiano cheese
2 Tbsp. butter
4 cups (4 oz.) packaged arugula, stemmed and very coarsely chopped

Stem tomatoes but do not peel. Halve tomatoes horizontally and squeeze halves to remove as many seeds as possible. Coarsely chop halves into ¾-inch chunks and place in a large mixing bowl.

Heat olive oil in heavy skillet over medium heat. Add onion, and sauté 1 minute longer. Stir in tomatoes and any other collected juices, ¾ teaspoon salt, and red pepper. Cook, stirring often, until tomatoes are broken down. The mixture is thick and most of the liquid will evaporate in 12 to 15 minutes. Try to leave it just a little juicy.

Cook penne; drain well. Return to pot where it was cooked. Add butter and ½ cup cheese. When melted, add tomato sauce and arugula, and toss until arugula wilts.

"He is The Bread sown in the virgin, leavened in the Flesh, molded in His Passion, baked in the furnace of the Sepulchre, placed in the Churches, and set upon the Altars, which daily supplies Heavenly Food to the faithful." ~St. Peter Chrysologus (400-450)

Our Lady of the Rosary
Feast Day ~ October 7

Pope Pius V established this feast in 1573 honoring Our Lady of the Rosary. Christians naval forces were fighting against the Turks. They were greatly outnumbered and the battle raged on for 5 hours. The pope encouraged everyone to pray the rosary, and a great miracle occurred: the Christian forces won the battle. The battle was very important as it marked the end of Turkish supremacy in the Mediterranean Sea and protected Rome from invasion. This feast day was also known as **Our Lady of Victory**. Pope St. Pius V promoted this feast day throughout the entire Church in 1716. The word rosary means crown of roses. Each Hail Mary is a rose for our Lady. It wasn't always said the way we know it today. Years ago, people would pray 150 Our Fathers counted on beads in imitation of the 150 psalms recited daily by monks. Today we say set prayers while meditating on key events in the lives of Jesus and Mary. As you pray the rosary, imagine that you are holding the hand of Mary as she leads you to her Son through all 20 Mysteries. There are 4 groups each containing 5 Mysteries: The Joyful, The Sorrowful, The Luminous and The Glorious Mysteries. See page 293 for an explanation on how to pray the rosary.

What will you do this week to help your family celebrate this feast? Why not draw some pictures of the Mysteries of the Rosary and say one decade before each meal this week?

Mac & Cheese

Good for Friday dinners! The kids can make a rosary out of the noodles on their plate!

2 Tbsp. butter or oil	Salt and pepper to taste
2 Tbsp. flour	Worcestershire sauce
1 cup milk	3-4 cups noodles
2 cups grated cheese, more or less	

Bring sufficient water to a boil. Cook noodles al dente. In frying pan, melt butter and whisk in flour. Allow to bubble and slightly brown. Pour in milk; whisk to combine and cook until thickened. Add salt, pepper, and Worcestershire sauce to taste. When noodles are done, drain and return to pot. Add white sauce to noodles and add roughly 2 cups shredded cheese. Stir to combine. Pour into 9x13-inch pan and bake at 350° for 30 to 45 minutes until bubbly.

Our family likes a combination of mostly sharp cheddar cheese, with some mozzarella added in (maybe 1 ½ cups of cheddar to ½ cup of mozzarella); but many cheeses besides these are delicious. The stronger the flavor of the cheese(s), the more "grown-up" the final flavor will be. I sometimes add in bits of leftovers or mashed up steamed cauliflower.

❧ **"In the sixth month, the angel Gabriel was sent from God to a town of Galilee called Nazareth, to a virgin betrothed to a man named Joseph, of the house of David, and the virgin's name was Mary. And coming to her, he said, "Hail, favored one! The Lord is with you."** Luke 1:26-28

"When Elizabeth heard Mary's greeting, the infant leaped in her womb, and Elizabeth, filled with the holy Spirit, cried out in a loud voice and said, "Most blessed are you among women, and blessed is the fruit of your womb." Luke 1:41-42

Nutritional Yeast Gravy

This gravy is delicious on mashed potatoes, steamed cauliflower, and as the sauce for a vegetable pot pie or Vegetarian Shepherd's Pie. Nutritional yeast flakes can be found in most health food stores.

¼ cup white flour
½ cup Nutritional Yeast Flakes
⅓ cup oil
Pepper to taste
1 ½ cups water
3 Tbsp. soy sauce

Measure oil and water to have ready quickly. Combine flour and yeast in saucepan over high heat; stir with whisk. When flour and yeast begin to have "nutty" smell, stir in the oil. After this is mixed well, add the water and pepper. When this thickens, add the soy sauce and turn down the heat. *Makes 1 ½ cups.*

Butter Herbed Baked Fish

½ cup butter or margarine
⅔ cup crushed saltines
¼ cup grated Parmesan cheese
½ tsp. each basil, oregano, and salt
¼ tsp. garlic powder
1 lb. frozen or fresh sole or flounder fillets

In 13x9x2-inch baking pan, melt butter in preheated oven, 5 to 7 minutes. Combine crackers, cheese, basil, oregano, salt, and garlic powder. Dip fish in melted butter, then in crumb mixture. Bake at 350° for 20 to 30 minutes or until fish is tender and flakes with a fork.

"The best way to economize time is to 'lose' half an hour each day attending Holy Mass." ~Blessed Frederic Ozanam

Savory Sole

3 oz. tomato juice
1 Tbsp. onion flakes
3 cloves garlic, crushed
1 bay leaf
Dash chili powder
¼ tsp. basil

½ tsp. oregano
1 pkg. instant chicken broth
Salt and pepper to taste
1 lb. filet of sole
1 cup sliced mushrooms
1 cup chopped fresh parsley

In a small bowl, combine tomato juice, onion flakes, garlic, bay leaf, chili powder, basil, oregano, broth mix, salt and pepper. Brown fillets on one side in skillet. Turn fish over. Pour juice mixture over fish. Add mushrooms and sprinkle with parsley. Simmer, uncovered, for 10 to 12 minutes.

Baked Haddock with Mushrooms

1 small onion, sliced
1 (4 oz.) can mushrooms
   (or fresh)
1 Tbsp. chopped parsley
1 clove garlic, minced
Salt and pepper to taste

1 cup nonfat milk
1 lb. haddock filets
2 Tbsp. lemon juice
2 Tbsp. grated Parmesan
   cheese

Sauté onion, mushrooms, parsley, and garlic over very low heat about 15 minutes. Stir in salt and pepper. Add milk slowly and heat. Place fish in Pam-sprayed baking dish and sprinkle with lemon juice. Pour onion mixture over fish and sprinkle with cheese. Bake at 350° for 30 to 40 minutes.

"For believing Catholics, the Eucharist is not a symbol, or rather, it's enormously more than a symbol. It's the literal, tangible body and blood of Jesus Christ."
~Most Reverend Charles J. Chaput, O.F.M. Cap.

Blessed Pier Giorgio Frassati (1901-1925)
Feast Day ~ July 4

Born in Italy to a father who was the founder of a newspaper and an influential politician, and to a mother who was a painter, Pier Giorgio was a sensitive child always thinking of others. His family was wealthy and enjoyed high social standing. He once took off his shoes and gave them to a poor child. When he was 17, he joined the St. Vincent de Paul Society and spent many hours helping the sick and poor as he saw the face of Jesus in all he encountered.

His mother went to Mass as an obligation, but Pier Giorgio went because he loved it. He would spend hours in front of the Blessed Sacrament. He was a fun child and enjoyed being active, climbing mountains and skiing. At 22, he joined the Dominican Third Order and loved praying the rosary. He also took an active part in protesting against Fascism and joined several groups actively trying to reform his country. Once, he found himself in jail after a demonstration, but he prayed the rosary and kept others upbeat and joyful. In 1925, Pier Giorgio became sick, most likely he contracted his illness from the poor he so willingly served. He didn't want anyone to know since his grandmother was also sick and needed to be cared for. His mother was disappointed that he was never around to help and he wasn't able to attend his grandmother's funeral. The day after his grandmother's funeral, Pier Giorgio died from polio. He was 24 years old. At his funeral, crowds of people attended, giving testimony to how Pier Giorgio had helped them. His parents were astounded; they had no idea that Pier Giorgio had taken care of so many people.

In 1984 his body was exhumed and found to be incorrupt. Pier Giorgio was declared a Blessed on May 20, 1990, 65 years after his death.

Without taking money (you may earn it) from your parents this week, how could you help a poor person?

Frassati's Fish Piccata

2 Tbsp. olive oil
4 filets – any kind of white fish, preferably sole
All-purpose flour

¼ cup dry white wine
2 Tbsp. (¼ stick) butter
1 Tbsp. drained capers
1 Tbsp. chopped fresh parsley

Heat oil in large nonstick skillet over medium-high heat. Sprinkle fish with salt and pepper; dust both sides with flour. Add to skillet; cook until browned and just opaque in center, about 2 minutes per side. Transfer fish to platter and cover with foil to keep warm.

Add wine and butter to same skillet. Bring mixture to a boil, whisking up any browned bits. Add capers and parsley. Simmer sauce until slightly thickened, about 3 minutes. Season to taste with salt and pepper. Spoon sauce over fish.

"Rich and poor have a common bond: the LORD is the maker of them all." Prov. 22:2

Cheesy Broiled Flounder

2 lbs. flounder filets
2 Tbsp. lemon juice
½ cup grated Parmesan
¼ cup butter, softened

3 Tbsp. mayonnaise
3 green onions, chopped
¼ tsp. salt
Dash of hot sauce

Place filets in a single layer on rack of greased broiler pan; brush with lemon juice. Combine next 6 ingredients in a small bowl and set aside.

Broil filets 4 to 6 minutes, until flaky. Remove from oven and spread with cheese mixture. Broil an additional 30 seconds, until cheese is brown and bubbly. Garnish with lemon and parsley.

Taku * Grilled Salmon

This is an awesome recipe for every day or for entertaining!

⅓ cup butter
⅔ cup brown sugar
2 Tbsp. lemon juice

1 Tbsp. dry white wine
1 (10-12 oz.) salmon filets

In a medium saucepan, melt butter over medium heat. Stir in brown sugar until dissolved. Add lemon juice and wine. Stir and heat through, about 5 minutes. Use half of the sauce for basting and reserve the rest for serving along with the grilled salmon.

Place filets in a well-greased grill basket. Grill on an uncovered grill directly over medium coals for 4 to 6 minutes per ½-inch thickness or until fish flakes when tested with a fork. Turn once during cooking; brush occasionally with basting sauce. *Makes 8 servings.*

*Taku Inlet is in Alaska, just southeast of the city of Juneau.

Poor Man's Lobster

1-2 lbs. haddock fillet
¼ cup vinegar
¼ tsp. red pepper

2 Tbsp. salt
1 bay leaf
Melted butter

Mix all ingredients with enough water to cover fish. Do not add fish yet. Bring to boil in frying pan. Add fish and poach fish for 8 to 10 minutes. Serve with melted butter and eat the way you would lobster.

Salmon with Brown Sugar & Mustard Glaze

3 Tbsp. brown sugar
1 Tbsp. honey
2 Tbsp. butter
¼ cup Dijon mustard
2 Tbsp. soy sauce
2 Tbsp. olive oil

1 Tbsp. freshly grated ginger
(be generous)
Vegetable oil
Salt and pepper
Salmon filets

Preheat oven to 400°. Melt brown sugar, honey, and butter in small sauté pan over medium-high heat. Remove from heat and whisk in mustard, soy sauce, olive oil, and ginger. Let cool.

Place salmon, skin side down, in baking dish; brush with vegetable oil, and season with salt and pepper. Pour sauce over fish.

Bake at 400° for approximately 20 minutes or until fish flakes easily when tested with fork (don't over cook). To serve, pour remaining sauce in pan over fish.

Delicious served with wilted spinach/tomatoes and teriyaki rice.

Grilled Rosemary Salmon Kabobs

2 tsp. minced fresh rosemary
2 tsp. extra-virgin olive oil
2 cloves garlic, minced
2 tsp. lemon juice
½ tsp. kosher salt
¼ tsp. freshly ground pepper
1 lb. center-cut salmon filet
   (remove skin and cut into
   1-inch cubes)
1 pint cherry tomatoes

Preheat grill to medium-high. Combine all ingredients except tomatoes and salmon in a bowl. Add the cubed salmon, and toss to coat. Place salmon on skewers alternating with cherry tomatoes, dividing among 8 skewers. Oil the grill rack. Grill the kabobs until cooked through, turning once. Serve on a bed of steamed brown rice.

Salmon Patties

1 (16 oz.) can salmon
1 small onion, finely grated
2 Tbsp. minced fresh parsley
Ground black pepper to taste
2 large eggs, well beaten
1 to 1 ½ cups fine dry
   breadcrumbs
3 Tbsp. olive oil or vegetable oil

Turn salmon and liquid into a mixing bowl. Flake with a fork, removing OR mashing any bones (they are edible). Mix in grated onion, parsley, and pepper. Mix beaten eggs with salmon. Add enough breadcrumbs, about ½ to ¾ cup, to make thick enough to shape into 12 small patties. Roll patties in ½ cup breadcrumbs.

In large heavy skillet, heat the oil over low heat; add patties. Fry patties slowly on one side; turn patties and fry until brown on the other side, slowly adding more oil *if needed*.

"Every Consecrated Host is made to burn itself up with love in a human heart." ~St. John Vianney

Shrimp Stir-Fry

3 Tbsp. cornstarch
1 ¾ cups chicken broth
1 Tbsp. soy sauce
½ tsp. sesame oil *(optional)*
2 Tbsp. vegetable oil
1 lb. fresh OR frozen medium shrimp, shelled and deveined

4 cups cut-up vegetables*
½ tsp. ground ginger
¼ tsp. garlic powder OR 1 clove garlic, minced
4 cups hot cooked rice

Mix cornstarch, broth, soy sauce, and sesame oil. Heat **half** the oil in skillet. Add shrimp and stir-fry until done. Remove shrimp.

Add remaining oil. Add vegetables, ginger, and baking powder, and stir-fry until tender-crisp. Add cornstarch mixture. Cook and stir until mixture boils and thickens. Return shrimp to skillet and heat through. Serve over rice.

*Tip: Use a combination of very thinly sliced carrots, green pepper cut in 2-inch strips, and green onion cut in 1-inch pieces.

Shrimp & Lobster Casserole

¼ cup butter
2 (4 oz.) cans button mushrooms
1 cup chopped celery
½ cup chopped onion
¼ cup wild rice, cooked
1 lb. cooked lobster

2 lbs. cooked shrimp
3 Tbsp. chopped pimento
½ cup chopped green pepper
2 (10 ¾ oz.) cans cream of mushroom soup
½ cup toasted, slivered almonds

Melt butter. Add celery and onions; cook 5 minutes. Combine all other ingredients except almonds. Put in greased casserole and sprinkle with nuts. Bake at 350° for 35 minutes. *Makes 8 to 10 servings.*

Crab Casserole

1 lb. lump or backfin crabmeat
2 Tbsp. butter
2 Tbsp. flour
1 cup milk
Salt and pepper
Pinch of cayenne
½ tsp. dry mustard
½ tsp. onion juice
1 wine glass sherry
1 hard-boiled egg
Bread or cracker crumbs

Make a cream sauce of butter, flour, and milk. Cook, adding seasoning, sherry, and chopped egg. Fold crab into sauce. Put in a lightly buttered casserole dish. Cover with buttered breadcrumbs. Bake at 350° for about 20 minutes.

Scalloped Oysters

1 quart oysters with liquor
1 cup crushed soda crackers
Salt and pepper to taste
Bits of butter
2 cups cream

Sprinkle ¾ crackers in bottom of buttered casserole. Add oysters and their liquor. Add salt and pepper. Pour in cream. Sprinkle on rest of cracker crumbs. Dot with butter. Bake at 350° for 45 to 50 minutes.

❧ *"The humility of Jesus can be seen in the crib, in the exile to Egypt, in the hidden life, in the inability to make people understand Him, in the desertion of His apostles, in the hatred of His persecutors, in all the terrible suffering and death of His Passion, and now in His permanent state of humility in the tabernacle, where He has reduced Himself to such a small particle of bread that the priest can hold Him with two fingers. The more we empty ourselves, the more room we give God to fill us."* ~Blessed Teresa of Calcutta

Spicy Tuna Melt

2 English muffins, split
¼ cup chopped green onions
¼ cup light mayonnaise
2 tsp. Worcestershire sauce
2 tsp. prepared horseradish
1 tsp. prepared mustard
⅛ tsp. red pepper flakes
9 oz. can solid white tuna in water, drained
4 (¼-inch thick) slices tomato *(optional)*
½ cup shredded sharp cheese

Preheat broiler. Place muffin halves on a baking sheet, and broil 5 inches from heat for 3 minutes or until lightly toasted.

Combine the onions and the next 6 ingredients in a medium bowl. Divide evenly among the muffin halves. Top each muffin half with a tomato slice, and sprinkle with cheese. Broil 5 inches from heat for 4 minutes or until golden brown. *Makes 2 servings.*

Fish Marinade

1 cup soy sauce
Juice of 1 lemon
¼ cup dry sherry
2 Tbsp. finely chopped fresh ginger
¼ cup chopped green onions
1 clove garlic, finely chopped
Pinch of cayenne pepper
2 Tbsp. freshly ground black pepper

1 lb. salmon or tuna

Combine ingredients in glass or ceramic dish. Add fish and marinate at least 5 hours or overnight in the refrigerator, turning periodically. Bring fish to room temperature before grilling. Also good with chicken.

St. Elizabeth Ann Seton (1774-1821)
Feast Day ~ January 4

Founder of the Sisters of Charity, (the first American religious community for women), Elizabeth opened the first American parish school and orphanage. This was no small feat for a woman with 5 children whose husband had just died. Elizabeth had been a rich young girl, who married a wealthy businessman, but his business failed and he died of tuberculosis. Elizabeth was 30, penniless and living in Italy where they had gone seeking better health for her husband. While there, she was drawn to Catholicism because of kindness shown toward her by Catholic friends, and subsequently converted through her belief in the Real Presence of the Eucharist, the Blessed Mother, and that the Church could be traced back to Peter and the apostles. Rejected by family and friends, she returned to America and opened a school in Baltimore where she led a heroic life of sanctity. Elizabeth was the first American-born saint. She is buried in Emmitsburg, Maryland.

Sometimes it is hard to stand up for something you believe in. At the table tonight discuss what's important to you and your family. What do you believe in? Why is being Catholic special to you?

St. Elizabeth's Old Bay Fish Batter

2 cups Aunt Jemima pancake mix
½ medium onion, diced fine

3 tsp. Old Bay seasoning
¾ can beer *(approximately)*

Stir together pancake mix, Old Bay, and beer until there are no lumps and it is the consistency of pancake batter. Add onion. Blend and deep fry dipped fish fillets in 1 inch of oil at 375°.

"God is everywhere, in the very air I breathe, yes everywhere, but in His Sacrament of the Altar He is as present actually and really as my soul within my body; in His Sacrifice daily offered as really as once offered on the Cross."
~St. Elizabeth Ann Seton

Disciplines of True Fasting
(Is 58:6-7)
True Fasting can also be a time of Feasting!

FAST from judging others;
 FEAST on Christ dwelling in them.
FAST from emphasis on differences;
 FEAST on the unity of all life.
FAST from apparent darkness;
 FEAST on the reality of all light.
FAST from thoughts of illness;
 FEAST on the healing power of God.
FAST from words that pollute;
 FEAST on phrases that purify.
FAST from discontent;
 FEAST on gratitude.
FAST from anger;
 FEAST on patience.
FAST from pessimism;
 FEAST on optimism.
FAST from worry;
 FEAST on God's providence.
FAST from complaining;
 FEAST on appreciation.
FAST from negatives;
 FEAST on affirmatives.
FAST from unrelenting pressures;
 FEAST on unceasing prayer.

FAST from hostility;
 FEAST on nonresistance.
FAST from bitterness;
 FEAST on forgiveness.
FAST from self-concern;
 FEAST on compassion for others.
FAST from personal anxiety;
 FEAST on eternal Truth.
FAST from discouragement;
 FEAST on hope.
FAST from facts that depress;
 FEAST on verities that uplift.
FAST from lethargy;
 FEAST on enthusiasm.
FAST from suspicion;
 FEAST on truth.
FAST from thoughts that weaken;
 FEAST on promises that inspire.
FAST from shadows of sorrow;
 FEAST on the sunlight of serenity.
FAST from idle gossip;
 FEAST on purposeful silence.
FAST from problems that overwhelm;
 FEAST on prayer that sustains.

Mother Nadine Brown, Intercessors of the Lamb

Desserts

"Jeffy's only kneeling on one knee again and saying half the Hail Mary."

DESSERTS INDEX

Agatha's Carrot Cake 203
Almond Cookies 255
Angel Fruit Whip 252
Anise Toast Cookies 257
Apple Crisp 246
Apple Crumb Pie 234
Applesauce Loaf 225
Bernadette's Almost
  Candy Bars 271
Bernard's Apple-Blueberry
  Cobbler 245
Best Brownies 267
Black Bottom Bars 266
Black Forest Truffle
  Cake 217
Blueberry Cake 207
Blueberry Nut Bread 226
Brenton Brittle 277
Butterfinger Bars 269
Chocolate Cherry Cake 214
Chocolate Cherry Dump Cake .. 213
Chocolate Chip Pound Cake 216
Chocolate Chip Zucchini Bread 227
Chocolate Éclair Cake 215
Chocolate Pie 236
Cobbler (Cherry, Blueberry,
  Peach) 243
Colonial Pumpkin Bars 273
Congo Bars 272
Creamy Icing 221
Dutch Miracle Bars 269
Easy Dessert 247
Easy Peach Cobbler 243
Easy Pumpkin Cupcakes 221
Easy Time Holiday Squares 277
Fantastic Fudge 276
Friendship Brownies 267
German Gingerbread 211
Gobs (Sandwich Cookie) 264
Golden Apple Cake 205
Gonzaga's Great
  Cookies 261
Heavenly Fruitcake 224
Hildabrotchen (German
  Cookies) 264

Hummingbird Cake 219
Ice Cream Cake 253
Ice Cream Sandwich Cake 253
Impossible Coconut Pie 235
Incredible Chocolate Chippers .. 266
Jewish Apple Cake 206
Julia's Decorator Icing 223
Juliana's Remarkable Fudge 275
Light Fruitcake 225
Lucy's Oat Cran Cookies 263
Marzipan Candy 273
Mom's Cut-Out Cookies 256
Mom's Fresh Blueberry Pie 233
Monster Cookies 265
No-Bake Cookies 265
Orange Crunch Cake 220
Out-of-This-World Cake 218
Peaches 'n Cream
  Cheesecake 242
Peanut Butter Pie 237
Perpetua & Felicity's Berry
  Puff 231
Prize-Winning Blondies 272
Queen of Pudding 252
Quick Apple Crisp 246
Rhubarb Cake 206
Rhubarb Custard Pie 235
Saintly Citrus Crosses 259
Sour Cream Chocolate Cake ... 213
Spiced Peaches 247
St. Brice's Pumpkin Dessert 249
St. Cecilia's Fudge Pies 241
St. Joseph's Cream Puffs 229
St. Margaret's Lemon Cake 209
St. Nick's Toll House Pie 239
Strawberry Pie 234
Sugared Pecans 276
Sunrise Cherry Pie 237
Tandy Cake 212
Texas Sheet Cake 201
The Cake That
  Doesn't Last 218
Unbeatable Pineapple Cake 212
Watergate Salad 247

Desserts

Texas Sheet Cake

2 cups sugar
2 cups flour
½ tsp. salt
2 sticks (1 cup) margarine
1 cup water
4 Tbsp. cocoa
2 eggs
½ cup sour cream
1 tsp. baking soda
1 tsp. vanilla
1 tsp. vinegar

Icing:
1 stick (½ cup) margarine
4 Tbsp. cocoa
6 Tbsp. milk
1 box powdered sugar
1 tsp. vanilla
¾ cup walnuts

In a large mixing bowl, mix sugar, flour, and salt; set aside. In a saucepan, combine margarine, water, and cocoa; boil until dissolved. Cool.

In a small bowl, mix eggs, sour cream, baking soda, vanilla, and vinegar. Add cooled cocoa mixture and egg mixture to the large mixing bowl that contains the flour and sugar mixture. Mix well. Pour into a greased and floured cookie sheet. Bake at 350° for 20 minutes or until cake tests done.

Icing: Mix all ingredients and put on cake when it comes out of the oven.

"Every member of the Church must be vigilant in seeing that this sacrament of love shall be at the center of the life of the people of God so that through all the manifestations of worship due to it, Christ shall be given back 'love for love,' and truly become the life of our souls." ~ Pope John Paul II

St. Agatha (died around 251)
Feast Day ~ February 5

Some Romans didn't like Christians. They considered Christians criminals and so they were permitted by law to do horrific things to them. Agatha was a beautiful young girl from a wealthy family who loved God with her whole heart and consecrated herself to Him. When Quintianus, a powerful man who governed Sicily in Italy, wanted her, she rejected him because she belonged to God. He was furious and punished her by having her stretched on a rack. When she refused him again and would not renounce her Faith, she was again tortured. As she lay unconscious in her prison cell, the jailers came and saw that she was alive and perfectly healthy. Her body had been restored! Quintianus immediately had her rolled in hot coals until she died. She is the patron saint of those with breast ailments including breast cancer.

Find someone you know who is sick this week and bring them dinner or help with an errand. Why not help make this delicious dessert and bring it to a sick person you know?

Agatha's Carrot Cake

The white icing is a symbol of Agatha's purity! The nuts remind us of the hot coals. Nothing could extinguish the love Agatha had for God!

2 cups sugar
1 cup oil
4 eggs
1 tsp. vanilla
½ tsp. salt
2 tsp. baking soda
1 tsp. baking powder
2 tsp. cinnamon
2 cups flour
3 cups grated carrots

Icing:
1 stick (½ cup) butter
1 (8 oz.) pkg. cream cheese
   (I use ⅓ less fat)
1 lb. 10X sugar
1 tsp. vanilla
1 cup chopped pecans

Beat and mix well the sugar, oil, eggs, and vanilla. Slowly add the combined dry ingredients. Fold in grated carrots. Pour into 3 well-greased 8- or 9-inch pans. Bake at 350° for 25 to 30 minutes. Combine icing ingredients and beat with mixer. Ice cake when completely cooled.

This is the best carrot cake I've ever tasted. We always have it on Easter and for many of the kids' birthdays. I finally bought a third pan so I can bake them all together. It only took me 20 years!

"On a man generous with food, blessings are invoked, and this testimony to his goodness is lasting." Sir. 31:23

St. John Chrysostom (344-407)
Feast Day ~ September 13

John was born in 344 in Antioch, Syria. When he was just a baby, his father died and his mother did not remarry but spent her time making sure he and his sister were well-educated. John was very smart and loved to give speeches. His last name, Chrysostom, means "*golden mouthed.*" After John was baptized at the age of 23, he became a priest and eventually a bishop. John spoke and people listened, and he soon gained a worldwide reputation. As he was speaking about excessiveness and extreme wealth, the Empress took this to mean that he was talking about her. This enraged her, and she and some very jealous men accused John of treason for protecting pious monks years before. He was exiled, but the people demanded his return, and he was brought back. He continued to preach, once telling the crowd that they needed to stop applauding in church, as it was vulgar and offensive and took away from the solemnity of Church services. John was banished from the city of Constantinople permanently when he spoke to the people about their excessive admiration after the unveiling of a statue of the Empress. When he died in Turkey in 407, a hailstorm bombarded the city of Constantinople, and the Empress died four days later. The son of the Empress honored St. John and was truly sorry that his mother had banished him. St. John is one of the great Doctors of the Church and is the TASTE program's patron saint!

This week why not work especially hard at being a good student and go beyond what your teacher expects from you! How about doing some extra math problems or helping someone who struggles with homework?

204 Desserts

Golden Apple Cake

You'll find this isn't a very sweet cake; therefore, it can be used as breakfast cake, snack cake, or dessert after dinner with ice cream. It makes a big cake, but it may disappear rather quickly!

- 3 medium apples, peeled and thinly sliced
- ¼ cup + 1 Tbsp. sugar
- 1 Tbsp. + 2 tsp. ground cinnamon
- 3 cups all-purpose flour
- 2 cups sugar
- 1 Tbsp. baking powder
- 1 tsp. salt
- 4 eggs, beaten
- 1 cup vegetable oil
- ¼ cup orange juice
- 1 Tbsp. vanilla extract
- Sifted powdered sugar (optional)

Combine first 3 ingredients, tossing well, and set aside. Combine flour, 2 cups sugar, baking powder, and salt in large mixing bowl. Combine next 4 ingredients; add to flour mixture, mixing well.

Pour **one-third** of batter into a greased and floured 10-inch tube pan. Top with **half** of the sliced apples, leaving a ½-inch margin around center and sides. Repeat layering, ending with batter on top.

Bake at 350° for 1 hour and 20 minutes, or until a toothpick inserted in center comes out clean. Cool in pan 10 to 15 minutes; then remove from pan and cool completely. Sprinkle with powdered sugar if desired.

"How many of you say: I should like to see His face, His garments, His shoes. You do see Him, you touch Him, you eat Him. He gives Himself to you, not only that you may see Him, but also to be your food and nourishment." ~St. John Chrysostom

Jewish Apple Cake

2 large *(or 4 small)* apples, peeled
2 Tbsp. sugar
2 tsp. cinnamon
3 cups flour
2 ½ cups sugar
1 cup oil
4 eggs
½ cup orange juice
3 tsp. baking powder
2 tsp. vanilla

Slice apples very thin; then add sugar and cinnamon. Set aside while preparing batter.

Combine all other ingredients thoroughly. Will make a very thick batter. Pour ¾ of batter into a greased tube pan. Add apple mixture on top of batter. Then pour remaining batter on top of apples. Preheat oven to 350° and bake in a fluted round pan for 1 hour 15 minutes.

Rhubarb Cake

This cake is a dessert with whipped cream, or is equally good for breakfast. Family favorite.

1 ½ cups brown sugar
½ cup shortening
2 cups flour
1 tsp. baking soda
1 egg, beaten in
   1 cup sour milk/buttermilk
½ tsp. salt
1 tsp. vanilla
3 cups rhubarb, cut up fine

Mix all ingredients and then add rhubarb. Pour batter into a 9x13-inch greased cake pan. Sprinkle pecans on top if desired; or mix ¼ cup sugar and ¾ teaspoon cinnamon, and sprinkle on top. Bake at 325° for 35 to 40 minutes.

Blueberry Cake

¼ cup butter
1 cup sugar
1 egg
2 ½ cups all-purpose flour
1 Tbsp. baking powder
1 cup milk
3 cups fresh blueberries

Cream Cheese Frosting:
8 oz. cream cheese, softened
½ cup powdered sugar
1 Tbsp. milk
½ tsp. vanilla extract

Cream butter; gradually add sugar, beating well. Add egg; beat well. Combine flour and baking powder. Add flour mixture alternately with milk to the creamed mixture, beginning and ending with flour mixture. Mix after each addition. Fold in blueberries.

Pour batter into a buttered Bundt pan. Bake at 350° for 45 to 50 minutes or until toothpick inserted in center comes out clean. Cool in pan 5 minutes. Remove from pan and let cool completely on a wire rack. Optionally, spread cream cheese frosting on top of cake.

Cream Cheese Frosting: Beat cream cheese at medium speed until light and fluffy. Add remaining ingredients; beat until smooth. *Makes 1 cup.*

"As the body cannot be sustained without corporeal food, nor continue in natural life, so without this life-giving food the soul cannot persist in the spiritual life of grace." ~Dionysius the Carthusian

St. Margaret Clitherow (1556-1586)
Feast Day ~ March 26

Margaret was born into a Protestant family and raised in Middleton, England. Her father was a rich candle maker. After marrying a well-to-do butcher, she had two children and became Catholic. She lived in England, but the law prohibited the practice of the Catholic Faith. Margaret loved God with her whole heart and wanted to receive Jesus in the Eucharist. The government punished her and put her in prison for two years. This didn't stop Margaret. When she came home, she started a school for Catholic children. She was fined for not going to Protestant services, but Margaret didn't care. She had a secret hiding place where priests would come and celebrate Mass with the faithful people.

When Margaret sent her oldest son to France to receive a Catholic education, she was put under house arrest for 18 months. Her house was raided one day and articles used by the priests to say Mass were found. She was quickly arrested and charged with hiding priests. They tried to force her to deny her Faith and tortured her, but Margaret could never have denied her God; so they killed her. She is a martyr who is honored for her strength in standing up for what is good and right.

What could you do this week to stand up for something you strongly believe in? Is there someone being picked on at school that you could protect? What about asking Father if you might be able to help out in your church? Maybe you could straighten up the pews without even being asked.

St. Margaret's Lemon Cake

St. Margaret never became discouraged. She spread sunshine wherever she went.

1 pkg. Duncan Hines Lemon Supreme cake mix
¾ cup oil
¾ cup apricot nectar
1 (3 oz.) box lemon Jell-O
4 eggs
1 tsp. lemon extract

Icing:
Juice of 2 lemons
1 cup confectioner's sugar

Mix cake mix, oil, apricot nectar, and Jell-O. Add eggs and lemon extract. Bake in 9x13-inch pan at 325° for 1 hour. Combine lemon juice and confectioner's sugar; pour over warm cake.

"Neither theological knowledge nor social action alone is enough to keep us in love with Christ unless both are proceeded by a personal encounter with Him. Theological insights are gained not only from between two covers of a book, but from two bent knees before an altar. The Holy Hour *becomes like an oxygen tank to revive the breath of the* Holy Spirit *in the midst of the foul and fetid atmosphere of the world,"* ~Archbishop Fulton J. Sheen

St. Peter Canisius (1521-1597)
Feast Day ~ Dec 21

Peter was born in Holland in 1521. His father wanted him to be a lawyer, but Peter wanted to be a priest so he joined the Society of Jesus. Peter worked hard to reform the universities in Germany. Students were being taught heresy, and Peter was responsible for getting the right information to the universities. He risked his life to travel and smuggle in books containing the correct information. He also cared for the sick during a plague and won people's hearts. Peter was so successful in preaching the Faith that he was asked to write a catechism. He wrote one in 1555 on wisdom and justice. Soon he wrote two more for children helping them choose good over evil. and another one with prayers. He is a Doctor of the Church.

Now would be a good time to get your catechism and read a few pages in it every day this week. After you learn something new about your Faith, write it down and share it this Friday with your whole family.

210 Desserts

German Gingerbread

Good warm or cold, served with lemon sauce, chocolate sauce, ice cream, or warm applesauce!

1 cup sugar
½ cup Crisco shortening
½ cup molasses
2 cups flour
1 tsp. cinnamon
1 tsp. ginger
½ tsp. cloves
½ tsp. salt
2 tsp. baking soda
1 cup boiling water
2 eggs, well beaten
½ tsp. vanilla

Cream together sugar, shortening, and molasses. Sift together flour, cinnamon, ginger, cloves, and salt; add to creamed mixture. Dissolve baking soda in boiling water. Add to previous mixture along with beaten eggs and vanilla. Bake in greased 9-inch square pan at 300° for 1 hour.

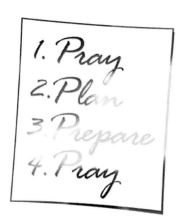

"Our holy mother, the Church, holds and teaches that God, the first principle and last end of all things, can be known with certainty from the created world by the natural light of human reason. Without this capacity, man would not be able to welcome God's revelation. Man has this capacity because he is created "in the image of God". ~Catechism of the Catholic Church CCC 36

Unbeatable Pineapple Cake

2 cups flour
1 ½ cups sugar
¼ tsp. salt
2 cups crushed pineapple
2 eggs
2 tsp. baking soda

Topping:
1 stick (½ cup) butter or margarine
1 small can evaporated milk
½ tsp. vanilla
⅔ cup sugar
½ cup coconut
½ cup chopped nuts

Blend all ingredients with a spoon. Do not beat. Bake in a greased and floured 9x13-inch pan at 350° for 35 to 40 minutes. Cool for 5 minutes, then spread with topping.

Topping: Cook first 4 ingredients until thickened, at least 10 minutes. Add coconut and chopped nuts. Cook 5 minutes more.

Tandy Cake

4 eggs
2 cups sugar
1 tsp. vanilla
2 cups flour
1 tsp. baking powder

1 cup milk
2 Tbsp. margarine
1 cup peanut butter
1 (8 oz.) Hershey Bar

Beat eggs, sugar, and vanilla until creamy. Add flour and baking powder. Scald milk and margarine. Add to mixture and beat (batter will be thin).

Grease and flour cookie sheet (with sides) or sheet pan. Bake at 350° for 20 to 25 minutes. Remove pan from oven and immediately spread peanut butter on top. Cool, refrigerate, or if in a hurry, put in freezer.

Melt Hershey Bar (in double boiler or in microwave), and spread over cold cake.

Sour Cream Chocolate Cake

2 sticks (1 cup) margarine
2 cups flour
4 Tbsp. cocoa
1 cup water
½ pint (8 oz.) sour cream
2 eggs
2 cups sugar
½ tsp. salt
1 tsp. baking soda

Icing:
1 stick margarine
4 Tbsp. cocoa
4-6 Tbsp. milk
1 (1 lb.) box powdered sugar

Bring margarine, cocoa, and water to boil. Mix remaining ingredients and add boiled mixture. Batter will be thin. Bake in a greased and floured 11x15-inch jelly roll pan at 350° for 20 to 25 minutes. While cake is baking, make icing.

Icing: Boil margarine, cocoa, and milk. Add powdered sugar to boiled mixture and frost hot cake. Icing sinks into cake, but cake is still frosted.

Chocolate Cherry Dump Cake

1 pkg. chocolate cake mix
1 (20 oz.) can cherry pie filling
3 eggs
Powdered sugar *(optional)*

Mix first 3 ingredients and bake according to instructions on the cake mix box. When baked, may sprinkle with powdered sugar or put a thin glaze on top.

Chocolate Cherry Cake

1 pkg. Pillsbury Plus dark chocolate or devils food cake mix
3 eggs
1 (21 oz.) can cherry fruit pie filling
1 tsp. almond extract

Glaze:
½ cup semi-sweet chocolate chips
1 Tbsp. margarine or butter, softened
1-2 Tbsp. milk
½ cup powdered sugar

Grease and sugar 12-cup fluted plastic or ceramic tube pan. In large bowl, blend first 4 ingredients until moistened. Beat 2 minutes at highest speed. Pour into pan.

To microwave, cook on low for 11 minutes, then on high for 6 minutes, or on high only for 13 minutes. Rotate pan ½ turn every 5 minutes.

Cool upright in pan 10 minutes; turn onto serving plate. Cool completely.

Glaze: In 2-cup glass measure, microwave first 3 ingredients for 2 minutes until chocolate chips melt. Stir in powdered sugar. Add additional milk if necessary for glaze consistency. Spoon over cooled cake. *Makes 10-inch ring cake.*

༄ "When we go before Jesus in the Blessed Sacrament we represent the one in the world who is in most need of God's Mercy." We "Stand in behalf of the one in the world who does not know Christ and who is farthest away from God and we bring down upon their soul the Precious Blood of The Lamb."
~Pope John Paul II

Chocolate Éclair Cake

Graham crackers
2 (3 oz.) pkgs. instant vanilla pudding
3 cups milk
9 oz. Cool Whip

Topping:
1 cup granulated sugar
⅛ tsp. salt
⅓ cup cocoa
¼ cup milk
¼ cup butter
1 tsp. vanilla

Grease a 9x13-inch pan with butter. Line with graham crackers. Mix pudding with milk. Mix pudding mixture with Cool Whip. Pour half of pudding mixture over crackers. Put another layer of graham crackers on pudding. Pour in rest of pudding. Cover with another layer of crackers.

Topping: Combine sugar, salt, cocoa, and milk together; bring to boil and cook for 1 minute or until soft ball stage. Do not over cook. Remove from heat and add butter and vanilla. Cool, then pour over cake. Refrigerate for a couple of hours before serving.

"Not as common bread or as common drink do we receive these.....We have been taught that the food that has been Eucharistized by the word of prayer, that food which by assimilation nourishes our flesh and blood, is the flesh and blood of the incarnate Jesus." ~St. Justin Martyr

Chocolate Chip Pound Cake

1 (18.25 oz.) yellow cake mix with pudding
1 (3.9 oz.) pkg. chocolate instant pudding mix
½ cup sugar
¾ cup vegetable oil
¾ cup water
4 large eggs
1 (8 oz.) carton sour cream
1 (6 oz.) pkg. semi-sweet chocolate chips (¾ cup)
Sifted powdered sugar

Combine first 3 ingredients, stirring with a wire whisk to remove large lumps. Add oil and next 3 ingredients, stirring until smooth. Stir in chocolate chips.

Pour into a greased and floured 12-cup Bundt pan. Bake at 350°* for 1 hour or until a wooden pick inserted in center of cake comes out clean. Cool in pan on a wire rack for 10 minutes; remove from pan, and cool completely on wire rack. Sprinkle with powdered sugar.

*If using a 9x13-inch pan, bake 45 minutes.

"We cannot separate our lives from the Eucharist; the moment we do, something breaks. People ask, 'Where do the sisters get the joy and the energy to do what they are doing?' The Eucharist involves more than just receiving; it also involves satisfying the hunger of Christ. He says, 'Come to Me.' He is hungry for souls."
~Blessed Teresa of Calcutta

Black Forest Truffle Cake

1 box chocolate cake mix
Kahlua liqueur *(however much you like)*
2 (yes, 2) 3 oz. boxes **instant** chocolate pudding
1 **large** container Cool Whip

4 crushed Skor toffee bars *(or Hershey toffee bars)*
1 (21 oz.) can cherry pie filling (optional) - *occasionally I add this to mine, after the pudding layer*

Bake chocolate cake in 8-inch round pans, as directed on package. Prepare pudding according to package directions.

In truffle dish, layer:
1 layer cake
Kahlua *(poke holes in cake and soak it in)*
½ pudding
½ Cool Whip
½ toffee bars, sprinkled

Repeat above layers. Refrigerate until ready to serve.

"Adoration will heal our Church and thus our nation and thus our world...Adoration touches everyone and everything...[because it touches the Creator, Who touches everything and everyone]...When we adore, we plug into infinite dynamism and power. Adoration is more powerful for construction than nuclear bombs are for destruction."
~Peter Kreeft, philosopher at Boston College

The Cake That Doesn't Last

3 cups flour
2 cups sugar
1 tsp. baking soda
1 tsp. salt
1 ½ cups vegetable oil
    (Mazola, Puritan, canola)
1 tsp. cinnamon
1 ½ tsp. vanilla flavoring
2 cups bananas, mashed
    (3 or 4 bananas)
8 oz. crushed pineapple, undrained
1 cup chopped nuts

Blend ingredients well. Do not use a mixer or blender! Use a wooden spoon to blend all of the above ingredients. Pour into a well-greased and floured Bundt pan. Bake at 350° for 1 hour and 20 minutes or until tester comes out clean. Let stand about 10 minutes, then turn out onto a rack. Sprinkle with powdered sugar when completely cooled.

Note: This cake is actually much better the day after it is baked.

Out-of-This-World Cake

1 yellow cake mix
1 (20 oz.) can crushed pineapple, undrained
3 cups milk
1 (6 oz.) pkg. vanilla instant pudding
1 tsp. vanilla extract
1 (8 oz.) pkg. cream cheese, softened
1 (12 oz.) container Cool Whip, thawed
1 cup shredded coconut
1 cup chopped pecans

Prepare cake in 9x13-inch pan. Pierce top of the cake with a fork. Pour the undrained pineapple over the cake. Mix the milk, pudding mix, and vanilla in a medium mixing bowl. Set aside.

Beat the cream cheese in a medium mixing bowl at high speed until light and fluffy. Add the pudding mixture, beating until smooth. Spread over cake. Top with Cool Whip. Sprinkle with coconut and pecans. Cover and chill for several hours.

Hummingbird Cake

3 cups all-purpose flour
2 cups sugar
1 tsp. baking soda
1 tsp. salt
1 tsp. cinnamon
2 cups chopped bananas
1 cup vegetable oil
1 ½ tsp. vanilla extract
1 (8 oz.) can crushed pineapple, undrained
3 eggs, beaten
1 cup chopped pecans

Cream Cheese Frosting:
1 (8 oz.) pkg. cream cheese, softened
½ cup butter or margarine, softened
1 (16 oz.) pkg. 10X sugar
1 tsp. vanilla

Combine first 5 ingredients in a large mixing bowl. Add eggs and oil, stirring until dry ingredients are moistened. Do not beat. Stir in vanilla, bananas, pineapple, and pecans.

Spoon batter into 3 greased and floured 9-inch cake pans. Bake at 350° for 25 to 30 minutes or until a wooden pick inserted in center comes out clean. Cool in pans 10 minutes; remove from pans and cool completely. Frost with Cream Cheese Frosting.

Cream Cheese Frosting: Combine cream cheese and butter, beating until smooth. Add 10X sugar and vanilla; beat until light and fluffy. *Makes frosting for one 3-layer cake.*

"As a man must be born before he can begin to lead his physical life, so he must be born to lead a Divine Life. That birth occurs in the Sacrament of Baptism. To survive, he must be nourished by Divine Life; that is done in the Sacrament of the Holy Eucharist."
~Bishop Fulton J. Sheen

Orange Crunch Cake

Crunch Layer:
1 cup graham cracker crumbs
½ cup firmly packed brown sugar
½ cup chopped walnuts (or pecans)
½ cup margarine or butter

Cake:
1 pkg. Pillsbury Plus yellow cake mix
½ cup water
½ cup orange juice
⅓ cup oil
3 eggs
2 Tbsp. grated orange peel

Frosting:
1 can Pillsbury Ready to Spread Vanilla Frosting Supreme
1 cup frozen whipped topping, thawed
3 Tbsp. grated orange peel
1 tsp. grated lemon peel

Decoration:
1 (11 oz.) can mandarin oranges, drained
Mint leaves

Preheat oven to 350°. Grease and flour two 8- or 9-inch round cake pans *(Use parchment paper because the crunch part will stick to your pans).* In small bowl, combine crunch layer ingredients until crumbly. Press half of crunch mixture into each prepared pan.

In large bowl, blend cake ingredients at low speed until moistened. Beat 2 minutes at highest speed. Pour batter evenly over crunch layer. Bake at 350° for 30 to 35 minutes or until toothpick inserted in center comes out clean. Cool 10 minutes; remove from pans. Cool completely.

In small bowl, beat frosting until fluffy; add whipped topping and continue beating until light and fluffy. Fold in orange and lemon peel. Place one layer, crunch side up, on serving plate; spread with ¼ of frosting. Top with remaining layer, crunch side up. Spread top and sides with remaining frosting. Arrange orange sections on top. Garnish with mint leaves.

Easy Pumpkin Cupcakes

1 box spice cake mix
1 cup pumpkin *(the kind to make pumpkin pie – 1 cup is about ½ the can, so I usually make 2 batches and freeze some)*

⅔ cup water
2 eggs

Beat all ingredients together until blended. Bake in muffin tins at 350° for 15 to 20 minutes. *Yes, use the dry cake mix, and there is no oil in this recipe.*

Creamy Icing

1 stick (½ cup) margarine
½ cup Crisco
1 cup granulated sugar

¾ cup scalded milk
1 tsp. vanilla

Beat together margarine, Crisco, and sugar. Add scalded milk gradually, beating after each small addition. Add vanilla and beat until smooth. *Great on chocolate cake!*

"How can this come about?" Mary asked. "The Holy Spirit will come upon you," the angel answered, "and the power of the Most High will cover you with its shadow." And now you are the one who puts the question: "How can bread become Christ and wine His Blood?" I answer: "The power of the Holy Spirit will be at work to give us a marvel which surpasses understanding."
~St. John Damascene (d. 749)

St. Julia (5th century)
Feast Day ~ May 23

Julia was born in North Africa to noble parents. While she was just a child, her city was invaded by barbarians in 489, and she was taken and sold as a slave. She accepted this as God's will and tried to do everything cheerfully. She was allowed to read her holy books, and she prayed to God every day. Her master decided to take a trip and took her with him. On their way to France, he stopped off on an island to go to a pagan festival. Julia stayed away because she knew there was only one God, and she didn't want to have anything to do with such a horrible spectacle. The governor was furious that Julia did not attend his festival and questioned her master. He explained that she was a Christian but that she was a wonderful servant, and he valued her tremendously. The governor offered four of his best servants for Julia, but he turned him down. "Nothing you have could ever make me give her up," he said. While he was sleeping, the governor took Julia and tried to make her sacrifice to his gods. He told her that he would set her free. Julia told him that she was already free as long as she could love God. Julia refused, and the governor killed her.

Would you be able to stand up for your faith at school, on the playground, or with your friends if you were going to be criticized or laughed at? Look around this week and see how you might be able to bring God with you wherever you go. Pray to the Blessed Mother and ask her to help you!

Julia's Decorator Icing

As you ice your cake with this delicious frosting, think of St. Julia, a precious pure young girl who loved God and wouldn't deny Him.

1 cup Wesson shortening
1 Tbsp. meringue powder added to powdered sugar
1 tsp. clear vanilla
½ tsp. almond extract
½ tsp. salt, dissolved in water
½ cup water
2 boxes 2 lbs. 10X sugar, sifted

Measure shortening and place in large mixing bowl. Sift the powdered sugar with the meringue powder into the shortening. Start adding the combined liquids to make it easier to mix. Whip with a mixer until light and fluffy. *Makes enough icing for two 9x13-inch cakes.*

"But even if you should suffer because of righteousness, blessed are you. Do not be afraid or terrified with fear of them." 1Pet. 3:14

Heavenly Fruitcake

1 cup butter
2 cups sugar
3 cups unsweetened applesauce
1 tsp. salt
4 ½ cups sifted flour
2 ½ tsp. cinnamon
1 tsp. nutmeg
1 tsp. allspice
½ tsp. ground cloves
1 Tbsp. baking soda
1 ½ lbs. candied fruit
½ lb. or more candied cherries
½ lb. or less candied pineapple
1 lb. dark raisins
1 lb. light raisins
3-4 cups coarsely chopped walnuts
3-4 cups coarsely chopped pecans
Brandy

Cream butter and sugar together in very large bowl. Add applesauce. Mix all dry ingredients, except fruit and nuts. Add flour mixture to sugar mixture and blend well. Add candied fruit and nuts and mix well.

Spray 6 regular size loaf pans with nonstick cooking spray and press mixture down into pans. Bake at 300° for 1 hour. Cover with parchment paper the last half hour. Test center for doneness with toothpick. Cool 20 minutes. Turn out on racks. Sprinkle brandy liberally or as desired all over loaves. When cool, wrap tightly in plastic wrap and then foil.

I bake three at a time. Place pans on cookie sheet. May take 15 minutes more to bake, but the bottoms aren't so brown when placed on cookie sheet.

"If I can give you any advice, I beg you to get closer to the Eucharist and to Jesus... We must pray to Jesus to give us that tenderness of the Eucharist." ~Blessed Teresa of Calcutta

Light Fruitcake

1 cup pecans
1 cup walnuts
1 cup Brazil or macadamia nuts
1 cup red candied cherries
1 cup pitted dates, halved

1 cup sugar
1 cup flour
4 eggs
1 tsp. vanilla
Brandy

Mix first 7 ingredients together. Add 4 egg yolks and vanilla. Stir up – will be lumpy. Beat 4 egg whites until fluffy and fold into above mixture.

Press into 2 foil loaf pans sprayed with nonstick cooking spray. Bake at 300° for 30 minutes. Cover with parchment paper and bake another 20 to 30 minutes. Test center. Cool 15 minutes; turn out onto racks. Apply brandy as desired when cool. Refrigerate for easy slicing.

Applesauce Loaf

½ cup shortening
1 cup sugar
2 eggs
1 ¾ cups sifted flour
1 tsp. salt

1 tsp. baking powder
½ tsp. baking soda
½ tsp. cinnamon
½ tsp. nutmeg
1 cup sweetened applesauce

Combine ingredients. Place in loaf pan and bake at 350° for 1 hour. Glaze with 10X sugar and water when cool.

Blueberry Nut Bread

Vegetable oil spray for greasing baking pan
1 cup soy flour
1 cup nuts *(walnuts or almonds)*, finely ground
1 cup Splenda or sugar substitute
1 ½ tsp. ground cinnamon

½ tsp. baking soda
½ tsp. baking powder
½ cup vegetable oil
1 cup egg beaters
1 (16 oz.) pkg. frozen blueberries, thawed and drained
1 tsp. vanilla extract

Preheat oven to 350°. Spray 8x4-inch loaf pan with oil spray.

In a large bowl, combine all dry ingredients and mix thoroughly. In a medium bowl, combine blueberries, vanilla, eggs, and oil. Pour liquid mixture into dry ingredients and mix thoroughly. Pour batter into prepared pan. Bake 1 hour. Cool in pan for 10 minutes before removing from pan. Use serrated knife when cutting. Serve with butter.

You can substitute berries with 1 medium zucchini, coarsely grated (1 ½ cups).

"O my soul, how can you refrain from plunging yourself ever deeper and deeper into the love of Christ, who did not forget you in life or in death, but who willed to give Himself wholly to you, and to unite you to Himself forever?" ~St. Angela Foligno

Chocolate Chip Zucchini Bread

¾ cup sugar
3 Tbsp. oil
2 large eggs
1 cup applesauce
2 cups flour
2 Tbsp. unsweetened cocoa
1 ¼ tsp. baking soda

1 tsp. cinnamon
¼ tsp. salt
1 ½ cups finely shredded zucchini *(about 1 medium)*
½ cup semi-sweet chocolate chips

Preheat oven to 350°. Place first 3 ingredients in a large bowl; beat mixture at low speed until well blended. Stir in applesauce.

Lightly spoon flour into dry measuring cup. Level with knife. Combine flour and next 4 ingredients (through salt), stirring well with a whisk. Add flour mixture to sugar mixture, beating just until moist. Stir in zucchini and chocolate chips.

Spoon batter into a well-coated 9x5-inch loaf pan. Bake 1 hour or until wooden pick inserted in center comes out clean. Cool in pan 10 minutes on wire rack. Remove from pan. Cool completely.

"We should never again use the expression, 'When Jesus was on earth' or think of Him as being only in heaven, Jesus is still on earth. While all the sacraments confer grace, the Eucharist contains the author of grace, Jesus Christ Himself."
~Fr. John Hardon, SJ.

St. Joseph (1st Century)
St. Joseph the Husband of Mary Feast Day ~ March 19
St. Joseph the Worker Feast Day ~ May 1

St. Joseph, the foster father of Jesus, was a kind and gentle man who loved Mary and Jesus very much. When he found out that Mary was going to have a baby, he wanted to protect her and keep her from harm. In those days, a woman found to be pregnant and not married could be stoned to death. Joseph was going to quietly let her go, but an angel appeared to him and let him know that Mary had conceived Jesus through the power of the Holy Spirit. They were poor, yet they were to raise the Son of God. We know they were poor because when Joseph went to the temple to have Jesus circumcised, he brought two turtledoves or a pair of pigeons. This was only permitted if the family could not afford an unblemished lamb. Joseph was always obedient to God's will. He left immediately when he was told by the angel to flee to a foreign land. He didn't stop to think of himself, but only wanted to protect Jesus and Mary. He immediately listened to God and left all his belongings and friends and moved to an obscure village in a foreign land to keep Jesus and Mary safe. He suffered with Mary when they lost Jesus for three days in the temple. Joseph loved his family and taught Jesus his woodworking skills. He is known as the first adorer of Jesus as he watched Jesus grow in Mary and was the first person to hold Him. He is known as the patron saint of the universal Church, carpenters, fathers and social justice.

This week ask your parents if you could visit someone who is lonely. Why not bake some cookies and bring them to an elderly person or someone you think might need some love.

St. Joseph's Cream Puffs

½ cup butter
1 cup water
¼ tsp. salt
1 cup all-purpose flour
4 eggs
1 tsp. vanilla
Filling such as pudding or whipped cream

Ricotta Crème:
¾ lb. ricotta cheese, preferably skim milk
¼ cup sugar
1 Tbsp. chopped candied fruit (optional)

Preheat oven to 400°. Place butter and water in a heavy saucepan over medium heat and bring to a boil. Remove from heat and quickly add the flour mixture and stir vigorously. Return to heat and stir constantly until the dough forms a thick, smooth ball. Allow to cool about 10 minutes.

Once the dough is lukewarm, add the lightly beaten eggs and continue to mix until you have a smooth thick paste. Drop by tablespoonfuls onto parchment paper-lined cookie sheet and bake.

Bake for 15 minutes and then reduce the oven temperature to 350°. Bake for an additional 30 to 40 minutes or until the shells are golden brown and are dry inside when split. Turn the oven off and, with the oven door slightly ajar, let the shells dry out for an additional 10 to 15 minutes. Remove from oven and let cool on a wire rack.

Fill with desired filling such as white pudding, whipped cream, or ricotta crème.

Ricotta Crème: (This must be made the day before using.) Drain the ricotta by placing it in a strainer set in a bowl. Refrigerate at least 2 to 3 hours or overnight. If the drained ricotta is lumpy, work in a food processor until smooth. Transfer ricotta to a bowl, add the sugar, and whip until light and fluffy. Stir in candied fruit. Cover and refrigerate until ready to use.

Sts. Perpetua and Felicity (died 203?) *Martyrs*
Feast Days ~ July 10 (P) March 7 (F)

Perpetua, the young daughter of a wealthy nobleman, lived in Africa and became a Christian. Felicity was her maid-servant and they became great friends. Both loved God with their whole heart. Perpetua's father begged her to renounce God as he was not a Christian and didn't want his child killed by the mean-spirited emperor. She was taken prisoner at the age of 22. Married and having to give up her child to go to prison, she still would not deny that God existed. Felicity was pregnant and had her baby a few days before both of them were killed by wild beasts at the games in the amphitheater. These brave girls went out together holding hands. They knew they would rather die than deny that Jesus existed. They are martyrs of the Church, and if you listen closely at Mass, sometimes you will hear their names mentioned in the litany of the saints.

How will you show the world that you are Christian? Do you say grace before you eat when you go out to a restaurant or before you eat at school? What will you do this week to show God that you are proud to be a Catholic and belong to His Church?

Perpetua & Felicity's Berry Puff

Follow the baking instructions closely and serve the dish immediately.

3 cups berries *(fresh or frozen – if frozen, be sure to thaw ahead of time!)*	1 cup milk
⅓ cup orange or berry marmalade	6 eggs
	1 cup flour
	½ tsp. salt
3 Tbsp. butter, melted and divided	2 Tbsp. powdered sugar

Preheat oven to 450°. Stir berries and marmalade together; set aside. Use a pastry brush to coat a deep-dish baking/casserole dish with 1 tablespoon butter. Combine milk, eggs, and remaining butter. Whisk in flour and salt until smooth.

Pour batter into baking/casserole dish. Bake for 13 minutes. Reduce oven temperature to 350°. Continue baking for 15 to 17 minutes or until sides are golden brown. Sprinkle with sugar and fill center with topping.

"The hidden treasure… is Jesus himself, the Kingdom in person. In the Sacred Host, he is present, the true treasure, always waiting for us. Only by adoring this presence do we learn how to receive him properly-we learn the reality of communion".
~Pope Benedict XVI, address Altotting, Germany, Sept. 11, 2006

"It is not the man who is responsible for the offerings as they become Christ's Body and Blood; it is Christ Himself who was crucified for us. The standing figure belongs to the priest who speaks these words. The power and the grace belong to God. 'This is My Body,' he says. And these words transform the offerings."
~St. John Chrysostom

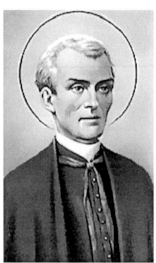

St. Peter Julian Eymard (1811-1868)
Feast Day ~ August 2

Peter grew up in a poor family during a difficult time in France. The French Revolution had changed things, and he grew up in the Age of Romanticism. The French people were very anticlerical--they didn't like priests. Peter wanted very much to serve God. His father didn't want him to be a priest but changed his mind. Though Peter went off to become a priest, he had to come home because he became ill; in 1834, his dream came true and he was ordained at the age of 23.

During this time, there was a heresy (false teaching) called Jansenism which taught that human beings were completely sinful, and totally unworthy to ever be in God's presence. Peter struggled with his own unworthiness, but 5 years after becoming a priest, he joined the Marist Congregation and took his vows of poverty, chastity and obedience. He grew to love preaching about the Eucharist and was very close to Our Lady. He asked if he could write a Eucharistic rule for the Third Order of Mary and was turned down. This didn't stop Peter. He prayed and worked hard. Eventually, Peter founded the Congregation of the Blessed Sacrament though it took many hardships to get it off the ground. His intense love for Jesus in the Blessed Sacrament swelled in his heart. A book about him called **Tomorrow Will Be Too Late: The Life of Saint Peter Julian Eymard**, **Apostle of the Eucharist**, is excellent and will help you understand his great love of the Eucharist.

This week take your entire family to Eucharistic Adoration and spend time with Jesus.

Mom's Fresh Blueberry Pie

As a reminder of how much St. Peter Eymard loved Jesus' Mother, this pie with its blue blueberries will remind you of Our Lady.

Baked pie shell
2-3 cups fresh blueberries
Juice of 1 lemon
1 cup sugar
3 Tbsp. cornstarch

Place 1 cup fresh blueberries in bottom of baked pie shell. Cook until thick: 1 cup blueberries, lemon juice, and cornstarch. Pour over berries in pie shell, then add more fresh berries on top Chill and serve.

☙ *Hear Mass daily; it will prosper the whole day. All your duties will be performed the better for it, and your soul will be stronger to bear its daily cross. The Mass is the most holy act of religion; you can do nothing that can give greater glory to God or be more profitable for your soul than to hear Mass both frequently and devoutly. It is the favorite devotion of the saints.*
~St. Peter Julian Eymard

☙ *"Today solemn exposition of the Blessed Sacrament is the grace and need of our time. Society will be restored and renewed when all its members group themselves around our Emmanuel."*
~St. Peter Julian Eymard

Strawberry Pie

1 cup sugar
2 Tbsp. cornstarch
2 cups water

1 small (3 oz.) pkg. strawberry Jell-O
2 pints strawberries, sliced
Whipped cream for topping

Boil sugar, cornstarch, and water until thick. Add package of strawberry Jell-O. When it begins to set, pour over sliced strawberries in pie shell. Refrigerate and serve with whipped cream! *Makes 8 servings.*

Apple Crumb Pie

5-7 tart apples or 2 cans sliced pie apples, drained
1 9-inch unbaked pastry shell *(use deep dish if frozen pie shell)*
⅓ cup sugar mixed with 1 tsp. cinnamon

Crumb Topping:
½ cup sugar
¾ cup flour
⅓ cup butter or margarine

Pare apples and cut into eighths or sixteenths. Arrange in pie shell. Sprinkle with sugar and cinnamon mixture. Mix the ½ cup sugar with flour; cut in butter until crumbly. Sprinkle evenly over apples. Bake at 400° for 40 minutes.

I make this pie in a 10-inch pie plate and use 7 or 8 large Granny Smith apples. Using a refrigerated Pillsbury ready-made pie crust and rolling it out to fit the 10-inch plate is an easy way to "make" the crust. Bake for about 50 minutes for a 10-inch pie.

Rhubarb Custard Pie

2 cups rhubarb
1 ¼ cups sugar
6 Tbsp. flour
2 eggs, separated

1 cup milk
1 tsp. vanilla
1 unbaked 9-inch pie shell

Mix rhubarb, sugar, and flour together. Slightly beat egg yolks, and stir in milk and vanilla. Add to rhubarb mixture. Beat egg whites until stiff; fold in slowly.

Pour into unbaked 9-inch pie shell and bake in slow oven at 325° for 45 minutes or until knife comes out clean.

Impossible Coconut Pie

2 cups milk
¾ cup sugar
½ cup Bisquick baking mix
¼ cup margarine or butter

4 eggs
1 ½ tsp. vanilla
1 cup flaked or shredded coconut

Preheat oven to 350°. Lightly grease a 9- or 10-inch pie plate. Place all ingredients in blender container. Cover and blend on high speed for 15 seconds. Pour into pie plate. Bake until golden brown and knife inserted in center comes out clean, about 50 to 55 minutes. Refrigerate any leftover pie.

Other Varieties of Impossible Pie

Impossible Chocolate Pie: Add 2 tablespoons cocoa.

Impossible Fruit Pie: Use 10-inch pie plates. Cool pie; spread 1 (21 oz.) can fruit pie filling over top. Refrigerate at least 2 hours.

Impossible Lemon Pie: Use 10-inch pie plate. Add ¼ cup lemon juice.

Impossible Macaroon Pie: Do not blend coconut; sprinkle over top of pie before baking.

Impossible Pumpkin Pie: Use 10-inch pie plate. Combine 2 cups milk, ¾ cup light brown sugar, ½ cup Bisquick, 4 eggs, 1 cup pumpkin, and 1 tsp. pumpkin pie spices in blender container. Blend until smooth. Pour into pie plate and bake as directed above.

Chocolate Pie

3 egg whites
¼ tsp. cream of tartar
⅛ tsp. salt
¾ cup granulated sugar
½ tsp. vanilla
1 cup chopped pecans

Filling:
1 (12 oz.) pkg. semi-sweet chocolate chips
¼ cup water
3 egg yolks
1 tsp. vanilla
1 cup whipped cream

Beat egg whites. Mix together next 4 ingredients. Fold in egg whites and nuts. Pour into buttered pie pan and bake at 275° for 45 minutes to 1 hour.

Filling: Add water to chocolate and melt; cool slightly. Beat in egg yolks and vanilla. Fold in 1 cup whipped cream and pour into pie shell. Add additional whipped cream on top if desired. Refrigerate.

"The Eucharist is at the very center of our life; such was the teaching of Jesus. When commenting on the miracle of the multiplication of the loaves He told His apostles that He Himself is the Living Bread that came down from heaven. He called on the twelve for an act of faith and it was Peter who answered in the name of all: 'Lord, to whom shall we go? You have the words of everlasting life. We have come to believe and know that you are the Holy One of God' (John 6:69). Christian faith is faith in the Eucharistic Christ." ~Fr. Jean Galot, S.J.

Sunrise Cherry Pie

This dessert is wonderful for summer, but the name reminds me of Easter.

1 (8 oz.) can crushed pineapple
1 (8 oz.) pkg. cream cheese, softened
½ tsp. vanilla extract
1 (21 oz.) can cherry pie filling
1 cup heavy cream
¼ cup confectioner's sugar
1 (6 oz.) graham cracker pie crust

Drain pineapple well; reserve 2 tablespoons of the juice. Combine softened cream cheese, vanilla extract, and the 2 tablespoons of juice until well blended. Stir in ¼ cup pineapple and ½ can cherry pie filling.

Gradually add sugar to cream, beating until soft peaks form. Fold into cream cheese mixture. Pour into crust. Top with remaining pineapple around edge of pie and fill in center with cherry pie filling. Chill until firm.

Peanut Butter Pie

½ cup crunchy peanut butter
¾ cup powdered sugar
1 (6 oz.) pkg. instant vanilla pudding and pie filling
Cool Whip
Pie shell

Bake pie shell and let cool. Mix peanut butter and powdered sugar until crumbly. Put ¾ of the crumbs in the baked pie shell.

Prepare pudding and pour over the crumb mixture. Top with Cool Whip and coat with remaining crumbs.

**St. Nicholas (270-343)
Feast Day ~ Dec 6**

When Nicholas was a young man, both his parents died leaving him great wealth. Nicholas did not use the money for himself, but gave it to the poor. The most famous story of his generous heart was when Nicholas heard about a man with 3 daughters who was poverty stricken and was going to have to give his daughters to men to make money, so he sneaked out late one night and dropped a bag of gold into this family's open window. This became the dowry of the oldest daughter. He did this with the second daughter as well. Upon doing it the third time, Nicholas was caught and the man thanked him and was very grateful. Nicholas did many other great and generous things.

He lived in a time when there was a powerful heresy called Arianism, and he did much to teach the people that Jesus Christ was fully divine and fully human. It is because of brave men like Nicholas that we have our true Faith. Nicholas also saved some men who had been falsely accused of a crime they didn't commit. He stood up for these men and had the accuser admit that he had taken money to get rid of the men. He was a great man of conviction who has thousands of miracles attributed to him.

Why not celebrate St. Nicholas' Feast Day by doing something nice for someone in your family and not letting them find out who did it?

St. Nick's Toll House Pie

2 eggs
½ cup flour
½ cup sugar
½ cup brown sugar

1 cup margarine, melted, room temperature
1 cup semi-sweet chocolate morsels
1 9-inch unbaked pie shell

Note: If using frozen pie shell, it's necessary to use deep-dish style.

Preheat oven to 325°. In large bowl, beat eggs until foamy. Add flour, sugar, and brown sugar. Beat until well blended. Blend in melted margarine. Stir in chocolate morsels. Pour into pie shell. Bake for 1 hour.

"[Or] am I not free to do as I wish with my own money? Are you envious because I am generous?" Matt. 20:15

"But as for the seed that fell on rich soil, they are the ones who, when they have heard the word, embrace it with a generous and good heart, and bear fruit through perseverance." Luke 8:15

"Tell them to do good, to be rich in good works, to be generous, ready to share." 1Tim. 6:18

**St. Cecilia (3rd Century)
Feast Day ~ November 22**

Cecilia was a beautiful young noblewoman who had given herself to Christ even though her father had given her in marriage to a youth named Valerian. Hearing music in her heart at the wedding, Cecilia told the youth she had a secret to share with him. She said she had an angel protecting her and that she had given herself to God. If Valerian would let her keep her promise to God, her angel would protect him, too. Valerian was so moved by this, that he became a Christian. When he came back from being baptized, he saw Cecilia praying. He also saw her angel holding two crowns with beautiful flowers, which were placed on their heads. When his brother came in and saw the flowers and smelled the beautiful fragrance, he was told the story and also became a Christian. Together they did many works of charity.

The brothers were arrested for being Christians, but they would not deny Jesus and were killed. Cecilia buried them and went out to preach some more. She converted over 400 people and was soon arrested herself. They put her in a fire where she was protected from the roaring flames. When Almachius, the ruler, heard she was still alive, he sent in a man to behead her. He struck her three times and was unable to cut off her head. She lived for three days and then died. As she lay dying, people from the village came to collect her blood and to hear her preach. She held out her hands holding up one finger of one hand and three in the other hand showing that there is one God and three persons in the Trinity. She died a virgin and a martyr. She is the patron saint of music.

God rewards those who faithfully follow Jesus, maybe not in this lifetime but certainly in heaven. Pick something this week that you are especially thankful for and do something to thank God. Maybe your parents are very good to you so you might want to surprise them and make their bed or help them in the kitchen. Whatever it is, do it with a happy heart for Jesus.

St. Cecilia's Fudge Pies

Pretend you are St. Cecilia and mix the 3 ingredients, the milk, chocolate chips, and marshmallows. Those three become one. Then pour it on top of the 1 ingredient, the ice cream. There are three persons in one God – God the Father, God the Son, and God the Holy Spirit!

1 cup evaporated skim milk
1 cup chocolate chips
1 cup miniature marshmallows
Dash salt

2 (9-inch) graham cracker crusts
½ gallon vanilla ice cream
Pecan halves *(optional)*

In heavy saucepan, stir evaporated milk, chocolate chips, marshmallows, and salt over medium heat until melted and mixture thickens, stirring constantly. Remove from heat and cool. Line bottoms of two 9-inch pie pans with graham cracker crusts or use two purchased graham cracker crusts.

Spoon half of the ice cream into the bottom of the two crusts, pressing down as flat as possible. Put half of chocolate mixture on top of ice cream. Spoon on another layer of ice cream, using all of it for the two pies. Then put the rest of the chocolate mixture on top. Freeze until firm, 3 to 5 hours, then cover with plastic wrap and aluminum foil or place in airtight keeper, and they'll keep for weeks.

Peaches 'n Cream Cheesecake

¾ cup flour
1 tsp. baking powder
½ tsp. salt
1 (3 ¼ oz.) pkg. dry vanilla pudding *(not instant)*
3 Tbsp. margarine, softened
1 egg
½ cup milk

1 (15-20 oz.) can sliced peaches or pineapple chunks, well drained; reserve juice
1 (8 oz.) pkg. cream cheese, softened
½ cup sugar
3 Tbsp. reserved juice
1 Tbsp. sugar
1 tsp. cinnamon

Combine first 7 ingredients in large bowl; beat 2 minutes. Pour into greased 9-inch deep pie pan. Place sliced peaches or pineapple chunks over batter.

Combine cream cheese, sugar, and reserved juice in small mixer bowl. Beat 2 minutes. Spoon to within 1 inch of edges of batter. Combine sugar and cinnamon. Sprinkle over cream cheese filling.

Bake at 350° for 30 to 35 minutes until crust is golden brown. Store in refrigerator.

❧ **"Do good to the just man and reward will be yours, if not from him, from the LORD."** Sir. 12:2

❧ **"But rather, love your enemies and do good to them, and lend expecting nothing back; then your reward will be great and you will be children of the Most High, for he himself is kind to the ungrateful and the wicked."** Luke 6:35

Easy Peach Cobbler

1 (29 oz.) can sliced peaches
1 butter recipe cake mix

2 sticks (1 cup) melted butter

Preheat oven to 350°. Pour peaches into large baking dish. Pour dry cake mix over peaches. Drizzle butter over top of cake mix. Bake 30 to 35 minutes or until brown.

Cobbler (Cherry, Blueberry, Peach)

2 Tbsp. margarine
½ cup sugar
¾ cup flour
1 tsp. baking powder
⅛ tsp. salt

¾ cup milk
1 cup prepared fruit pie filling, or use 1 ½ to 2 cups fresh fruit with ⅓ to ½ cup sugar

Melt margarine in 8x8x2-inch glass dish. Mix dry ingredients in bowl. Add milk and mix. Pour over melted margarine but don't mix. Spoon fruit in mounds on top of batter and bake at 350° for 35 to 40 minutes.

To double, use 9x13-inch pan and double ingredients. Bake a little longer, until golden brown on top.

"When you look at the Crucifix, you understand how much Jesus loved you then. When you look at the Sacred Host you understand how much Jesus loves you now." ~Blessed Teresa of Calcutta.

St. Bernard (1090-1153)
Feast Day ~ August 20

Bernard had six brothers and sisters who all loved God very much. When his mother died, he was 17 years of age and very sad. His sister took him in and cheered him up. Bernard had many friends and was enjoying his life. There was a very strict way of life in the Cistercian Order, and Bernard felt drawn to it. No one could believe that he wanted to live this way so they tried to talk him out of it. Amazingly, Bernard ended up convincing his uncle, his brothers and 26 friends to join, too! His youngest brother was to inherit all the land and wealth of the family, but when he was old enough, he also joined Bernard. It was said that he looked at Bernard and said, "What! Will you take heaven and leave me the earth? Do you call that fair?" After 3 years Bernard was sent to Clairvaux to become the abbot. He stayed there for the rest of his life. He became very influential and advised the pope and made peace between rulers. He loved the Blessed Mother so and would go past her statue and say, "*Hail Mary.*" Legend says that once the Blessed Mother responded with, "*Hail Bernard,*" to show her love for him. This man never wanted to be famous but only to love God. He changed thousands of people's lives by saying "yes" to God. He is a Doctor of the Church.

Have you ever thought of what you wanted to be when you grow up? Ask God if he would like you to be a priest, a nun or missionary. Maybe God is calling you. Try listening to God and thinking about how you might want to serve Him when you get older.

Bernard's Apple-Blueberry Cobbler

When putting the blueberries into the bowl, it might be fun to count them. Bernard brought 30 people with him when he joined the Cistercian order.

1 (21 oz.) can apple pie filling
1 (14 oz.) pkg. frozen blueberries
1 cup sugar, divided
1 (18.25 oz.) pkg. white cake mix
½ cup butter or margarine, melted
1 cup chopped pecans or walnuts

Spread apple pie filling on bottom of lightly greased 9x13-inch pan. Toss together frozen blueberries and ¾ cup sugar; spoon over filling. Sprinkle cake mix evenly over fruit and drizzle with melted butter. Sprinkle with chopped nuts and remaining ¼ cup sugar. Bake at 350° for 45 to 50 minutes or until golden and bubbly.

> What is impossible with men is possible with God
> Luke 18:27

"Do not grow slack in zeal, be fervent in spirit, serve the Lord." Rom. 12:1

Apple Crisp

2 cups quick oats
¼ cup melted butter or margarine
½ cup brown sugar
4 medium apples, cored and sliced
1 Tbsp. lemon juice
½ cup honey
2 Tbsp. hot water
Dash salt

Mix together oats, butter, or margarine, and brown sugar to make a crumbly topping. Mix apples with lemon juice, honey, and hot water. Salt very lightly and spread in a lightly greased 8-inch square baking pan.

Cover with oat mixture and bake, uncovered, at 375° for 30 to 35 minutes or until apples are tender. Serve with ice cream, whipped cream, or yogurt topping.

Quick Apple Crisp

5 Granny Smith apples, peeled, cored, and sliced
1 butter cake mix
2 Tbsp. sugar
1 Tbsp. ground cinnamon
⅓ cup butter or margarine, melted
¼-½ cup raisins, nuts, and/or oats *(optional)*

Preheat oven to 350°. Place apples in pie dish. Sprinkle dry cake mix over apples. Combine sugar and cinnamon (also raisins, nuts, and oats, if desired), and sprinkle over cake mix. Drizzle with butter and bake 30 to 35 minutes. Serve warm.

Variation: If desired, use spice cake mix in place of butter cake mix.

Spiced Peaches

2 (29 oz.) cans peach halves in heavy syrup
1 tsp. cornstarch
½ tsp. cinnamon
¼ tsp. grated orange rind
⅛ tsp. ground cloves
⅛ tsp. ground nutmeg
½ tsp. whole cloves

Drain peaches; reserve syrup – set aside.

Combine cornstarch and spices in medium saucepan; add reserved syrup and mix well. Place over medium heat and bring to boil, stirring constantly. Add peaches, reduce heat, and cook 1 minute longer.

Watergate Salad

1 (3.4 oz.) box pistachio pudding
1 large (12 oz.) container Cool Whip
1 (16-22 oz.) can crushed pineapple, undrained
½ cup walnuts
1 cup mini marshmallows

Combine all ingredients in order listed until thoroughly mixed. Chill until serving time.

Easy Dessert

1 (20 oz.) can cherry pie filling
1 (20 oz.) can pineapple chunks, drained
1 (14 oz.) can Eagle Brand sweetened condensed milk
1 cup chopped walnuts
1 cup coconut
1 (8 oz.) container Cool Whip

Mix all ingredients. May be frozen.

**St. Brice (370-444)
Feast Day ~ Nov. 13**

Brice was an orphan who was extremely mischievous. As he grew, he became proud, wild, and arrogant and some said he was possessed. Martin of Tours took him in and raised him, but the child was unbearable. He became a priest but didn't change his ways. Martin told people that, "Jesus had Judas and I have Brice." When Martin died, Brice rightfully succeeded him but the townspeople threatened to stone him, so he fled. After 30 years, Brice came to his senses and repented, so when Martin's successor died, Brice came back to take his place, but was again thrown out of town. Another ten years passed, and finally the town's people, seeing that he really had changed, allowed him to come back and he became Bishop of Tours until he died. He is the patron saint of those with stomach diseases.

Patience is a virtue. What will you do this week to forgive someone who is constantly trying to annoy you?

"Stop judging and you will not be judged. Stop condemning and you will not be condemned. Forgive and you will be forgiven." Luke 6:37

St. Brice's Pumpkin Dessert

1 (15 oz.) can pumpkin
1 (12 oz.) can evaporated milk
3 eggs
1 cup white sugar
4 tsp. pumpkin pie spice
1 (18.5) box yellow cake mix
1 stick (½ cup) melted butter
1 ½ cups chopped walnuts

Preheat oven to 350°. Grease a 9x13-inch baking pan. Mix pumpkin, milk, eggs, sugar, and spices well. Pour into the pan. Sprinkle dry cake mix over the top and drizzle with the melted butter. Top with walnuts.

Bake at 350° for approximately 40 to 45 minutes until a toothpick inserted in the center comes out clean. Serve with ice cream or whipped cream.

"If we acknowledge our sins, he is faithful and just and will forgive our sins and cleanse us from every wrongdoing."
1John 1:9

"When you stand to pray, forgive anyone against whom you have a grievance, so that your heavenly Father may in turn forgive you your transgressions." Mark 11:25

"Then Peter approaching asked him, "Lord, if my brother sins against me, how often must I forgive him? As many as seven times?" Jesus answered, "I say to you, not seven times but seventy-seven times." Matt. 18:21-22

St Jerome (circa 342-420)
Feast Day ~ September 30

Jerome was born to Roman Christians and was home schooled for many years. He was sent to a pagan school to learn from the best teachers. There he soon found some holy friends and was baptized in 360. He went off after his education and lived all alone in the desert, promising God he would never marry, where he prayed and learned to discipline himself for 4 years. He taught himself Hebrew. Legend claims that a lion befriended him after he removed a thorn from his paw. That is why you always see pictures of him with a lion. He went to Antioch and became a priest and was asked to settle doctrinal disputes in the Church because he studied hard and could translate different documents. He became secretary to Pope Damasus. He was able to translate the Bible into Latin so that everyone could understand it. It was called the Vulgate and was used by the Church for 1000 years. This was a great work because more people could read it and learn the Faith. He also taught others that you need to be very careful how you act because you might be the only Bible that a person ever reads. He spent the last 34 years of his life in Bethlehem where he prayed, studied and wrote many teachings explaining the Faith. He is both a Doctor and Father of the Church.

What could you do this week to imitate Jerome? Every night this week get your Bible and read a passage or have mom or dad read a passage to you. Discuss what God is trying to tell you. Try to memorize one sentence and keep it in your head all day long. At dinner see who can remember their Bible verse and where it came from in the Bible.

250 Desserts

Jerome's Lion Claws

1 (8 oz.) can refrigerator crescent dinner rolls
2/3 cup confectioners sugar
1/2 cup almond paste
Dash of salt
1 egg, slightly beaten
2 Tbsp. sliced almonds

Heat oven to 375°. Unroll dough to form 2 rectangles, seal perforations. Combine 2/3 cup confectioners sugar, almond paste, salt and 2 tablespoons egg in bowl. Beat until smooth. Spread lengthwise down center of rectangles. Fold dough to enclose filling, sealing edges. Cut each strip into 4 pastries. Cut 4 slashes into each cut pastry to resemble a lion's paw. Place seam side down on greased baking sheet. Brush with remaining egg; sprinkle with confectioners sugar. Bake in oven for 13-15 minutes. While still warm put a toothpick into each lion's paw and have the kids pull out the toothpick (thorn). A great way for kids to remember the story of St. Jerome!

"Ignorance of Scripture is ignorance of Christ". ~ St. Jerome

Some verses to memorize!

"Your word is a lamp for my feet, a light for my path. Psa. 119:105

"If you love me, you will obey what I command. " John 14:15

"Whoever eats my flesh and drinks my blood remains in me and I in him." John 6:56

"You shall love the Lord your God with all your heart, with all your soul, with all your mind, and with all your strength." Mark 12:30

Angel Fruit Whip

Angel food cake, cubed
1 (3 oz.) pkg. vanilla pudding, prepared
1 (16 oz.) can pineapple chunks, drained *(juice reserved)*
1 (12 oz.) container Cool Whip
Sliced strawberries
Sliced kiwi
Red and green grapes

In trifle bowl, layer angel food cubes. Drizzle with pineapple juice. Add vanilla pudding, fruit, and top with Cool Whip. Repeat layers to top of dish, ending with Cool Whip. Garnish with sliced strawberries. Chill until serving.

Note: You may use your favorite fruit (bananas, apples, peaches, berries…)

Queen of Pudding (or Ice Box Cake)

2 ¼ lbs. German sweet chocolate
3 Tbsp. granulated sugar
3 Tbsp. water
4 or 5 eggs
1 tsp. vanilla
Lady fingers
Whipped cream

Melt chocolate, sugar, and water in a double boiler. Remove from heat and add beaten egg yolks. Beat whites separately until stiff; add vanilla. Fold into chocolate mixture.

Line deep baking pan with lady fingers up the side. Pour in chocolate mixture and let stand in refrigerator for 24 hours. Serve with whipped cream topping.

Ice Cream Cake

30 Oreo cookies, divided 20 and 10
1 stick (½ cup) butter or margarine
3 squares (3 oz.) unsweetened chocolate
3 eggs
2 cups sifted confectioner's sugar
½ gallon ice cream *(cookies and cream, or your choice)*
¼ gallon ice cream *(coffee or your choice)*
Cinnamon

Crush 20 Oreo cookies *(I put in Ziploc bag and use rolling pin to smash them into crumbles)*. Sprinkle cookies in bottom of 9x13-inch Pyrex baking dish.

Melt margarine and chocolate in double boiler. Mix in sifted sugar and eggs. Stir until very smooth. Pour chocolate mixture over crumbled cookies. Freeze 40 minutes. Meanwhile, let ice cream soften.

Spread ½ gallon of your choice ice cream over frozen cookie mixture. Sprinkle with cinnamon. Spread ¼ gallon ice cream of your choice over cinnamon. Sprinkle with remaining 10 Oreo cookie crumbs. Freeze. *Enjoy!*

Ice Cream Sandwich Cake

24 ice cream sandwiches
12 oz. Cool Whip
Hot fudge topping

Layer ice cream sandwiches tightly in a 9x13-inch pan. Top ice cream sandwiches with hot fudge topping. After hot fudge topping, spread with Cool Whip. Repeat with ice cream sandwiches, hot fudge, and Cool Whip, and keep in freezer until ready to serve. *Easy dessert. Can be done ahead, and is a crowd pleaser!* ☺

St. Francis of Assisi (1181-1226)
Feast Day ~ October 4

Born in Assisi and baptized Giovanni after St. John the Baptist, the future saint was renamed by his father when he returned from a business trip to France. He called his infant son Francis, which means, "man of France." Francis grew up spoiled and carefree. Though very well-liked, he was often rude to others. He did poorly in school, was a daydreamer and a picky eater. As a teen he was the leader of the "in crowd" and since he was rich, he had wild parties and lived in sin. Francis dreamed of being a knight. When Assisi went to war with Perugia, Francis went to fight but was taken prisoner and kept in a dark dungeon for a year. This dreadful experience might have changed him, but it didn't. When he was ransomed, he went right back to his sinful life.

Francis still desired to seek glory and when the call went out for him to become a knight he had a suit of armor made with gold trim and a cloak to adorn him along with an expensive horse. As he rode off, he dreamed of becoming a prince. When Francis went to sleep that night after a one-day journey under his belt, he had a dream. In the dream God spoke to him and told him he was to return home. The entire town laughed at him and Francis started to spend time in prayer. As Francis was riding his horse one day, a man passed him who was a leper. Francis was repulsed at his deformity, but suddenly he got off his horse and gave the man a kiss. When the kiss was returned from the leper, Francis felt joy throughout his entire body. When he turned around to wave, the leper was gone. Francis thought that this was a test from God which he had passed.

As Francis searched for meaning in his life, he found himself drawn to an old, run-down church called San Damiano. While he was praying there, Christ spoke to Francis and said, "Francis, repair my Church." Francis thought he understood what Jesus was asking, and he took some fabric from his father's shop and used the money to rebuild the church. Upset, his father had Francis taken to the bishop, and Francis renounced everything including the clothes on his back, and went out to really begin what God would have him do for the rest of his life. He had misunderstood what Jesus meant. Jesus wanted Francis to rebuild His Church, the Catholic Church, not just one little chapel, so Francis listened and began the Franciscan Order.

There is much more to this story so ask your parents to get a good book for you to read about St. Francis. If you can't read yet, have mom or dad read it to you. What a wonderful thing to do before you go to bed every night this week!

Almond Cookies

A young widow befriended Francis after she heard him preach and would make almond cookies for him. She sensed one day that Francis was sick and dying and brought to him, among other things, her almond cookies. Try this version of almond cookies, they're delicious!

1 cup butter softened	2 ½ cups flour
1 ½ cups confectioner's sugar	1 tsp. baking soda
1 egg	1 tsp. cream of tartar
1 tsp. vanilla	1 cup crushed almonds
1 tsp. almond extract	granulated sugar for sprinkling

Heat oven to 375°. Mix together the butter, sugar, egg, vanilla and almond extract. Sift the flour, baking soda and cream of tartar into the butter mixture and stir until mixed. Add crushed almonds and spoon onto cookie sheet. Sprinkle lightly with sugar and bake for 7 to 8 minutes. Makes 5 dozen 2 inch cookies.
You may omit the almonds and sprinkled sugar and simply spread frosting on these cookies too. Yum!

Mom's Cut-Out Cookies

1 cup shortening *(or 2 sticks margarine)*
4 cups all-purpose flour
½ tsp. salt
2 eggs
1 cup sugar
4 Tbsp. milk
1 tsp. vanilla
1 tsp. baking soda
Confectioner's sugar
Colored sugar

Cut shortening into flour (like when making pastry) and add salt. Combine eggs and sugar; beat well. Combine milk, vanilla, and baking soda; add to eggs and sugar. Then add mix to flour mixture and mix in with a big spoon. Divide into 4 parts; flatten out. Put in plastic bag and refrigerate.

Roll out ¼-inch thick on floured board and cut with fancy cookie cutters. Place on ungreased pan and bake in preheated oven at 400° for about 10 minutes or so. Frost with confectioner's sugar and sprinkle with colored sugar. Can also use dough for filled cookies, heavy jam, and nut pastries.

Anise Toast Cookies

6 cups flour
1 tsp. salt
2 tsp. baking powder
1 cup Crisco, margarine, or butter
1 ¾ cups sugar
6 eggs

2 tsp. vanilla
2 ½ Tbsp. anise seed *(can use ground anise seed also – flavor will be more intense)*
2 ½ oz. slivered/sliced almonds *(almost 1 cup)*

Cream shortening and sugar together. Add eggs, one at a time, beating a little after each one, until all are added. Add vanilla and anise seeds. Add flour (do not add all the flour at one time), leaving some out to knead in, salt, and baking powder. Add almonds in with the flour.

Knead until smooth – just like bread, but only as much flour and as long as it takes to become nice and smooth. Then roll into logs. *Recipe says 5 logs, 2 ½ inches wide – I really do not follow that. I just roll them into logs and put them on ungreased cookie sheets.*

Bake at 350° for 20 minutes – may not look done. Take them out, let cool a few minutes, and then cut, using a serrated edge knife, on the diagonal. Put back in oven – stand them up – for roughly 10 minutes. Watch so they do not get too brown.

"Certainly amongst all devotions, after that of receiving the sacraments, that of adoring Jesus in the Blessed Sacrament holds the first place, is the most pleasing to God, and the most useful to ourselves. Do not then, O devout soul, refuse to begin this devotion; and forsaking the conversation of men, dwell each day, from this time forward, for at least half or quarter of an hour, in some church, in the presence of Jesus Christ under the sacramental species. Taste and see how sweet is the Lord."
~St. Alphonsus Ligouri

Blessed Mary MacKillop (1842-1909)
Feast Day ~ August 8

Mary was born in Melbourne, Australia, the oldest of 8 children. Her parents were devout Catholics. Mary began working as a governess at 16 to help support her family. She met Fr. Woods, a priest who had a great love for teaching. His parish was enormous and the outback covered 22,000 square miles. Eventually Mary, who was greatly inspired by Fr. Woods, and two of her sisters, opened St. Joseph's School in Penola. Together the Mackillop's opened the school and taught 50 children. Mary loved the poor and worked tirelessly to teach and spread the Faith. As more women came to join her, she became the superior of the Sisters of St. Joseph. She was the very first sister of a new convent founded by an Australian. In two years the convent grew to seventy sisters and there were several schools all dedicated to the poor and neglected. She also opened orphanages and cared for the homeless and poor regardless of age. No one was an outcast as she gave ex-prisoners and ex-prostitutes a second chance, bringing them back to the Faith and caring for their needs. She underwent many disappointments trying to do the right thing while some people tried to dissuade her and get her into trouble. Mary forgave them and never held a grudge. She went to Rome to ask that her order be recognized. Upon her return she brought back many new sisters, new materials, and recognition for her order, the Josephites known affectionately in Australia as the "Brown Joeys". By 1877 they staffed more than 40 schools. Mary had much to suffer but God protected her work and many children were taught the Faith. Despite her failing health the sisters wanted her to continue to lead the order, and elected her once again to lead them. She lived for 7 more years getting around in a wheelchair. When she died, her body was brought to a vault near the altar of the Mother of God Memorial Chapel, on Mount Street in Sydney. The Sisters of St. Joseph continue their work today, helping the less fortunate get an education and understand the Faith. Mary was declared a Blessed by John Paul II in 1995.

Make up some fun puzzles, crosswords, and other activities, and help your younger brothers and sisters learn about God. Mary showed us that one person can make a difference.

"Have courage no matter what your crosses are." ~Mary MacKillop

Saintly Citrus Crosses Mary MacKillop Commemorative Biscuits

½ cup butter
1 cup super fine sugar
1 tsp. grated lemon rind
1 tsp. grated lime rind
2 tsp. lime juice
1 egg lightly beaten
1 cup all-purpose flour
1 cup self rising flour
2 tsp. ground ginger

½ cup coconut flakes
⅓ cup chocolate chips
½ cup finely chopped pistachio nuts

Lemon Icing:
1 ½ cups powdered sugar
3 ½ Tbsp. softened butter
1-2 Tbsp. lemon juice

Beat sugar, rinds, juice and egg until light and fluffy. Add sifted flours, ginger and coconut; mix to a soft dough. Knead gently on lightly floured surface until smooth. Cover, refrigerate for 20 minutes. Roll out dough between 2 sheets of parchment paper to ⅛ inch. Cut crosses from dough. Re-roll dough and cut out crosses until all dough is used. Place cookies 1 inch apart on lightly greased baking sheet. Place a chocolate chip in the center of each cookie. Bake at 350° for 10 minutes or until light brown. Loosen with spatula and let cool. Lemon Icing: Combine powdered sugar and butter and stir in lemon juice to make a smooth paste. Spoon icing into a piping bag fitted with a medium, plain tube and pipe onto cookies. Top with nuts.

St. Aloysius Gonzaga (1568-1591)
Feast Day ~ June 21

Born to a prince, Aloysius grew up wealthy and was expected to take his father's place one day and be a military hero. As a young boy of 7, he experienced God in his life and decided to devote himself to the Lord. By the age of 11, he was teaching the catechism to children. He worked in the royal courts as a page of Philip II. He didn't like it and started reading books on the saints. One book really caused him to want to become a priest, and he joined the Jesuits. His father objected but eventually allowed Aloysius to renounce his inheritance. Aloysius was full of zeal and he was ready to dedicate his life to God, but the young nobleman was seen as someone who needed to learn obedience and humility, so he was sent to a city hospital where he had to care for the sick and dying. He despised his work, and it took great strength to get through each day. In 1591 an epidemic blanketed Rome, and the hospitals were overflowing, so the monasteries opened their doors to the sick and dying. Aloysius worked with great zeal to help the many thousands of people who were critically ill. Nothing could stop him in his service to God. He found beds for them, bathed them, told them about God, and prayed with them. He became very sick and died soon after. He was only 23 when he died, but he had done God's will and not what he wanted to do.

How many times have we made decisions not asking God first what He wants? This week work on saying no to yourself and yes to God!

Gonzaga's Great Cookies

St. Aloysius helped thousands of people who were very sick. Think about what a treat it would have been to be able to make these cookies for someone you love. Why not share these delicious cookies with your whole family tonight!

2 sticks (1 cup) butter
2 eggs
1 ½ cups brown sugar
½ cup sugar
1 ½ tsp. vanilla
2 cups flour
1 tsp. baking soda
½ tsp. salt
½ tsp. cinnamon
2 cups quick oats
1 cup coconut
1 cup chocolate chips

Beat softened butter with eggs and vanilla. Stir in brown and white sugar. In separate bowl add flour, soda, salt, cinnamon and add to butter mixture. Stir in oats, coconut and chocolate chips. Bake in 350° oven for about 10 minutes.

"The center of devotion to the Sacred Heart of Jesus is the Enthronement of the image of the Sacred Heart in the home. By the Enthronement of the Sacred Heart, we link the tabernacle of our parish church to our home, inviting our Lord to be our constant and most intimate companion. The Enthronement is a way of life. It means that Christ is King of our hearts, and we desire Him to be present with us always." ~Most Reverend Raymond L. Burke, Prefect of the Supreme Tribunal of the Apostolic Signatura

St. Lucy (284-304)
Feast Day ~ Dec 13

St. Lucy was a young girl who loved Jesus with her whole heart and wanted to give herself totally to Him. Her mother suffered from bleeding and was frequently ill, so Lucy decided to take her to the shrine of St. Agatha and ask for healing. Her mother was healed. Lucy asked her if she could belong to God and not be the wife of a pagan, and her mother consented. The man she was supposed to marry was furious and accused Lucy of being a Christian. He threatened her and told her he would have her tortured. He punished Lucy for loving God by blinding her, but God restored Lucy's eyes. Then he threatened to make her live with sinful women. As men went to pick her up and carry her away, her body became like lead and they couldn't move her. In 304 he finally succeeded in killing Lucy. She loved God so much that she wouldn't deny her Faith. She died a martyr for Jesus and is the patron saint of blindness.

What will you do this week as we prepare to celebrate Jesus' birthday? What could you give to Jesus to help Him know that you love him?

Lucy's Oat Cran Cookies

2 cups quick cooking oats
½ cup whole wheat flour
½ cup all-purpose flour
1 tsp. baking soda
6 Tbsp. Promise spread stick
 (or any other, I'm sure)

1 ¼ cups firmly packed light brown sugar
1 egg
1 tsp. vanilla extract
1 cup dried cranberries
½ cup toasted finely chopped pecans

Preheat oven to 375°. Grease baking sheets and set aside. In medium bowl, combine oats, flours, and baking soda; set aside.

In large bowl with electric mixer, beat Promise spread stick and brown sugar on medium speed for 3 minutes or until creamy. Beat in egg and vanilla until blended. Gradually mix in oat mixture on low speed just until blended. Stir in dried cranberries and pecans.

On prepared sheets, drop dough by 2 tablespoons 4 inches apart. Bake 12 minutes or until edges are golden and centers are set. Cool 2 minutes on wire rack; remove from sheets and cool completely. *Makes 28 servings.*

"And Joseph too went up from Galilee from the town of Nazareth to Judea, to the city of David that is called Bethlehem, because he was of the house and family of David, to be enrolled with Mary, his betrothed, who was with child. While they were there, the time came for her to have her child, and she gave birth to her firstborn son. She wrapped him in swaddling clothes and laid him in a manger, because there was no room for them in the inn." Luke 2:4-7

Hildabrotchen (German Cookies)

3 cups flour
1 tsp. baking soda
1 cup sugar

1 cup butter
1 egg
1 tsp. vanilla

Sift together flour and baking soda. Add sugar, vanilla, and egg. Mix well, then cut in butter. Cut until the batter is fine (can use electric beater), then knead. Roll out very thin. Cut half the dough into 2-inch circles and the remaining dough into smaller circles with 3 holes. Bake on cookie sheet at 375° for approximately 5 to 8 minutes.

Spread larger cookie with currant jelly. Put smaller cookie on top and dust with powdered sugar. *Very bland cookie without the jelly!* Can freeze without jelly.

Gobs (Sandwich Cookie)

½ cup shortening
2 cups sugar
1 cup buttermilk
2 eggs
2 tsp. baking soda
4 cups flour
½ tsp. baking powder
½ tsp. salt
¾ cup boiling water
½ cup cocoa
1 tsp. vanilla

Filling:
1 cup milk
5 Tbsp. flour
1 cup powdered sugar
1 cup shortening
1 tsp. vanilla
¼ tsp. salt

Cream together shortening and sugar; then add buttermilk, eggs, baking soda, flour, and salt. Mix together boiling water, cocoa, and vanilla. Add to mixture. Drop by teaspoon on ungreased cookie sheet. Bake at 450° for 6 to 10 minutes.

Filling: Cook milk and flour together until thick; set aside to cool. Mix remaining ingredients together well. Add flour and milk mixture (which you have cooled). Beat with electric mixer until light and fluffy. Spread between Gobs and sprinkle top with powdered sugar.

Monster Cookies

6 eggs
1 lb. brown sugar
2 cups white sugar
2 tsp. vanilla
2 tsp. white Karo
4 tsp. baking soda

½ lb. margarine
1 ½ lbs. peanut butter
9 cups quick oatmeal
1 (12 oz.) pkg. chocolate chips
1 lb. M&M's candy

Mix ingredients in a large bowl (about 2-gallon size) in the order given. Drop by well-rounded teaspoonfuls and flatten with fork. Bake at 350° for about 12 minutes until done. *Makes about 12 dozen cookies.*

No-Bake Cookies

4 cups sugar
½ lb. margarine (2 sticks)
1 cup milk
½ cup cocoa

1 cup peanut butter
2 tsp. vanilla
¼ tsp. salt
6 cups quick cooking oats

Combine first 4 ingredients in saucepan. Bring to a boil and boil for 3 minutes, stirring occasionally. Remove from heat. Immediately add peanut butter, vanilla, and salt. Stir well. Add oats and stir again.

Spread in a 9x13-inch pan or cookie sheet. Let cool completely and cut in squares.

Incredible Chocolate Chippers

1 cup butter
1 cup sugar
1 cup brown sugar
2 eggs
½ tsp. vanilla
2 cups flour
2 ½ cups oatmeal, (*ground to powder in food processor*)
½ tsp. salt
1 tsp. baking powder
1 tsp. baking soda
1 (6 oz.) Hershey Bar, grated
12 oz. chocolate chips
1 cup nuts

Cream together butter and sugars. Add eggs and vanilla. Mix together flour, oatmeal, salt, baking powder and baking soda. Combine with creamed mixture. Add chocolate chips and nuts. Place cookies (1 heaping Tbsp.) 2 inches apart on ungreased cookie sheet and bake at 375° for 6 minutes.

Black Bottom Bars

Crust
1 cup all purpose flour
¼ cup packed brown sugar
½ cup butter softened
¾ cups semi sweet chocolate chips melted

Filling
½ cup sugar
½ cup packed brown sugar
½ cup butter softened
8 oz. pkg. cream cheese, softened
1 cup flour
¼ tsp salt
1 tsp. rum extract
1 Tbsp. vanilla extract

Glaze
¼ cup semi sweet chocolate chips
1 Tbsp. rum extract
1-2 tsp. water

Preheat oven to 325°. In large bowl combine the flour and remaining crust ingredients. Press mixture into 9 inch square pan or 11x7 pan. In large bowl beat sugar, butter and cream cheese until smooth. Add remaining filling ingredients; blend well. Spread over crust. Bake at 325° for 40 minutes until edges are lightly browned. Cool 30 minutes. In a saucepan over low heat melt glaze ingredients stirring constantly until smooth. Drizzle over warm bars. Refrigerate for at least 1 hour before serving. Store in refrigerator.

Friendship Brownies

1 large Mason jar
16-inch square of material
Raffia or twine
Blank index card

1 ⅓ cups flour
½ tsp. baking powder
¼ tsp. salt
¾ cup cocoa
1 cup brown sugar, loosely packed
Chocolate chips or nuts

In the jar, layer the following: flour, baking powder, salt, cocoa, brown sugar, and chocolate chips (or nuts).

Place lid of jar down and use pinking shears to cut fabric in a circle about 2 inches larger than the lid. Fold index card in half and use decorative scissors to cut along the edges. Punch a hole in the folded corner. On the front of the card write, "Friendship Brownies." On the inside, write: "To dry ingredients add ¾ cup oil, 1 tsp. vanilla, and 3 eggs. Mix well. Bake at 350° for 27 to 32 minutes in a 9x13-inch pan. Share with friends."

Best Brownies

A family favorite for over four generations.

2 cups sugar
½ cup butter
¾ cup unsweetened cocoa
4 eggs, beaten

1 cup flour
1 ½ tsp. salt
1 cup chopped nuts (optional)
2 tsp. vanilla

Cream butter and sugar. Add cocoa and cream well. Add beaten eggs, followed by rest of ingredients. Bake in a 9x13-inch pan sprayed with oil at 350° for 25 minutes. Frost with chocolate frosting.

St. Ludwina (1380-1433)
Feast Day ~ April 22

Ludwina's name actually means "suffering". She was from Holland and at the age of 15, dedicated herself to God. While she was skating with her friends one day, she slipped and fell on the ice. She broke a rib and was in pain. Ludwina got worse instead of better. She had very bad headaches and pain throughout her entire body. She cried to her father and said she couldn't take it anymore. Her parish priest came to visit her and explained to Ludwina that she could be just like Jesus and suffer as He had. She changed that day as she realized that she could keep Jesus company in her sufferings. Her sufferings went on for a very long time - 38 years. For the last 19 years, she could only eat Holy Communion and this nourished her. It was a gift from God. She is the patron saint of ice skaters!

Remember St. Ludwina the next time you fall down. Offer your pain to Jesus and unite yourself to His suffering and be strong.

"For to this you have been called, because Christ also suffered for you, leaving you an example that you should follow in his footsteps." 1Pet. 2:21

Dutch Miracle Bars

Ludwina survived on nothing but the Eucharist for 19 years. The name of this treat reminds us of this great miracle.

½ cup butter
1 ½ cups graham cracker crumbs
14 oz. sweetened condensed milk
6 oz. semi-sweet chocolate chips
6 oz. butterscotch chips
1 ⅓ cups flaked coconut
1 cup chopped walnuts or pecans

Preheat oven to 350°. Melt butter in 9x13-inch pan in the oven. Sprinkle crumbs over butter; mix together and press down in pan. Pour milk evenly over crumb mixture. Top evenly with other ingredients. Bake 25 to 30 minutes until slightly browned. Cool thoroughly, cut into squares, and serve.

Butterfinger Bars

4 cups uncooked Quaker Oats
1 cup brown sugar
1 cup white sugar
2 sticks (1 cup) soft butter
1 (6 oz.) bag of milk chocolate morsels
1 cup peanut butter *(crunchy is best!)*

Mix or use hands to combine first 4 ingredients. Mixture will be loose, like pie crust. Press into a greased cookie sheet and bake at 350° for 10 to 15 minutes. Cool.

Melt chocolate morsels and peanut butter in a double boiler. Spread over cooled crust; cut into squares and refrigerate.

Our Lady of Lourdes
Feast Day ~ February 11

St. Bernadette (1844-1879)
Feast Day ~ April 16

Little Bernadette Soubirous was a sickly child and lived in a former pigsty. One day she, her sister and a friend went to gather some wood for the fire. As the girls all ran to get wood, Bernadette stopped to take off her stockings. She wasn't allowed to get wet since she was always getting sick and had asthma. As she was preparing to cross a stream, she heard a rustling sound and turned, but saw nothing. She heard it again and rubbed her eyes. There was a beautiful Lady up on the rocks and Bernadette took out her rosary, knelt down and began praying. When the girls noticed her kneeling, they wondered what she saw because they saw nothing. Bernadette was having a conversation with the Blessed Mother. She didn't know who the Lady was at the time, and when she was questioned, she was laughed at. The local priest questioned her many times and asked Bernadette to ask the Lady who she was. When Bernadette finally asked Our Lady, she was told to go tell the bishop, "I am the Immaculate Conception." Bernadette repeated it over and over to herself because she did not know what it meant.

When she went to the priest and told him, he hugged her and finally believed that the child was telling him the truth since she could not possibly have made that up. Bernadette was forbidden to go back since many people thought she just wanted to get attention; but she would sneak out to see Our Lady. Finally, the Blessed Mother asked Bernadette to eat some grass and the village people laughed at her and called her a cow. She was told to dig, and she obeyed the Lady. Her parents were embarrassed and they took her away. Water started to bubble from the hole that she dug with her hands. The townspeople started building a circle with bricks around the hole but the water kept flowing. As they tried to contain the water, a woman's crippled hand was suddenly cured. It seemed that everyone who touched the water was being healed. Thousands started coming to Lourdes. Today, water still flows from the hole and millions of people visit Lourdes each year. There have been many miracles at Lourdes. Bernadette went on to become a nun and died of tuberculosis. She was a simple girl who loved God with all her heart. Many were jealous that she had been chosen to see our Lady. Do you get jealous sometimes?

This week, work on being happy for someone who wins or gets a better grade than you do. Next time try harder, but don't spoil the other person's happiness. Congratulate them and be happy that they won!

Bernadette's Almost Candy Bars

1 box chocolate cake mix
1 stick (½ cup) butter or margarine
1 cup butterscotch morsels
1 (6 oz.) pkg. chocolate chips
1 cup nuts, finely chopped
1 cup flaked coconut
1 can sweetened condensed milk

Combine *dry* cake mix with stick of butter using a pastry blender; when blended, spread in an ungreased 10x15-inch jelly roll pan. Press down lightly *(it looks like you're spreading dirt just like Bernadette did)*.

One at a time, sprinkle chocolate chips, butterscotch morsels, nuts, and coconut over top.

Slowly pour condensed milk over all ingredients. It will seem like a big area to cover, but it does tend to spread out to cover the entire pan. *I pour it in rows and leave some space between them, and go back and try to fill in the light spots. You can't spread it with a spoon – it makes a big mess!*

Bake at 350° for about 20 to 25 minutes. Cool completely before cutting into squares. *Enjoy!* Can be stored in airtight container.

Prize-Winning Blondies

¾ cup Crisco shortening
3 eggs
2 ½ tsp. baking powder
1 tsp. vanilla
1 cup chopped walnuts

1 pkg. dark brown sugar
2 cups flour
½ tsp. salt
1 pkg. semi-sweet chocolate chips

Preheat oven to 350°. Cream together Crisco, eggs, vanilla, and dark brown sugar. In medium bowl, combine flour, baking powder, and salt. Mix contents of the two bowls together until creamy. Stir in the chocolate chips and walnuts. Bake 35 to 40 minutes or until toothpick in center comes out clean.

Congo Bars

2 ¼ cups flour
2 tsp. baking powder
⅛ tsp. salt
½ cup (1 stick) + 2 Tbsp. butter, cut into chunks

1 (16 oz.) box light brown sugar
3 large eggs
12 oz. semi-sweet chocolate chips

Preheat oven to 350°. Grease a 9x13-inch baking pan. Combine flour, baking powder, and salt. Set aside.

In a glass bowl, microwave butter until melted. Stir in brown sugar until dissolved and mixture is smooth. Stir in eggs, 1 at a time. Stir in dry ingredients. Mix in chocolate chips.

Bake 30 minutes or until tester comes out clean in the center. Begin checking at 20 minutes. Cool to room temperature.

Colonial Pumpkin Bars

¾ cup butter or margarine
2 cups sugar
4 eggs
1 (15 oz.) can pumpkin
2 cups flour
2 tsp. baking powder
½ tsp. baking soda
1 tsp. cinnamon
½ tsp. salt

¼ tsp. nutmeg
1 cup chopped walnuts

Vanilla Frosting:
1 (3 oz.) pkg. cream cheese
⅓ cup butter or margarine
1 tsp. vanilla
3 cups confectioner's sugar

Cream butter and sugar until light and fluffy. Add the eggs, 1 at a time, and mix well. Add pumpkin and mix well. Combine next 6 dry ingredients and mix well; add to liquid mixture. Stir in walnuts. Spread mixture into a greased and floured 15½ x 10½-inch jelly roll pan. Bake at 300° for 30 to 40 minutes or until a dry toothpick comes out clean. Cool before frosting.

Vanilla Frosting: Combine the cream cheese, butter, and vanilla until well blended. Add sugar gradually, mixing well after each addition.

Bars can be made ahead and frozen. Thaw and cut to serve.

Marzipan Candy

2 ½ cups powdered sugar
3 oz. Philadelphia Cream Cheese

Food coloring
Flavoring

Mix powdered sugar and cream cheese well; separate into 4 balls. Add food coloring and flavoring, 1 drop at a time. Roll in sugar and press into small fancy shaped candy molds. Set out to dry. *Makes 50 pieces.*

St. Juliana Falconieri (1270-1341)
Feast Day ~ June 19

Juliana was the daughter of very wealthy and devout parents. She grew up with many holy people who became saints themselves. If you are ever in Florence, Italy, the Church of the Santissima Annunziata — the Most Holy Annunciation, was built by Juliana's parents. She became a nun, and her mother purchased a palace for her because there were no convents in Florence at the time. Many women came and joined the order. Nuns of the middle ages were usually cloistered, but Juliana had an innovative approach to life. The Servite nuns included prayer and meditation, as well as going out to help others. They also had a strong devotion to the Blessed Mother. They encouraged Catholics to be strong in their faith and to repent of their sins. At times their work was dirty as they went out to help the poor and homeless, so Juliana shortened their sleeves to help them work more effectively. This lifestyle had women flocking to the order to become nuns.

St. Juliana is the patron saint of those suffering from chronic illnesses because she suffered from severe stomach ailments. When she was dying, she was vomiting violently, and the priest could not give her Holy Communion. She asked him to cover her chest with a corporal and he placed the host over her heart. Minutes later, the host disappeared. Juliana is buried in the church her parents built.

This week work on "getting dirty!" Do something for someone that's not your favorite thing to do. Clean a bathroom or scrub out something that's dirty! Offer up the smell or your distaste to Jesus.

Juliana's Remarkable Fudge

St. Juliana worked hard doing dirty work. After you finish doing something distasteful, enjoy this special treat.

4 cups sugar
1 (14 ½ oz.) can evaporated milk (1 ⅔ cups)
1 cup butter or margarine
1 (12 oz.) pkg. (2 cups) semi-sweet chocolate pieces
1 pint marshmallow crème
1 tsp. vanilla
1 cup broken California walnuts *(optional)*

Butter sides of heavy 3-quart saucepan. In it combine sugar, milk, and butter. Cook over medium heat to soft-ball stage (236°), stirring frequently.

Remove from heat; add chocolate, marshmallows crème, vanilla, and nuts. Beat until chocolate is melted and blended. Pour into a buttered 13x9x2-inch pan. Score in squares while warm, and if desired, top with walnut halves; cut when firm.

❧ **"We have come to know and to believe in the love God has for us. God is love, and whoever remains in love remains in God and God in him."** 1John 4:16

275 Desserts

Fantastic Fudge

2 sticks (1 cup) butter
4 cups sugar
1 cup milk
25 large marshmallows

12 oz. semi-sweet chocolate chips
13 oz. Hershey chocolate bar
1 cup chopped nuts *(optional)*

Melt butter, sugar, and milk; stir until warm, not hot. Add marshmallows and bring to a slight boil; remove from heat. Add chips and broken pieces of Hershey bar; stir. Add nuts if desired.

Line a 9x13-inch pan with waxed paper and grease with butter. Pour fudge into pan and chill in refrigerator overnight.

Cut first few pieces out of pan. *You may have to eat them because they come out all messy!* Cut fudge into approximately 2x6-inch chunks. Wrap individually in waxed paper and then in foil. Store in the refrigerator or freezer. Slice into smaller pieces for serving.

Sugared Pecans

2 cups pecans
1 cup sugar
1 ½ tsp. vanilla

¼ tsp. salt
5 Tbsp. water
½ tsp. cinnamon

Bake pecans at 325° in a flat pan until toasted. Cook next 5 ingredients over medium heat and boil until it hairs. Pour nuts into mixture and toss. Cool on waxed paper.

Easy Time Holiday Squares

1 cup sugar
1 cup butter
4 eggs
1 ½ tsp. baking powder
1 Tbsp. lemon extract
1 cup cherry pie filling
2 cups flour
Powdered sugar

Gradually add sugar to butter in a large bowl. Cream at medium speed until fluffy. Add eggs and beat well at medium speed. Add flour and extract, and pour into a 15x10x2-inch sheet pan.

Mark off into 24 squares and place 1 teaspoon of cherry pie filling in the center of each square. Bake at 350° for 30 minutes. While hot, sprinkle with powdered sugar. Cut into 24 squares.

Brenton Brittle

Brenton or saltine crackers
1 cup sugar
1 cup butter
1 tsp. vanilla
1 ½ cups semi-sweet chocolate chips *(Toll House or Ghirardelli)*
Chopped nuts

Line jelly roll pan with aluminum foil. Spray pan with oil. Layer crackers over entire pan.

Boil sugar, butter, and vanilla for 3 minutes. Pour over crackers. Place in 450° oven for 8 minutes. Turn off oven.

Sprinkle chocolate chips over crackers. Place pan in oven for 5+ minutes until chocolate chips are melted. Sprinkle with chopped nuts. Refrigerate. Remove from pan. Break into pieces. Keep in refrigerator.

Palachinke (Croatian for Crepes)

Palachinke Batter:
2 eggs, beaten
1¼ cup milk
1 cup all-purpose flour
1 tsp. sugar
½ tsp. vanilla extract
¼ tsp. salt

Sweet Cheese Filling:
2 eggs, beaten
¼ cup sugar
3 Tbsp. cream
16 oz. cottage cheese

Topping:
¼ cup cream
1 egg yolk
1 Tbsp. sugar

Batter: In medium bowl, whisk eggs and milk together while gradually adding the flour to blend into a smooth cream consistency. Stir in sugar, vanilla and salt. (Let sit in fridge covered for 30 minutes.) In a nonstick (approx. 8 inch) sauté pan brush or spray 1 tsp. vegetable oil. (Stir batter before each scoop) and pour ¼ cup of batter into hot pan, swirling it around to evenly coat the bottom of the pan. Place pan on medium-high heat and when the top is dry (about 30 seconds) flip the crepe over for an additional 15-30 seconds until both sides show golden brown marbled pattern. Stack one on top of each other, about 10 crepes. (At this point you can enjoy the crepes as is or fill them with jam, Nutella, or fresh fruit. For savory crepes omit the vanilla and sugar in the batter and fill with chicken, cheese or ham.)

Filling: Stir together sweet cheese ingredients and place two heaping tablespoons of filling on one edge of crepe. Roll crepe and place in a greased baking pan a little smaller than the length of the crepe so the filling doesn't fall out. Do this for remaining crepes and pour topping mixture over all the crepes to keep them moist while baking in a 350° oven for 20-30 minutes.

> "The holy Eucharist contains the whole spiritual treasure of the Church, that is, Christ himself.... He who is the living bread, whose flesh, vivified by the Holy Spirit and vivifying, gives life to men," ~Vatican II

This & That

"Do caterpillars know they're going to be butterflies, or does God surprise them?"

THIS & THAT INDEX

Caramel Corn 283
Dog Biscuits 284
Homemade French
   Dressing 281
Hot Mulled Wine 281
Hot Spiced Wine Punch . 279
Lemon Berry Crush
   Smoothy 280
Marriage Cake 284
Mocha Punch 280
Sticky Popcorn 281

This and That

Hot Spiced Wine Punch

This makes up very easily in a crockpot, and is a warm tasty treat for a party.

2 (3-inch) cinnamon sticks
6 whole cloves
3 whole allspice
2 cups water

¾ cup sugar
2 cups apple cider
2 cups red burgundy wine
1 cup dry sherry

Tie spices in cheesecloth bag or put into tea ball, breaking cinnamon sticks as needed. In large saucepan*, combine water, sugar, and spice bag; bring to a boil over medium-high heat. Reduce heat; simmer 10 minutes. Remove spice bag. Stir in cider, wine, and sherry. Heat thoroughly. Serve warm. *Makes 14 (½-cup) servings.*

*I heat the water, sugar, and spices in a small saucepan while the cider, wine, and sherry are warming in my crockpot on high. After the sugar water has simmered, I add it and the spice ball to the crockpot. After the punch seems heated through, I turn the crockpot down to low. When I put it away for the night in the refrigerator, I remove the spice ball and discard it.

"*He remains among us until the end of the world. He dwells on so many altars, though so often offended and profaned.*"
~St. Maximilian Kolbe

Mocha Punch

1 ½ quarts water
½ cup instant chocolate drink mix
½ cup sugar
¼ cup instant coffee granules

½ gallon vanilla ice cream
½ gallon chocolate ice cream
Whipped cream, chocolate curls *(optional)*

In large saucepan, bring water to boil; remove from heat. Add drink mix, sugar, and coffee, stirring until dissolved. Cover and refrigerate for 4 hours, or overnight.

About 30 minutes before serving, pour into punch bowl. Add ice cream by scoopfuls; stir until partially melted. Garnish with dollops of whipped cream and chocolate curls, if desired. *Makes 20 to 25 servings (about 5 quarts).*

Note: *I make this for First Communions, Confirmations, etc. I make up 2 batches of the chocolate/coffee concoction, and when the punch is half gone, I add the second batch, but don't need to add anymore ice cream.*

Lemon Berry Crush Smoothy

1 ½ cups fat-free milk
1 ½ tsp. Crystal Light lemonade flavor low-calorie soft drink mix

1 (8 oz.) container vanilla yogurt *(fat-free or original)*
1 cup fresh or frozen blueberries
1 cup ice cubes *(6 to 7)*

Place ingredients in order listed in a blender and cover. Blend on high speed until smooth. Serve immediately. *Makes four 1-cup servings.*

Hot Mulled Wine

2 cups water
½ rind of 1 orange
1 cup sugar
½ rind of 1 lemon
12 whole cloves
Juice of 1 lemon
1 cinnamon stick
2 cups orange juice
6 whole cloves allspice
1 bottle of burgundy

Simmer all ingredients for about 15 minutes. Can use crockpot to keep warm. *Nice for a cold evening and makes your house smell wonderful! Serve in mugs.*

Homemade French Dressing

1 cup tomato soup
1 cup oil
¾ cup vinegar
½ cup sugar
¾ Tbsp. salt
¾ tsp. pepper
1 Tbsp. onion powder
1 tsp. paprika
1 Tbsp. dry mustard or regular yellow mustard
1 Tbsp. Worcestershire sauce

Combine all ingredients and beat well with an electric beater. Store in refrigerator in 2 carafes or containers.

Sticky Popcorn

3-4 quarts popped popcorn
½ cup white sugar
¼ cup corn syrup
1 ½ tsp. vinegar
3 Tbsp. butter
1 tsp. baking soda

Cook sugar, corn syrup, vinegar, and butter to boiling. Let boil a minute or so. Add baking soda and mix well. The mixture will become foamy white. Pour over popcorn and mix. *Enjoy!*

St. Teresa of Avila (1515-1582) *Virgin*
Feast Day ~ October 15

Teresa was born in 1515 in Avila, Spain to rich parents. Her brother and she would read the lives of the saints and martyrs and would want to imitate them. Since becoming a martyr was the fastest way to get to heaven, they decided to run away to a far away land and die for Christ. Their uncle caught them and brought them back home. They decided to go out to their garden and become hermits, but they didn't have enough stones to build their huts.

As Teresa grew she read romance novels and lost her devotion to prayer. She wanted pretty dresses and fancy things. She became ill and while she was recovering, she read a book about St. Jerome. It changed her life. Her mother died when she was 12 years of age, and she asked Our Lady to be her mother. She wanted to become a Carmelite and did so in 1536. She found her life hard. She couldn't concentrate on praying and she was sickly. She also loved to talk and spent a long time having useless conversations. This too changed when she was in front of a picture of Jesus and she began to have great sorrow that she didn't love God as she should. This was a great turning point in her life for now she really loved God. He rewarded her with visions, and she was able to hear Jesus speaking to her. She opened 16 convents that were known for a stricter way of living than the one in which she originally lived. She also wrote **The**

Way of Perfection and **Interior Castle** both classics of spirituality. She was and still is a wonderful example of how God can change you if you only listen and cooperate with His will. She died in 1582 and was declared a saint in 1622. In 1970 she was declared the first woman Doctor of the Church by Pope Paul VI.

When you are little you daydream about what you might be when you grow-up. Try and be serious for a minute and really think about what God wants you to be. Think of a person who does what you want to do. After you decide ask your parents to get you a book on someone you've chosen to be like.

Caramel Corn

¾ cup unpopped popcorn
1 stick (½ cup) unsalted butter
¼ cup light Karo syrup
½ tsp. salt
½ tsp. baking soda
½ tsp. vanilla

Preheat oven to 250°. Spray a turkey roaster pan with nonstick spray. Fill with 15 cups air-popped popcorn (¾ cup unpopped).

In a medium pan, melt butter. Add Karo syrup and salt. Bring to a hard boil. Remove from heat and add baking soda and vanilla. Pour hot caramel mixture over popcorn and mix. Bake for 1 hour, stirring every 15 minutes. Cool, then store in a tin. *Share with friends!*

"When I came to the spring today, I prayed: 'LORD, God of my master Abraham, may it be your will to make successful the errand I am engaged on!'" Gen. 24:42

"Let nothing disturb thee, nothing frighten thee; all things pass away, but God never changes. Patience obtains all things."
~St. Teresa of Avila

Dog Biscuits

2 cups whole wheat flour
1 cup cornmeal
⅔ cup brewer's yeast flakes
2 tsp. garlic powder

1 egg
1 bouillon cube, dissolved in 1 ½ cups of boiling water

Mix all ingredients in a large bowl. Roll out portions of dough about ⅜-inch thick. Using a sharp knife, cut into strips or desired shapes. Bake on greased cookie sheet at 375° for 20 minutes. Turn off oven and leave biscuits in oven until cool.

Marriage Cake (Make Often)

3 bushels Love
2 cups Understanding
1 cup Sense of Humor
1 tsp. Teasing
2 tsp. Spunk

4 cups Patience
1 ½ cups Sharing
2 Tempers, separated
Spices of your own choice

Sift Understanding once through the groom's Love, once through the bride's Love, and once through the Love of Christ. Add Teasing and Spunk; sift once more. Separate Tempers into two (2) different bowls; beat his on high until tender; beat hers until light and frothy. To his, add Patience and Sharing, then blend in all the Understanding and Sense of Humor. Take her light and frothy Temper and fold it into his mixture, adding Spices of your own choice. (This can be varied from time to time, for variety is the spice of life!)

Handle all ingredients tenderly. Bake in four loving arms, well prepared with forgiveness at a pleasant temperature. Put layers together with love and kisses. Slice in generous slices and serve often.

Blessings

A Prayer For All Priests

O Jesus, Eternal Priest, keep your priests within the shelter of your Most Sacred Heart, where none can touch them. Keep unstained their anointed hands, which daily touch your Sacred Body. Keep unsullied their lips, daily tinged with your Precious Blood. Keep pure and unworldly their hearts, sealed with the sublime mark of the priesthood. Let Your Holy Love surround and protect them from the world's harmful ideas and practices. Bless their labors with abundant fruit, and may the souls to whom they minister be their joy and consolation here, and their everlasting crown in the hereafter. Amen.

~St. Thérèse of Lisieux

"As sacrament, the Holy Eucharist is the body and blood, together with the soul and divinity, of our Lord Jesus Christ, and therefore the whole Christ who is truly, really and substantially present (cf Council of Trent: DS 1651). We receive Him in Holy Communion." ~Francis Cardinal Arinze, Eucharistic Congress Washington D.C. September 25, 2004

The Cardinal Newman Prayer
The Missionaries of Charity (Mother Teresa's nuns) pray this prayer everyday

Jesus, help me to spread your fragrance wherever I am.

Fill my heart with your Spirit and your life.

Penetrate my being and take such hold of me that my life becomes a radiation of your own life.

Give your light through me and remain in me in such a way that every soul I come in contact with can feel your presence in me.

May people not see me, but see you in me.

Remain in me, so that I shine with your light, and may others be illuminated by my light.

All light will come from you, O Jesus. Not even the smallest ray of light will be mine. You will illuminate others through me. Place on my lips your greatest praise, illuminating others around me.

May I preach you with actions more than with words, with the example of my actions, with the visible light of the love that comes from you to my heart. Amen.

Remember to thank Jesus before ALL of your meals. That means if you are over at a friend's house for dinner or out in a restaurant, bow your head, make the Sign of the Cross and say a prayer.

Grace Before Meals

Bless us, O Lord, and these Thy gifts, which we are about to receive from Thy bounty, through Christ our Lord. Amen.

Guardian Angel Prayer

Angel of God, my Guardian dear, to whom God's love commits me here, ever this day (or night) be at my side, to light and guard, to rule and guide. Amen.

Morning Offering

O Jesus, through the Immaculate Heart of Mary, I offer You my prayers, works, joys and sufferings of this day for all the intentions of Your Sacred Heart, in union with the Holy Sacrifice of the Mass throughout the world, in reparation for my sins, for the intentions of all my relatives and friends, and in particular for the intentions of the Holy Father. Amen.

Morning Offering For Child

Father in Heaven I give You today, All that I think, do and say. And I unite it with what was done, by Jesus Christ your dearest Son.

The Angelus

This prayer reminds us of Jesus' Incarnation. Traditionally it is said at 6 a.m., noon and at 6 p.m.

V- The Angel of the Lord declared unto Mary.
R- And she conceived by the Holy Spirit. (Hail Mary....)
V- Behold the handmaid of the Lord.
R- Be it done unto me according to thy word. (Hail Mary....)
V- And the Word was made Flesh.
R- And dwelt among us. (Hail Mary....)
V- Pray for us, O Holy Mother of God.
R- That we may be made worthy of the promises of Christ.

LET US PRAY:
Pour forth, we beseech Thee, O Lord, Thy grace into our hearts; that, we to whom the Incarnation of Christ, Thy Son, was made known by the message of an Angel, may by His Passion and Cross, be brought to the glory of His Resurrection through the same Christ our Lord. Amen.

"Hail, full of grace, the Lord is with you" (Lk 1:28)

"Blessed are you among women, and blessed is the fruit of your womb" (Lk 1:42)

Act of Contrition

O my God, I am heartily sorry for having offended Thee,
and I detest all my sins because of Thy just punishment,
but most of all because I have offended Thee my God,
Who is all good and deserving of all my love.
I firmly resolve, with the help of Thy grace,
to sin no more, and to avoid the near occasion of sin. Amen.

The Serenity Prayer

God grant me the SERENITY to accept the
things I cannot change; COURAGE to change the things I can;
and WISDOM to know the difference.

Prayer To The Holy Spirit

Come, Holy Spirit, fill the hearts of Your faithful.
And kindle in them the fire of Your love
V: Send forth Your Spirit and they shall be created
R: And You shall renew the face of the earth

Let us Pray: O God, Who instructed the hearts of the faithful by the light of the Holy Spirit, Grant us in the same Spirit to be truly wise and ever rejoice in His consolation. Through Christ, our Lord. Amen.

The Angel's Prayer at Fatima

Most Holy Trinity, Father, Son, and Holy Spirit, I adore Thee profoundly. I offer Thee the Most Precious Body, Blood, Soul and Divinity of Jesus Christ, present in all the tabernacles of the world, in reparation for the outrages, sacrileges and indifference by which He is offended. And through the infinite merits of His Most Sacred Heart, and the Immaculate Heart of Mary, I beg of Thee the conversion of poor sinners.

The Anima Christi

Soul of Christ, sanctify me
Body of Christ, save me
Blood of Christ, inebriate me
Water from Christ's side, wash me
Passion of Christ, strengthen me
O good Jesus, hear me
Within Thy wounds hide me
Suffer me not to be separated from Thee
From the malicious enemy defend me
In the hour of my death call me
And bid me come unto Thee
That I may praise Thee with Thy saints
and with Thy angels
Forever and ever. Amen.

Memorare

Remember, O most gracious Virgin Mary, that never was it known that any one who fled to thy protection, implored thy help or sought thy intercession, was left unaided. Inspired by this confidence, We fly unto thee, O Virgin of virgins my Mother; to thee do we come, before thee we stand, sinful and sorrowful; O Mother of the Word Incarnate, despise not our petitions, but in thy mercy hear and answer them. Amen.

Prayer of Saint Francis of Assisi

Lord, make me an instrument of your peace.
Where there is hatred, let me sow love;
where there is injury, pardon;
where there is doubt, faith;
where there is despair, hope;
where there is darkness, light;
and where there is sadness, joy.
O Divine Master, grant that I may not so much seek
to be consoled as to console;
to be understood as to understand;
to be loved as to love.
For it is in giving that we receive;
it is in pardoning that we are pardoned;
and it is in dying that we are born to eternal life. Amen.

Try to pray The Divine Mercy Chaplet at 3 p.m. every day.

See Page 24 about Saint Faustina.

The Divine Mercy Chaplet

1. Begin with the Sign of the Cross, 1 Our Father, 1 Hail Mary and The Apostles Creed.
2. On the Our Father Beads say the following: Eternal Father, I offer You the Body and Blood, Soul and Divinity of Your dearly beloved Son, Our Lord Jesus Christ, in atonement for our sins and those of the whole world.
3. On the 10 Hail Mary Beads say the following: For the sake of His sorrowful Passion, have mercy on us and on the whole world.(Repeat step 2 and 3 for all five decades.)
4. Conclude with: Holy God, Holy Mighty One, Holy Immortal One, have mercy on us and on the whole world. Say three times.

Jesus said later to Sister Faustina:

"Say unceasingly this chaplet that I have taught you. Anyone who says it will receive great Mercy at the hour of death. Priests will recommend it to sinners as the last hope. Even the most hardened sinner, if he recites this Chaplet even once, will receive grace from My Infinite Mercy. I want the whole world to know My Infinite Mercy. I want to give unimaginable graces to those who trust in My Mercy...."

"....When they say this Chaplet in the presence of the dying, I will stand between My Father and the dying person not as the just judge but as the Merciful Savior".

Jesus, I trust in You!

The Rosary

In 1917, Our Lady appeared six times to three shepherd children near Fatima, Portugal. She delivered a divine message for our time. What was the message? That Christ founded His church to save souls from the fires of hell through the intercession of His Immaculate Mother. Each time Mary spoke to the children, she asked them to say the Rosary daily. She also asked that they offer themselves to God and accept the suffering He sent to them, in reparation and supplication for poor sinners. Let us do likewise!

Pope John Paul II in his Apostolic Letter on the Rosary encouraged God's people by saying, "I look to all of you, brothers and sisters of every state of life, to you, Christian families, to you, the sick and elderly, and to you, young people: confidently take up the Rosary once again. Rediscover the Rosary in light of Scripture, in harmony with the Liturgy and in the context of your daily lives."

1. Holding the crucifix; make the Sign of the Cross and recite the **Apostles Creed**.
2. Recite the **Our Father** on the first large bead.
3. Recite a **Hail Mary** on each of the next three beads in turn for an increase of faith, hope and charity.
4. Holding the fourth bead up from the crucifix, announce the first mystery and recite the Our Father.

5. On each of the adjacent ten small beads (also referred to as a decade) recite a Hail Mary while reflecting on the mystery.
6. Recite the "**Glory Be**" (no bead) and **The Fatima Prayer**.
7. Each succeeding decade is prayed in the same manner by reciting the mystery and praying the Our Father, ten Hail Mary's, Glory Be and Fatima Prayer.
8. When the fifth mystery is completed the **Hail, Holy Queen** is said ending with the Sign of the Cross.

Prayers of the Rosary

Sign of the Cross: In the Name of the Father, and of the Son, and of the Holy Spirit. Amen.

Apostles Creed

I believe in God, the Father Almighty, Creator of heaven and earth; and in Jesus Christ, His only Son, our Lord; Who was conceived by the Holy Spirit, born of the Virgin Mary, suffered under Pontius Pilate, was crucified, died, and was buried. He descended into hell; the third day He arose again from the dead. He ascended into heaven, and sits at the right hand of God, the Father Almighty; from thence He shall come to judge the living and the dead. I believe in the Holy Spirit, the Holy Catholic Church, the communion of Saints, the forgiveness of sins, the resurrection of the body and life everlasting. Amen.

Our Father

Our Father, who art in heaven; hallowed by Thy name; Thy kingdom come; Thy will be done on earth as it is in heaven. Give us this day our daily bread; and forgive us our trespasses as we forgive those who trespass against us, and lead us not into temptation; but deliver us from evil. Amen.

Hail Mary
Hail Mary, full of grace, the Lord is with thee; blessed art thou among women, and blessed is the fruit of thy womb, Jesus. Holy Mary, Mother of God, pray for us sinners, now and at the hour of our death. Amen.

Glory Be
Glory be to the Father, and to the Son, and to the Holy Spirit. As it was in the beginning, is now, and ever shall be, world without end. Amen.

Hail Holy Queen
Hail, Holy Queen, Mother of Mercy! our life, our sweetness and our hope! To thee do we cry, poor banished children of Eve; to thee do we send up our sighs, mourning and weeping in this valley of tears. Turn then, most gracious advocate, thine eyes of mercy toward us, and after this our exile, show unto us the blessed fruit of thy womb, Jesus. O clement, O loving, O sweet Virgin Mary!
V. Pray for us, O Holy Mother of God.
R. That we may be made worthy of the promises of Christ.

Let us pray. O GOD, whose only begotten Son, by His life, death, and resurrection, has purchased for us the rewards of eternal life, grant, we beseech Thee, that meditating upon these mysteries of the Most Holy Rosary of the Blessed Virgin Mary, we may imitate what they contain and obtain what they promise, through the same Christ Our Lord. Amen.

Fatima Prayer

"O my Jesus, forgive us our sins, save us from the fires of hell, lead all souls to Heaven, especially those who have most need of your mercy."

JOYFUL MYSTERIES
Mondays and Saturdays, and the Sundays of Advent until Lent

Mystery	Scripture Verse	Fruit of the Mystery
1. The Annunciation	Luke 1:26-38	Humility
2. The Visitation	Luke 1:39-56	Love of Neighbor
3. The Nativity	Luke 2: 1-20	Poverty
4. The Presentation	Luke 2 22-38	Obedience
5. Finding Jesus in the Temple	Luke 3:41-52	Joy in Finding Jesus

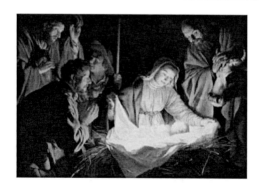

LUMINOUS MYSTERIES Thursdays		
Mystery	**Scripture Verse**	**Fruit of the Mystery**
1. The Baptism of Christ	Matthew 3:13-17	Openness to the Holy Spirit
2. The Wedding Feast of Cana	John 2:1-11	To Jesus through Mary
3. The Proclamation of the Kingdom	Mark 1:15; 2:3-13	Repentance and Trust in God
4. The Transfiguration	Matthew 17:1-8	Desire for Holiness
5. The Institution of the Eucharist	Matthew 26:26-32	Adoration

SORROWFUL MYSTERIES
Tuesdays and Fridays, and the Sundays of Lent

Mystery	Scripture Verse	Fruit of the Mystery
1. The Agony in the Garden	Luke 22:39-46	Sorrow for Sin
2. The Scourging at the Pillar	Mark 15:6-15	Purity
3. The Crowning with Thorns	John 19:1-8	Courage
4. The Carrying of the Cross	John 19:16-22	Patience
5. The Crucifixion	John 19:25-30	Perseverance

GLORIOUS MYSTERIES
Wednesdays and Sundays

Mystery	Scripture Verse	Fruit of the Mystery
1. The Resurrection	Matthew 28:1-10	Faith
2. The Ascension	Acts 1:6-11	Hope
3. The Descent of the Holy Spirit	Acts 2:1-13	Love
4. The Assumption of Mary	Revelation 12:1-3, 13-18	Grace of a Happy Death
5. The Coronation of Mary	Revelation 12:1-5	Trust in Mary's Intercession

Blessings 299

The Five First Saturdays

Mary's Great Promise at Fatima

Mary said to Lucia:

"I shall come to ask... that on the First Saturday of every month, Communions of reparation be made in atonement for the sins of the world."

This devotion and the promises associated with it were Mary's promise to be with us at the hour of our death. Lucia was told by the Blessed Mother "*I promise to assist, at the moment of death, with all the graces necessary for salvation, all those who on the First Saturday of five consecutive months shall:*

1. Go to Confession (can be up to 8 days following the first Saturday) and Receive Communion in a state of grace.

2. Recite five decades of the Rosary: Joyful, Luminous, Sorrowful, or Glorious Mysteries while meditating on the Mysteries.

3. Keep Mary company for fifteen minutes in addition to the Rosary while meditating on several Mysteries of the Rosary, with the intention of making reparation to offences committed against the Immaculate Heart of Mary.

Metric Conversion Chart
Cooking Measurements

1 tsp. =	5 ml
1 Tbs. =	15 ml
1/8 cup =	30 ml
1/4 cup =	60 ml
1/3 cup =	80 ml
1/2 cup =	120 ml
2/3 cup =	160 ml
3/4 cup =	180 ml
1 cup =	240 ml
1 stick butter =	8 Tbsp., 4 ozs. or 113 grams

Weights

American Standard	Metric
1/2 ounce =	15 grams
1 ounce =	30 grams
2 ounces =	57 grams
3 ounces =	85 grams
4 ounces =	115 grams
6 ounces =	170 grams
8 ounces =	225 grams
12 ounces =	340 grams
16 ounces or 1 pound =	453 grams

Oven Temperature Conversions

Fahrenheit	Celsius
300 =	149
325 =	163
350 =	177
375 =	190
400 =	204
425 =	218
450 =	323

Different Terminology

American	British
all purpose flour	plain flour
baking sheet	baking tray
baking soda	bicarbonate of soda
bouillon cube	stock cubes
bread flour	strong flour
candied fruit	glacé fruits
cilantro	coriander, fresh
cookies	biscuits
confectioners'/powdered sugar	icing sugar
cornstarch	cornflour
cream, heavy	double cream
cream, light, half-and-half	single cream
eggplant	aubergine
extract (vanilla, etc.)	essence
flank steak	skirt steak
graham crackers	digestive biscuits
ground meats	minced meats
ham	gammon
light corn syrup	golden syrup
molasses	treacle
papaya	paw paw
raisins/seedless, golden	sultanas
sausages	bangers
shredded coconut	desiccated coconut
slice	rasher
strain; strainer	sieve
(to) strain	(to) sift
Sugar, superfine	castor sugar
sweet or bell peppers	capsicums
zucchini	courgette
Bisquick substitute	See pg. 91

INDEX

Appetizers

Artichoke Dip 2
Asian Roll Ups 15
Baked Cheese Bread Dip .. 1
Baked Crab Dip 7
Cranberry Dip 7
Grandma's Cheese Balls .. 11
Katharine's Hot Crab Dip ... 5
Margaret's Spinach Balls ... 9
Marinated Pretzels 15
Mexican Dip 6
Olive Dip 1
Philly Chili Cheese Dip 5
Ruben Dip 7
Salmon Dill Sauce 16
Salsa 10
Sausage Dip 6
Spinach & Artichoke Dip 3
Spinach Squares 11
Spinahoke Dip 2
St. Basil's Vegetable
   Cheese Squares 13
Sweet Corn and Pepper
   Salsa 10
Veggie Bars 14
Zucchini Rounds 14

Soups and Salads

Black Bean and Corn
   Salad 39
Broccoli Orange Salad 38
Broccoli Salad 38
Chicken Noodle Soup 30
Colorful Fresh Vegetable
   Salad 35
Crab Bisque 32
Crunchy Asian Salad 41
Cucumber and Onion
   Salad 34
DeSales Dinner Salad 37
Easy Fruit Salad 44
Easy Vegetable Soup . 17, 19
Grape Salad 46
Great Greek Salad 32
Irish Potato Soup 23
Mandarin Salad 44
Neumann's Philly 43
Overnight Salad 46
Pennsylvania-Dutch
   Cucumbers & Dressing. 34
Polish Black-Eyed Pea
   Soup 25
Polish Sausage Soup 27
Ramen Noodle Salad 41
Rotini Salad 40
Seven-Layer Salad 35
Shrimp Bisque 31
Southwest Bean and Corn
   Salad 39
Spaghetti Salad 40
Spinach Salad 33
St. Peter's Lentil Soup 21
Strawberry Pretzel Salad .. 45
Strawberry Spinach Salad 33
Tortellini Soup 29
Tortellini Spinach Salad 40
Turkey Tortellini Soup 30
Vegetable Soup 19

Bread and Breakfast

Absolutely Incredible
   Muffins 54
All-Bran Muffins 54

INDEX

Angel Pumpkin Muffins 53
Banana Nut Bread 51
Banana Nut Muffins 51
Bannock Bread 49
Blueberry Muffins 55
Breakfast Casserole 60
Christmas Morning
  Breakfast 60
Croissant French Toast 57
Egg Casserole 59
Egg Lasagna 61
Herb Rolls 50
Overnight Eggs 61
St. Gerard's Delicious
  Dough for Shaping 48
Sticky Buns 55
Versatile Egg Casserole ... 58
Zucchini Bread (In a Can). 50

Vegetables and Side Dishes

Bail-Out Beans 77
Broccoli Casserole 63
Carrots Supreme 64
Cauliflower Bake 65
Cheesy Broccoli 63
Corn Pudding 65
Deer Hunter Beans 78
Do-Ahead Mashed
  Potatoes 73
Elkridge Tomatoes 66
Fiore di Zucca Fritta 64
French Fried Onions 67
Grandmal's Turkey
  Dressing 80
Grilled Portabella
  Mushrooms 67

Harvard Beets 67
Hot Potato Casserole 73
Juan Diego's Guacamole
  Mexican Recipe 69
Maria's Sweet Potato
  Crunch 75
Praline Topped Sweet
  Potatoes 76
Quick & Easy Rice 78
Roasted Red Potatoes 72
Savory Apple Casserole ... 79
Sweet Potato Casserole ... 76
Thanksgiving Potatoes 72
Vianney's Potato Bake 71
Yummy Corn Pudding 66
Vegetable Soup 19

Main Dishes

"Heavenly" Bagel Pizzas 153
Augustine's Jerk Chicken 115
Australian Meat Pie 106
Baked Maple Pork
  Chops 147
Baked Parmesan
  Chicken 109
Benedict's Italian
  Lasagna 157
Bulgoki (Korean Steak) ... 159
Catherine's Chili 101
Catherine's Sloppy Joe's
  in the Crockpot 105
Chicken Tetrazzini 119
Chicken Casserole 108
Chicken Franchaise 116
Chicken Pot Pie 137
Chicken Pie 138
Chicken Stew 138

INDEX

Chicken Swiss 117
Chicken-Italian Dressing
   Bake 111
Clare's Chicken
   Casserole 127
Cornish Pastries 85
Crescent Roll Pizza 149
Crispy Crunchy Chicken . 108
Crispy Garlic Chicken 109
Crockpot Kraut 148
Crunchy Chicken
   Casserole 106
Cuban Potted Steak 84
Cuban Style Pot Roast 84
Curry Chicken 133
Dominic's Turkey
   Meatballs and Pasta ... 143
Easy Chicken a la King ... 121
Easy Feta Chicken Bake 117
Easy Layered Taco Pie 93
Easy Meatloaf 94
Easy Stromboli 151
Elegant Chicken Breasts 116
Elizabeth's Easy Beef
   Stroganoff 97
English Muffin Pizza 153
Gianna's Garlic Chicken . 113
Harvest Pork Roast 146
Hearty Bosco's Chicken
   Pot Pie 135
Jambalaya 148
Josemaria's Burrito Bake .. 91
Layered Enchilada Bake ... 89
Layered Zucchini Bake ... 149
Marinated Flank Steak 81
Marsala Chicken with
   Sage 118
Meatball Stew 102
Mexican Chicken Delight 107

Nana's Barbecue 103
Oven Fried Chicken 108
Pasta & Veggie Bake 124
Pizza Burgers 103
Possenti's Pasta with
   Feta and Tomatoes 155
Rita's Creamy Baked
   Chicken Breast 123
Ro-Tel King Ranch
   Chicken 125
Rouladen (Stuffed Beef
   Roll) 95
Santa Fe Taco Casserole
   Bake 92
Shepherd's Pie 81
Simple Salsa Chicken 136
Slow Cooked Italian
   Chicken 119
Spaghetti Sauce 97
Spicy Beef Rolls 94
St. Anthony's Italian
   Noodles 99
St. Paul – Gyros of
   Corinth 145
St. Zita's Baked Ziti 141
Steak Fajitas 88
Stuffed Chicken
   Crescents 136
Swiss and Chicken
   Casserole 125
Texas Straw Hat 93
Tom's Summa Ribs
   Alogica 83
Turkey Enchiladas 107
Turkey Tortilla Casserole 139
Upside Down Pizza 87
Vincent's Chicken
   Enchiladas 131
Xavier's Dream Chicken

INDEX

Rice Salad 129

Fantastic Fridays

Baked Haddock with Mushrooms 189
Baked Tomatoes with Orzo and Olives 165
Blessed Kateri Tekakwitha Sweet Corn Cakes 163
Bridget's Vegetable Lasagna Bake 173
Butter Herbed Baked Fish 188
Cheesy Broiled Flounder 192
Crab Casserole 196
Disciplines of True Fasting 200
Fish Marinade 197
Frassati's Fish Piccata 191
Greek Quesadillas 176
Grilled Rosemary Salmon Kabobs 194
Heavenly Stuffed Zucchini 161
Homemade Spaghetti Sauce 179
Jane's Creamy Vegetable Lasagna 171
Mac & Cheese 187
Macaroni Casserole 184
Martin's Black Bean Lasagna 175
Mexican-Style Cheese Tortillas 177
Nutritional Yeast Gravy ... 188
Penne with Fresh Tomato Sauce, ... 185
Phillip's Light Fettuccine Alfredo 181
Poor Man's Lobster 193
Salmon Patties 194
Salmon with Brown Sugar & Mustard Glaze 193
Savory Sole 189
Scalloped Oysters 196
Shrimp & Lobster Casserole 195
Shrimp Stir-Fry 195
Spaghetti and Sand 184
Spicy Tuna Melt 197
St. Elizabeth's Old Bay Fish Batter 199
St. Julie's Quickie Quiche 169
St. Peter's Shrimp 183
Taku Grilled Salmon 192
Vegetarian Pot Pie 167
Vegetarian Shepherd's Pie 167
Zucchini Casserole 166

Desserts

Agatha's Carrot Cake 203
Almond Cookies 255
Angel Fruit Whip 252
Anise Toast Cookies 257
Apple Crisp 246
Apple Crumb Pie 234
Applesauce Loaf 225
Bernadette's Almost Candy Bars 271
Bernard's Apple-Blueberry Cobbler 245

INDEX

Best Brownies 267
Black Bottom Bars 266
Black Forest Truffle
   Cake 217
Blueberry Cake 207
Blueberry Nut Bread 226
Brenton Brittle 277
Butterfinger Bars 269
Chocolate Cherry Cake .. 214
Chocolate Cherry Dump
   Cake 213
Chocolate Chip Pound
   Cake 216
Chocolate Chip Zucchini
   Bread 227
Chocolate Éclair Cake 215
Chocolate Pie 236
Cobbler (Cherry,
   Blueberry, Peach) 243
Colonial Pumpkin Bars ... 273
Congo Bars 272
Creamy Icing 221
Dutch Miracle Bars 269
Easy Dessert 247
Easy Peach Cobbler 243
Easy Pumpkin Cupcakes 221
Easy Time Holiday
   Squares 277
Fantastic Fudge 276
Friendship Brownies 267
German Gingerbread 211
Gobs (Sandwich Cookie) 264
Golden Apple Cake 205
Gonzaga's Great
   Cookies 261
Heavenly Fruitcake 224
Hildabrotchen (German
   Cookies) 264
Hummingbird Cake 219

Ice Cream Cake 253
Ice Cream Sandwich
   Cake 253
Impossible Coconut Pie .. 235
Incredible Chocolate
   Chippers 266
Jewish Apple Cake 206
Julia's Decorator Icing 223
Juliana's Remarkable \
   Fudge 275
Light Fruitcake 225
Lucy's Oat Cran Cookies 263
Marzipan Candy 273
Mom's Cut-Out Cookies . 256
Mom's Fresh Blueberry
   Pie 233
Monster Cookies 265
No-Bake Cookies 265
Orange Crunch Cake 220
Out-of-This-World Cake .. 218
Peaches 'n Cream
   Cheesecake 242
Peanut Butter Pie 237
Perpetua & Felicity's
   Berry Puff 231
Prize-Winning Blondies .. 272
Queen of Pudding 252
Quick Apple Crisp 246
Rhubarb Cake 206
Rhubarb Custard Pie 235
Saintly Citrus Crosses 259
Sour Cream Chocolate
   Cake 213
Spiced Peaches 247
St. Brice's Pumpkin
   Dessert 249
St. Cecilia's Fudge Pies .. 241
St. Joseph's Cream
   Puffs 229

INDEX

St. Margaret's Lemon
  Cake 209
St. Nick's Toll House Pie 239
Strawberry Pie 234
Sugared Pecans 276
Sunrise Cherry Pie.........237
Tandy Cake 212
Texas Sheet Cake 201
The Cake That
  Doesn't Last...............218
Unbeatable Pineapple
  Cake 212
Watergate Salad.............247

This & That

Caramel Corn 285
Dog Biscuits....................286
Homemade French
  Dressing 283
Hot Mulled Wine 283
Hot Spiced Wine Punch..281
Lemon Berry Crush
  Smoothy 282
Marriage Cake................286
Mocha Punch..................282
Sticky Popcorn................283

These Cookbooks have been prepared for families who want to incorporate good values and wholesomeness into their everyday lives. Raising children to be holy is our goal as we all struggle to be saints. We were made holy and by striving to be holy, we are fulfilling our purpose. We must always try to do God's Will and not our own will.

Individual copies may be purchased at many Catholic bookstores as well as online at www.catholicfamilycookbook.com. For any questions please contact info@catholicfamilycookbook.com.

If you would like to raise money for your school or parish by selling these cookbooks please contact Kathy LeFevre at Friends and Family Cookbook Publishers. You may contact Kathy by calling 888-872-8202 or you may write or email her for information and an order form:

>Friends and Family Cookbook Publishers
>6480 N. Lostcreek-Shelby Rd.
>Fletcher, Ohio 45326
>Kathy@friendsandfamilycookbooks.com

For more information about The TASTE Program go to their website at www.tasteprogram.com or email info@tasteprogram.com

This book was published especially for *The Taste Program* by Friends and Family Cookbook Publishers. We publish fundraising and family cookbooks for all occasions. Everyone should make a family cookbook! We make it easy for you—you don't have to type your recipes. We'll add a personal touch and generate interest by adding your stories and up to 70 photographs. We accept orders as small as 50 books. For information, contact Kathy LeFevre at 888-872-8202. You may also visit our website at:

www. friendsandfamilycookbooks.com

Proudly Made in the USA